God and Human Wholeness

God and Human Wholeness

Perfection in Biblical and Theological Tradition

KENT L. YINGER

CASCADE Books • Eugene, Oregon

GOD AND HUMAN WHOLENESS
Perfection in Biblical and Theological Tradition

Copyright © 2019 Kent L. Yinger. All rights reserved. Except for brief quotations in critical publications or reviews, no part of this book may be reproduced in any manner without prior written permission from the publisher. Write: Permissions, Wipf and Stock Publishers, 199 W. 8th Ave., Suite 3, Eugene, OR 97401.

Cascade Books
An Imprint of Wipf and Stock Publishers
199 W. 8th Ave., Suite 3
Eugene, OR 97401

www.wipfandstock.com

PAPERBACK ISBN: 978-1-5326-1826-0
HARDCOVER ISBN: 978-1-4982-4368-1
EBOOK ISBN: 978-1-4982-4367-4

Cataloguing-in-Publication data:

Names: Yinger, Kent L.

Title: God and human wholeness : perfection in biblical and theological tradition. / Kent L. Yinger.

Description: Eugene, OR: Cascade Books, 2019. | Includes bibliographical references and index.

Identifiers: ISBN 978-1-5326-1826-0 (paperback) | ISBN 978-1-4982-4368-1 (hardcover) | ISBN 978-1-4982-4367-4 (ebook)

Subjects: LCSH: Perfection—Religious aspects—Christianity—History of doctrines. | Bible—Criticism, interpretation, etc. | Perfection—Biblical teaching.

Classification: BT766 Y56 2019 (print) | BT766 (ebook)

Manufactured in the U.S.A.   OCTOBER 15, 2019

Scripture quotations are from New Revised Standard Version Bible, copyright © 1989 National Council of the Churches of Christ in the United States of America. Used by permission. All rights reserved worldwide.

For Gordon Fee and Andrew Lincoln
who ignited in me a spark that still burns.

Contents

Preface xi
Acknowledgments xiii
Abbreviations xiv

1. Introduction and Definition 1
    Definition (Engl.) of Perfect/Perfection 3
    Written for Whom? 5
    A Roadmap 6
    A Funny Thing Happened on the Way To . . . 6

PART 1: THE JEWISH FOUNDATION OF WHOLENESS-PERFECTION

2. Now You See 'Em, Now You Don't: Perfect People in the OT 11
    Perfect People in the First Testament 12
    The Disappearance of All Those Perfect People 13
    t-m-m and Cognates 14
    sh-l-m 17
    Righteousness and Related Terms 18
    Summary 20
    A Note on OT Translations 20
3. Probing the Boundaries of Human Wholeness 23
    Covenantal View: Only Two Options 24
    Humanly Attainable? 26
    By What Power? 28
    The 100 Percent Obedience Issue Once Again 28
    What Level of Obedience if Not 100 Percent? 33
    Christian Theological Queries 35

4. Expanding the Foundation: Wholeness in Jewish Tradition 39
   Does the LXX Change the Picture? 40
   The Dead Sea Scrolls and Perfection 42
   Other Second Temple Voices 47
   Philo 60
   Entering the World of the Rabbis 61
5. Perfection in Hellenistic Tradition 65

PART 2: THE NEW TESTAMENT AND WHOLENESS-PERFECTION

6. Jesus and Perfection 73
   Jesus preaches human wholeness for Israel (Matt 5:48) 73
   EXCURSUS: *Who Is Jesus Addressing in the Sermon?*
   EXCURSUS: *Jesus's Problem with the Pharisees*
   Translating "Be Perfect" in Matt 5:48 82
   Matthew 19:21 86
7. Finding Perfection in Gal 3:10, or Maybe Not? 93
   Who Are the "Works of Law" Group? 96
   Why Are the "Works of Law" Group Under a Curse? 97
   Paul's Reasoning in Gal 3:10 101
   Was Luther All Wrong? 103
8. Human *Teleios* Throughout the Pauline Letters 104
   1 Corinthians 2:6 ("Among the *Teleioi* We Speak Wisdom") 105
   1 Corinthians 14:20 ("In Thinking Be *Teleioi*) 107
   Philippians 3:12–16 ("Not That I Have Already . . . Reached the Goal") 107
   Galatians 3:3 109
   Wholeness-Perfection in the Disputed Letters 110
   EXCURSUS: *Wholeness-Perfection and Judgment According to Works*
   Some Remaining "Perfect" Odds and Ends 117
   Summary 120
9. Cracking Some Tough Theological Nuts Raised by Paul's Use of *Teleios* 122
   Sweeping Away a Misunderstanding: By Whose Power? 123
   Can Human Beings Keep the Law? 124

Contents

    Doesn't Romans 3 Assert that No One Can Keep Torah (Perfectly)? 133
    Romans 7: Every Human's Losing Battle with Sin? 137
    Then Why Did Christ Have to Die for Sinners? 138
10. Wholeness-Perfection in Other Apostolic Voices 141
    Completion-Perfection in Hebrews 141
    Wholeness-Perfection in James 149
    Perfection in 1 John 152

PART 3: THE CHURCH'S PURSUIT OF PERFECTION

11. The Reception of Perfection in Christian History and Theology 161
    The Decisive Turn: Patristic Voices on Perfection 162
    The Alexandrian Seed Flowers in the Desert:
        Ascetic Monasticism 171
    EXCURSUS: *Windisch and Early Perfection Teaching*
    Augustine 174
    Medieval Perfection 176
    Perfection in Orthodox Spirituality 177
    A New Chapter: Reformation Voices on Legal Perfection 177
    Christian Perfection Finds a Home:
        John Wesley and Perfect Love 180
    Fringe Groups: Perfection as Freedom to Sin 181
    Recent Developments and Summary 182
12. Righteous Imperfection: Conclusions and Reflections 183
    Suggestion for Further Reflection 187

Bibliography 189
Subject Index 203
Author Index 206
Ancient Sources Index 208

Preface

For years I simply assumed the OT Law demanded perfect obedience for the award of the label "righteous." There were ten *commandments*, right, not *suggestions*! A holy God would expect nothing less than full compliance, right? During my early years of teaching and writing, this topic kept cropping up. Again and again small bumps in the road of my Bible reading raised questions. How could Job and Noah be called perfect? Did Paul really mean he lived with a "clear conscience before God" (Acts 23:1)? And what about the many Psalms whose authors talk as though they're obedient enough (e.g., Ps 24:20–24)?

If memory serves, it was probably E. P. Sanders's comments on this topic in *Paul and Palestinian Judaism* that first raised for me a serious challenge. It soon became clear from my own research, as well as from a wave of biblical studies, that neither the OT nor much of Jewish tradition accepted my perfect-obedience assumption. This early awakening was over twenty-five years ago.

As things stand today most biblical scholars are well aware of what I had begun to discover. There remain, of course, some who continue to push back, either simply assuming a perfect law-keeping requirement like I had earlier, or, less commonly, actually arguing for it. In church circles it seems I hardly go a month without experiencing a sermon or lay Bible discussion in which someone simply assumes in passing "none of us is righteous, *since no one can measure up to God's standard of perfect obedience.*"

This book is the result of my lengthy attempt to get to the bottom of this widespread assumption. My wife and golf buddies will be elated I can finally quit bringing the subject up. Readers will now have to judge whether this answers their questions as well.

Acknowledgments

Special thanks to those friends who read this manuscript and offered suggestions that made this a better book: Daniel Brunner, Rodney Duke, Don Garlington, Roger Newell, and Carole Spencer. More than a thank you to my wife, Debi, who could hardly begin to count the hours we've spent at our dining room table discussing the ins and outs of this topic. And gratitude to Chris Spinks, my editor at Cascade Books, who seemed to think this idea might work.

Abbreviations

AB	Anchor Bible
ad loc.	*ad locum*, at the place discussed
ACCS	Ancient Christian Commentary on Scripture
ANF	*Ante-Nicene Fathers*
BBR	*Bulletin for Biblical Research*
BCE	before the Common Era (= BC)
BDAG	Danker, et al., *Greek-English Lexicon*, 3rd ed.
BDB	Brown, et al., *A Hebrew and English Lexicon*
Bib	*Biblica*
BZAW	Beihefte zur Zeitschrift für die altestamentliche Wissenshaft
ca.	circa, about
CE	Common Era (= AD)
CEB	Common English Bible
CEV	Contemporary English Version
ch(s).	chapter(s)
DSS	Dead Sea Scrolls
ESV	English Standard Version
ET	English translation
GNB	Good News Bible
HCSB	Holman Christian Standard Bible
ICC	International Critical Commentary
JBL	*Journal of Biblical Literature*

Abbreviations

JSNT	*Journal for the Study of the NT*
JSNTSup	Journal for the Study of the NT, Supplement
JSOT	*Journal for the Study of the OT*
JSOTSup	Journal for the Study of the OT, Supplement
KJV	King James Version
LSTS	Library of Second Temple Studies
LXX	Septuagint
MS(S)	manuscript(s)
MT	Masoretic text
n(n).	note(s)
NAB	New American Bible
NASB	New American Standard Bible
NET	New English Translation
NIBC	New International Biblical Commentary
NICNT	New International Commentary on the NT
NIGTC	New International Greek Testament Commentary
NJPS	*Tanakh: The New JPS Translation*
NKJV	New King James Version
NLT	New Living Translation
NRSV	New Revised Standard Version
NTS	*New Testament Studies*
NovT	*Novum Testamentum*
p(p).	page(s)
par.	parallel(s)
PNTC	Pillar NT Commentary
RSV	Revised Standard Version
SBL	Society of Biblical Literature
SJT	*Scottish Journal of Theology*
s.v.	*sub verbo*, under the word
TDNT	*Theological Dictionary of the New Testament*

Abbreviations

TDOT	*Theological Dictionary of the Old Testament*
TynBul	*Tyndale Bulletin*
v(v).	verse(s)
WBC	Word Biblical Commentary
WUNT	Wissenschaftliche Untersuchungen zum Neuen Testament
ZNW	*Zeitschrift zum neutestamentlichen Wissenschaft*

Chapter 1

Introduction and Definition

> Spare me perfection. Give me instead the wholeness that comes from embracing the full reality of who I am, just as I am. Paradoxically, it is this whole self that is most perfect. As it turns out, wholeness, not perfection, is the route to the actualization of our deepest humanity.[1]

"What in the world does God want? What do I have to do for him to be satisfied?" Such questions will be heard in many a pastor's or counselor's office. If we're honest, most of us wonder from time to time what God thinks of us. Are we doing OK? Is he satisfied, happy, bothered? Traditionally, the church's answer has been tied to the idea of perfection. Christ has lived a perfect life of obedience and offers it to God in place of one's paltry behavior. However, that still leaves us with a nagging question about our own lives. But what about *my life and behavior*? I know by faith he accepts Christ's work on my behalf, but "is he satisfied with *me*?" This book tries to answer that question. What is God after with his human creation? What sort of person will satisfy him? After creating the world, he said "it's good." What sort of person would get the same "that's good" from God? Is perfection the only acceptable standard, or is he after something else?

The greatest problem in writing a book about perfection in biblical and theological tradition is the need to use the English word "perfect." If I had my druthers, I'd have avoided it altogether . . . and this for one simple reason: The Bible nowhere uses "perfect" in the sense we English-speakers

---

1. Benner, *Human Being and Becoming*, 11.

normally assume (flawless conformity to a norm, sinless). It nowhere advances the notion that such flawless obedience is expected or required of human beings at any time. Nevertheless, this book will have to use the word for at least two reasons. First, readers may miss the connection to specific Bible verses if we don't use "perfect." For instance, when I discuss Jesus's call to be whole, readers will likely fail to hear Matt 5:48 ("be therefore perfect") unless I use the traditional word. And second, it would be impossible to discuss any number of related theological and historical developments without using this word. Just imagine discussing Wesleyan distinctives without referring to "perfect love," or Roman Catholic spirituality without the "counsels of perfection."

The English adjective (perfect) and noun (perfection), along with the associated concept of human perfection, occupy an often overlooked but central role in the Christian biblical and theological tradition. From Noah who is called perfect (Gen 6:9, KJV) to Jesus ("be perfect," Matt 5:48)[2] the term crops up more than the casual reader of the Bible might suspect. Protestant thought on salvation pivots on the Old Testament's supposedly impossible demand for perfection, as every Lutheran child knows from the catechism.

> Question: "What was the original design of the law?"
>
> Answer: "To secure perfect obedience to all its precepts, and thus confer eternal life."
>
> Question: "Can any man be saved by the law?"
>
> Answer: "He cannot; because no man has perfectly obeyed."[3]

John Wesley's movement was both renowned and reviled for its insistence on Christian perfection, and Roman Catholic spirituality wrestles with the attainment of spiritual perfection, whether via the monastic counsels of perfection (chastity, poverty, and obedience) or the ascetic quest for perfection via elimination of the bodily passions. These are only the more well-known tips of the perfectionist iceberg. As we will see in subsequent chapters, there are many more.

As fascinated as humans seem always to have been with making themselves perfect, it is a deeply problematic endeavor. On the one hand, reaching for it would seem to be mandated in Scripture.

---

2. Unless noted, English Scripture quotations are from the NRSV, or are the author's own.

3. Luther and Conrad, *Luther's Small Catechism*, 49–50.

Introduction and Definition

- Walk before me, and be thou perfect. (Gen 17:1, KJV)
- Be perfect, therefore, as your heavenly Father is perfect. (Matt 5:48, NRSV)

Yet the Bible seems equally clear-eyed that humans are incapable of reaching perfection.

- The LORD saw that the wickedness of humankind was great in the earth, and that every inclination of the thoughts of their hearts was only evil continually. (Gen 6:5)
- There is no one who does good, no, not one. (Ps 14:3)

With or without the Bible, we all know that "nobody's perfect" and that being a "perfectionist" is usually not healthy.[4]

But that leaves a nagging question: What will we do with all those verses that seem to take human perfection seriously? Answering that question will occupy our attention in subsequent chapters. For the moment, let me simply suggest that a good deal of the problem lies in the very use of the word "perfect" in these contexts. What if God's expectation of his human creation is not, in fact, that they be perfect, but something else . . . something he created these lumps of clay to be able to attain? Suddenly, that which was so deeply problematic—be perfect/nobody can be perfect—may turn out to contain a call to a form of human living that is within our grasp. His call to Abraham to "walk before me, and be *tamim*," or Jesus's call to disciples to "be *teleios*," could become a key to a realistic vision of the human life envisioned by the creator himself, rather than simply an impossibly high bar. Perhaps we have been missing the best while focusing on the perfect.

Definition (Engl.) of Perfect/Perfection

Since we will be talking much about perfection, one of our first tasks is to figure out just what we English-speakers mean when we use this word, and, thus, what we think biblical texts mean when they use this word in translation. An easy place to start is with a truism common to all of us

---

4. Psychologists and counselors typically view perfectionism, the "combination of excessively high personal standards and overly critical self-evaluations," as a danger to human mental and emotional health. Curran and Hill, "Perfectionism," 1. Such perfectionism can lead to depression or even suicide.

who have grown up speaking English: "nobody's perfect." That is, everyone messes up, makes mistakes, fails to live without sin or error.

Roy Williams, coach of the North Carolina 2017 NCAA basketball championship team, was asked during the tournament if he was ever satisfied with his teams' performances. In one sense, he replied, the answer is "Of course. We just won the national championship for heaven's sake!" But in another sense the answer is "No. We are always looking for that elusive perfect game . . . that game with not a single mistake."

This street-level understanding of perfection sits well with Webster's "being without fault or defect."[5] The queen of English dictionaries, the *Oxford English Dictionary*, expands, "In the state of complete excellence; free from any flaw or imperfection of quality; faultless."[6] Growth, addition, or improvement is ruled out; the person or thing is at the pinnacle or end-point of all possible development.[7] When applied to persons and their moral performance, such are "of supreme moral excellence; righteous, holy; immaculate."[8] This is why readers of "be perfect" in the Sermon on the Mount predictably respond, "that's impossible."

Some may object that there are, in fact, other nuances of perfect that imply something less than this absolutely flawless or error-free perfection.[9] Thus, the preamble to the US Constitution speaks of forming "a more perfect Union," which in that historical context meant a form of federal government *more suited* to governing the states than the previous Articles of Confederation. A well-mannered little boy can be a "perfect gentleman." An obnoxious dinner companion can be a "perfect bore," that is, a complete lout, who in respect to "borishness" truly fits the bill, but it does not imply that they are *never* nice, kind, etc. Here, perfect functions as an intensifier, someone or something is truly, really, fully a representative of a particular quality. Similarly, to say that someone is in perfect health, does not mean that no x-ray or full-body scan would find any single thing amiss, but means that they are in top-notch health . . . there is nothing noticeably unhealthy about them. We can even use the term in exasperation, "Now that's just perfect!"

---

5. *New Merriam-Webster Dictionary*, 541.

6. Simpson and Weiner, *Oxford English Dictionary*, 11:534a, 536.

7. "What is perfect cannot be improved." J. H. Newman, cited in Simpson and Weiner,*Oxford English Dictionary*, 11:536.

8. Simpson and Weiner, *Oxford English Dictionary*, 4b.

9. The *Oxford English Dictionary* provides a multitude of such nuances *in nonmoral contexts*.

Introduction and Definition

Thus, the objection that perfect has various meanings is correct as far as it goes. However, when we speak of the *moral character and conduct* of individuals, such as one's "perfect obedience" (i.e., without lapse) or "perfect righteousness" (i.e., without any admixture of unrighteousness), the flawlessness of that character and conduct are front-and-center. This will be richly confirmed later when we examine predominant interpretations of biblical texts using the word "perfect."

Thus, when modern English-speakers hear or read "perfect" in relation to human moral behavior, they will inevitably understand flawless, sinless, error-free performance. But this presents readers of this book with an important caution. They will have to be on their toes as to precise meaning whenever the word "perfect" comes up in relation to human behavior (and that will be a lot). Since we will be considering a wide array of views and texts, some of them will use the word in the sense of faultlessness or sinlessness, so the Lutheran catechism cited above. Others will use it in a restricted sense as Wesley apparently did. While I will generally try to use the word in its natural sense of flawlessness, readers will quickly notice that it becomes impossible to achieve perfect lexical consistency, such as when quoting and interacting with those who use it in a different sense, for example. As said, readers will need to be on their toes to discern the precise nuance of the term at any given point in the discussion.

Written for Whom?

This book is not written primarily for Bible scholars. Most of the individual topics covered in this book have illustrious precedent in scholarship.[10] There have been definitive word-studies of the key Hebrew and Greek terms underlying our key biblical texts. Previous commentators have pointed out that many of the key verses do not actually speak of perfection, but of something else. And the history of Christian reflection on this perfection tradition has been covered well by others.[11] Readers wanting to pursue this further will find bibliographic detail in the notes to subsequent chapters. For most of the academic world of biblical studies, many elements of this book's argument will not sound novel, though

---

10. The standard treatment of the topic is Du Plessis, *Teleios*; along with LaRondelle, *Perfection and Perfectionism*.

11. See esp. Flew, *Idea of Perfection*.

I suspect a few points may still raise controversy. And there still remain some Bible scholars and theologians who resist these widely acknowledged results on perfection. New, however, in this book is the bringing together of lexical, exegetical, historical, and theological elements into a single volume tracing the perfection tradition in Bible and theology.[12]

If you consider yourself in some sense a student of the Bible and of Christian theology, this book is for you. Pastors, cross-cultural Christian workers, home Bible-study leaders, college and seminary students, and anyone reading a text like "be, therefore, perfect" and seriously wondering, "Now what is that supposed to mean?" . . . this book is for you.

A Roadmap

Our path to understanding perfection is straightforward. In three chapters we will lay out the OT and early Jewish understanding. This is the crucial starting point, I hope to show, because it will remain the stable foundation for the understanding of the topic in the NT. Rather than a legalistically rigorous picture of perfection, this literature will be found to yield an inviting portrait of human wholeness suited perfectly to the weak lumps of clay called humanity.

After a brief foray into Greek views of human perfection, five chapters will unfold the various voices in the NT on this subject. Special emphasis accrues to Jesus's Sermon on the Mount (esp. Matt 5:48) and to the apostle Paul's writings, since these have formed the chief battlefields in the past in many discussions of perfection. A careful look at how the church following the apostles handled this topic rounds out the treatment, and a concluding chapter summarizes the results. Those not quite ready for the whole meal could sample as an overview the chapters on the OT (chs. 2 and 3), Jesus (ch. 6), and Gal 3:10 (ch. 7). The heart of the exegetical work is contained in these chapters.

A Funny Thing Happened on the Way To . . .

Research for this book hit an unexpected speed bump at one point. I seemed unable to find ancient rabbis or modern Jewish scholars discussing

---

12. LaRondelle's work (see note above) comes closest, but is more oriented to scholarly discussion within the biblical theology movement, and less oriented toward lexical and exegetical treatments.

Introduction and Definition

an alleged Torah requirement of perfect obedience. Jewish encyclopedias apparently consider this idea too insignificant for comment, and treatments of relevant OT texts by Jewish biblical scholars generally head in other directions.[13] So, I contacted a Jewish colleague and asked him to point me toward Jewish discussions of perfect obedience to Torah. His initial reaction was that Jewish scholars take it for granted that the God of Israel did not expect perfection in the sense I was indicating. When I later spoke with him at a conference, his response was even more revealing: What a silly idea! We will unpack this further in the chapter covering Jewish tradition. In short, who would ever think that God would create weak and frail creatures of dust and then expect them to be perfect?[14] As my colleague responded spontaneously, how silly!

---

13. No entry for "perfect," "perfection," or "(perfect) obedience" is found in either Wigoder, *New Standard Jewish Encyclopedia*; or Hurvitz and Karesh, *Encyclopedia of Judaism*.

14. As a Jewish blogger put it, "perfection is not the goal of Judaism or God." http://blog.aaronedelheit.com/2008/07/25/jewish-perfection/.

Part One

The Jewish Foundation of Wholeness-Perfection

Chapter 2

Now You See 'Em, Now You Don't: Perfect People in the OT

No matter how great and important we think ourselves to be, we are still animals, fallible creatures fated to fall short of ever having it "all together."[1]

Recent debates over perfection, or better, Judaism and perfect law-keeping, took off with the publication of E. P. Sanders's *Paul and Palestinian Judaism*.[2] As mentioned in the introduction, for Luther and most of the Protestant theological traditions in his wake, one of the chief problems with salvation[3] according to the OT law was that no one had kept, or could keep, its commandments sufficiently to be considered righteous. Nearly all were agreed this was because the law required flawless or perfect obedience to all its commands. Since all are sinners, such a demand for perfect obedience returns a guilty verdict upon every single human being. The reformational reading of texts like Gal 3:10 or Rom 3:20 made Paul a further Jewish witness to this position. However, Sanders argued that this was a complete misreading of Jewish soteriology. For the most part, Jews did not think Torah required of them a perfect,

---

1. Hyde, *Perfection*, 2.

2. Earlier, usually overlooked, voices stating the same were: Moore, *Judaism*, 1:494–95 ("no suggestion of sinless perfection"; "God was too good, too reasonable, to demand a perfection of which he had created man incapable."); and earlier, Montefiore, *Judaism and St. Paul*, esp. 33–37.

3. Since terms like "salvation" and "save" are mainstays in the Bible and in theology, we will employ them. However, readers should be aware that OT texts usually mean something a bit different than modern church folk might think. Rather than "going to heaven," "living forever," or the like, OT texts usually intend "deliverance of a people or an individual from a threatening situation." Light, "Salvation," 1153.

unerring obedience. "Human perfection was not considered realistically achievable by the Rabbis, nor was it required."[4] In fact, as Stendahl had proposed earlier, Paul had no great problem at all with keeping the law adequately. "As to righteousness under the law," he thought he was "blameless" (Phil 3:6b).[5]

Thus, one important element of our agenda is clear: Did Jewish tradition (Torah itself and Jewish thinkers up to and around the time of the New Testament) teach that one had to keep Torah's commands flawlessly in order to be considered righteous? We will first investigate what the Jewish Scripture has to say, followed by analysis of Jewish writings up to the Common Era and finishing with a brief look at rabbinic thought.

However, there is an even more important issue to be probed in Jewish tradition; one that is usually short-circuited by the focus on perfect law-keeping. If Jews did not think their God was looking for perfection, what was he looking for? With what sort of person would he be satisfied? What was his aim for the people of Israel and for the humanity he had created? And how does Torah fit into all this? If not fixated on perfect obedience, what was its vision for Israel and for human persons?

In turning to the Old Testament on the subject of perfection, readers are in for two big surprises. First, there are quite a host of perfect people in the King James OT. And second, all these perfect people disappear depending on what English translation one reads.

Perfect People in the First Testament

English-speaking Bible-readers raised on the belief in the sinfulness of all human beings and convinced of the truism that "nobody's perfect," may be surprised to find quite a few perfect people in the Old Testament.

> Noah was a just man and perfect in his generations, and Noah walked with God. (Gen 6:9, KJV)

> Asa's heart was perfect with the LORD all his days. (1 Kgs 15:14, KJV)

---

4. Sanders, *Paul and Palestinian Judaism*, 137. Sanders acknowledged isolated texts with such perfect obedience expectations (e.g., 4 Ezra), but argued that these are exceptions to the widespread pattern of non-perfectionistic covenantal nomism. Sanders, *Paul and Palestinian Judaism*, 409, 414–18. For those not familiar with this terminology, "nomism" (from Greek *nomos* [law]), as Sanders uses it, refers to life governed by law, and "covenantal" to the divine-human relationship initiated by God's grace.

5. Stendahl, "Apostle Paul," 78–96.

> There was a man in the land of Uz, whose name was Job; and that man was perfect and upright, and one that feared God, and eschewed evil. (Job 1:1, KJV; cf. also 1:8; 2:3)

And these were not just the few exceptional individuals; ancient Israel was full of such perfect people.

> All these men of war [over 200,000!], that could keep rank, came with a perfect heart to Hebron, to make David king over all Israel: and all the rest also of Israel were of one heart to make David king. (1 Chr 12:38, KJV)

In fact, *all* those devoted to the God of Israel were considered perfect.

> That they may shoot in secret at the perfect [i.e., all the pious in Israel]. (Ps 64:4, KJV)

> For the upright shall dwell in the land, and the perfect shall remain in it. (Prov 2:21, KJV)

So, if "nobody's perfect" and everyone's a lost sinner, what are we to make of so many perfect people in the OT?

The Disappearance of All Those Perfect People

A first step is simply to read a different Bible. The King James translation of the OT uses various forms of the English word "perfect" (perfection, perfectly, etc.) sixty-eight times.[6] If we switch to the New Revised Standard Version, this drops to twenty; or in the New International Version, to twenty-one.[7] Even the New King James translation has eliminated nearly half, with thirty-eight remaining.[8]

There are, in fact, in the newer translations *no longer any perfect people*! Readers of these translations will still find that sacrificial animals must be perfect (Lev 22:21), the law of the Lord is still perfect (Ps 19:7), and, of course, the God of Israel remains perfect in his ways (2 Sam 22:31; Ps 18:30). However, Noah, Job, and many others have ceased to be perfect.

---

6. Only somewhat less (fifty-two) in the Roman Catholic Douay-Rheims version.

7. The 2011 revision of the NIV dropped an additional two of these, totaling now nineteen.

8. Counts in other translations include the NET (eighteen), ESV (nineteen), NJPS (twenty), NAB (twenty-three), NASB (twenty-four), and the NLT (thirty-three).

Instead, Noah is now "blameless" (Gen 6:9, NRSV and most other ETs). Job is likewise "blameless" (Job 1:1, NRSV) or "pure" (NET). Asa's heart is no longer described as perfect (1 Kgs 15:14), but is now "true" (NRSV), "wholly devoted" (NASB), "fully committed" (NIV), or "loyal" (NKJV). Similarly, devoted and faithful Israelites are no longer perfect (Prov 2:21) but "innocent" (NRSV), "honest" (NAB), "blameless" (NASB, NIV), or people "with integrity" (NET, NLT).

The careful reader will realize this hardly resolves the issue. True, the OT no longer teaches that humans can be perfect, but now it asserts they can be "pure," "blameless," "innocent," "fully committed," "wholly devoted," "true," etc. Although the English term "perfect" is no longer used, what remains doesn't sound all that different, and these descriptions still don't make them sound like sinners. To get to the bottom of this, we will have to dig more deeply into the meaning of the two main Hebrew roots in these texts.

t-m-m and Cognates[9]

The primary word-group used in the OT to speak of this wholeness, intactness, perfection of human beings in their relationship with God are the various forms of the stem *t-m-m* and their cognates.[10] These words in their various forms occur over two hundred times in the Hebrew text. They all indicate that a thing, person, or action is complete, entire, whole. *It fulfills its purpose and is intact, sound or mature.* This is easily seen in texts referring to non-personal objects. Thus, the sun stands still for "a whole [*tamim*, i.e., entire, complete] day" (Josh 10:13). Moses writes all the words of Torah "to the very end ['*ad tummam*]" (Deut 31:24), i.e., until they were completed. The Lord instructs Israel to wait a specified period of time, "you shall count off seven weeks; they shall be complete [*tamim*]" (Lev 23:15), i.e., finished.

The word-group is used about fifty times for sacrificial animals, which must be "without blemish [*tamim*]" (Exod 12:5). That is, they must

---

9. A brief but helpful overview of Hebrew terms lying behind this perfection tradition in the OT is, Turner, *Vision Which Transforms*, 41–45. More detailed treatment will be found in the standard Hebrew lexica as well as in Kedar-Kopfstein, "*Tamam, etc.*," 15:699–711; Olivier, "*Tamam*," 4:306–8; Shults, "Shalem and Thamim"; Dickson, "Idea of Perfection"; and Edlund, *Das Auge der Einfalt*, 27–50.

10. Included here are the adjectives *tamim* and *tam*, along with the nouns *tom* and *tummah*, as well as the verb *tamam*.

be whole or sound, not defective or disfigured in any of the specified ways forbidden in Torah (Lev 22:20–25).[11]

This same semantic range of that which is complete, whole, wholehearted, genuine, and mature, but not necessarily morally or otherwise perfect, holds true when the OT speaks of persons and their behavior.

> Noah was a righteous man, *tamim* in his generation; Noah walked with God. (Gen 6:9)

This is a description of Noah's general lifestyle and behavior, his "walk," which marked him out as a righteous person rather than a wicked one, as one whose life as a whole was in line with his talk. He was a blameless or genuine human being rather than being a hypocrite or blameworthy person; one whose aim was to adhere to God rather than to turn from him. Rather than suggesting Noah never sinned, this verse describes him as a person who is what God wants him to be, a complete and whole God-aimed human being, warts and all.[12] God was satisfied.

The same explanation applies to the description of Job:

> There was once a man in the land of Uz whose name was Job. That man was *tam* and upright, one who feared God and turned away from evil. (Job 1:1)

And it applies equally to all the godly who are wise and upright:

> For the upright will abide in the land, and the innocent[13] [*temimim*] will remain in it. (Prov 2:21)

> Happy are those whose way is blameless [*tamim*], who walk in the law of the LORD. (Ps 119:1)

---

11. This is parallel to the language of blemish or disfigurement (Hebrew *mum*). Most important is that the animals be complete and not disfigured, that they "conform to the class to which they belong." Douglas, *Purity and Danger*, 51–53, quotation 53.

12. Carol Kaminski's recent treatment of Noah's "finding favor" with God focuses on divine agency (God showed unmerited favor to Noah) rather than on Noah's behavior or character. She is particularly opposed to "the view that Noah *deserves* the favour he finds or that God is in some sense *obligated* to show him favour." Kaminski, *Was Noah Good?*, 110, original emphasis. Her point is well-taken that God's favor is always *unconditioned* (i.e., given without pre-conditions). However, she overlooks that such divine favor is not *unconditional* (i.e., given with no expectation/obligation of return); see Barclay, *Paul and the Gift*. Thus, to say Noah was "righteous," "found favor," and *tamim*, means he walks in the ways expected of one who has been shown such divine favor. Her study would be strengthened by giving greater attention to the language of "Noah walked with God" (only p. 195 and n. 95 as far as I can see) and his "blamelessness" (no treatment).

13. NIV: the blameless; ESV, NLT: those with integrity.

Thus, to say that someone is *tamim* marks them as upright, genuine, and complete in behavior, but does not imply they are perfect. This completeness involves the fear of the Lord, shunning evil and ordering one's behavior according to God's Torah (instruction, law). It "means to belong to him wholeheartedly, without practicing idolatry, sorcery, and other abominations (cf. [Deut] 18:9–12)."[14] Such a person avoids "great transgression" (Ps 19:13), rejection of God and his covenant, and can be described near-synonymously as "righteous [*tsaddiq*]" or "upright [*yashar*]." One who enters into Yahweh's presence must "walk *tamim* (with integrity, genuineness)" and "do *tsedeq*" (Ps 15:2). It is hard to improve on Deut 10:12–13 as a summary of this OT expectation: "So now, O Israel, what does the LORD your God require of you? Only to fear the LORD your God, to walk in all his ways, to love him, to serve the LORD your God with all your heart and with all your soul, and to keep the commandments of the LORD your God and his decrees that I am commanding you today, for your own well-being."

Notice, although this integrity referred typically to one's observable behavior (one's "way") it was certainly not limited to a mere external conformity. Such wholeness demanded that one's very heart, one's most essential inner being, thoughts, desires, and motivations, also be *tamim*, that is, whole and complete, conforming to the divine aim for humanity, where inner and outer reality combine in genuine integrity. Rabbi Harold Kushner gets it right when he summarizes:

> [I]f we want to know what God expects of us . . . my candidate for the most important single word in the Bible occurs in Genesis 17:1, when God says to Abraham, "Walk before Me and be *tamim*." What does that word mean?
>
> [M]ore recent translations . . . have backed away from the notion of God demanding that Abraham . . . be perfect and without flaw. . . . Contemporary scholars take the word *tamim* to mean something like "whole-hearted." My own study of the verse leads me to conclude that what God wants from Abraham . . . is not perfection but integrity. God wants Abraham to strive to be true to the core of who he is, even if he strays from that core occasionally.[15]

Moving on now to the second most frequent Hebrew term for our study,[16] we read,

---

14. Schnackenburg, *Christian Existence*, 1:162.
15. Kushner, *How Good Do We Have to Be?*, 169–70.
16. In addition to the two main Hebrew word-groups, forms of the stem *k-l-l* are

> And may you be wholehearted [or wholly devoted, NAB] (*lēb shalem*) with the LORD our God, to walk in His ways and keep His commandments, even as now. (1 Kgs 8:61, NJPS)

sh-l-m

Much like *tamim*, the adjective *shalem* denotes "totality, wholeness" as when a stone is *shalem* ("unhewn," Deut 27:6), or a people's guilt is not *shalem* ("full" or "complete," Gen 15:6; 25:15).[17] Often in the OT it occurs in combination with "heart" denoting that one's inmost being is undivided or totally devoted. Thus, Hezekiah reminds the Lord that he has walked before him "with a whole [*shalem*] heart" (Isa 38:3) [KJV: perfect heart; NIV: with wholehearted devotion], and the Chronicler comments that Asa's heart was true (NRSV), blameless (NASB), undivided (NAB), perfect (KJV) his entire life (2 Chr 15:17). As with *tamim*, it would be misleading to think of these as having a perfect heart, i.e., with no shadow, error, or evil thoughts. The point is that they are true and wholehearted in their devotion to Yahweh, as opposed to being half-hearted or hypocritical. This is clear in the account of King Asa just mentioned (1 Kgs 15:9–24; par. 2 Chr 14:1—16:14). After stressing his similarity to King David (15:11) and his positive deeds such as removing idols from the land (15:12–13), a negative trait, a particularly evil deed for a king, is mentioned: "the high places were not taken away" (15:14a). Yet, even with this imperfection, this wicked behavior, the narrator continues: "Nevertheless the heart of Asa was true to the LORD all his days" (15:14b).[18]

---

occasionally found behind texts translated with perfect in the KJV (e.g., Isa 47:9), but these add little to our study.

17. On this term, see Illman, "ŠLM," 15:97–105; and Nel, "Sh-L-M," 4:130–35. See esp. Eisenbeis, *Die Wurzel* שלם *im Alten Testament*, 339–41, although his treatment of the formula in Chronicles unnecessarily imports a legalistic assumption (347–48).

18. The flip side of this coin is seen in the narrative of King Amaziah, who is explicitly stated *not* to have a whole heart (2 Chr 25:2b; see 2 Kgs 14:1–22). Although he performed in many ways well as a king ("did what was right," 2 Chr 25:2a), his reign was full of "incongruity and disparity: because the king did not act 'with a blameless heart' (v. 2), his actions were incongruous with his role as king of God's people, and there was often disparity between the king's intentions and his achievements." Graham, "Aspects of the Structure," 85. Thus, the opposite of a whole heart is lasting hypocrisy.

Righteousness and Related Terms

Since we have spoken of righteousness in connection with this wholeness, perhaps a brief word on the meaning of this and other central covenantal terms is in order. While the human heart and behavior are the focus of the *tamim* and *shalem* word-groups, a closely related set of terms focuses on the covenantal relationship itself. Premier among these is "righteous/righteousness," Hebrew *tsaddiq, tsedaqah*.[19]

Out of chaos the God of the Bible created order . . . an order that was to result in goodness, life, and blessing for the creation. This went awry early on with the rebellion of the first couple, and the story seemed to be heading for a bad end until the appearance of Noah, "a righteous [*tsaddiq*] man, blameless [*tamim*] in his generation" who seemingly alone among all humans then living "walked with God" (Gen 6:9; cf. 7:1). At this first occurrence of the word in the canon, righteousness refers to a life in accord with the order God had originally desired, and it belongs to God's covenant or agreement with Noah (6:18). Largely overlapping with this, *tamim* marks Noah as a substantially mature or complete, though certainly not perfect, specimen of what God had intended for human life; and both are summed up in terms of Noah's relationship to this creator God: "Noah walked with God."

The next occurrence of righteousness comes in the account of Abram. As far as we can tell, Abram's family took part in the polytheistic milieu of the Chaldeans, but Yahweh's call and promise sets him on a path that will eventually lead to the establishment of the people of Israel. Although Abram apparently knows little about this God, he follows him to Canaan and trusts his promise of a large family and inheritance. This loyal trust and obedient adherence is "reckoned . . . to him as righteousness [*tsedaqah*]" (Gen 15:6). That is, Abram is considered to be in line with the order of the world and human life which this God desires. This, too, is part of the covenant God makes with Abraham (Gen 15:18). As such, he is also called to the human wholeness [*tamim*] that forms part of that order (Gen 17:1). Again, we see how closely related and largely overlapping these two concepts are.

Finally, we reach the heart of the OT story of God's establishing the desired order for his creation, but now centered on one people, Israel. They are the *tsaddiqim* (Ps 1:5) to whom alone among the nations on

---

19. The academic literature on this central topic is immense, but seems to have settled somewhat for our purposes. See Scullion, "Righteousness (OT)," 5:724–36.

earth has been revealed God's guidance (Torah/Law), whose detailed ordinances "are true and righteous altogether" (Ps 19:9). Now righteousness reaches its fullest, covenantal, and Torah-centered meaning. To be one of the righteous is to live in accord with the way of life detailed in Torah, conforming not necessarily perfectly, of course, but authentically, substantially, from the heart.

And it is this covenantally ordered *tsaddiq* lifestyle, along with closely related terms like "uprightness" (*yashar*) and "fidelity" (*'emunah*), which repeatedly overlap with *tamim* and *shalem*.[20]

> As for you, if you will walk before me, as David your father walked, with integrity [*tam*] of heart and uprightness [*yashar*], doing according to all that I have commanded you, and keeping my statutes and my ordinances. (1 Kgs 9:4)
>
> Judge me, O LORD, according to my righteousness [*tsaddiq*] and according to the integrity [*tam*] that is in me. (Ps 7:8)
>
> Mark the blameless [*tam*], and behold the upright [*yashar*], for there is posterity for the peaceable [*shalom*]. But transgressors shall be altogether destroyed; the posterity of the wicked shall be cut off. The salvation of the righteous [*tsaddiqim*] is from the LORD; he is their refuge in the time of trouble. (Ps 37:37–39)
>
> The righteousness [*tsidqath*] of the blameless [*tamim*] keeps their ways straight, but the wicked fall by their own wickedness. The righteousness [*tsidqath*] of the upright [*yesharim*] saves them, but the treacherous are taken captive by their schemes. (Prov 11:5–6)

Thus, it turns out that *tamim*, the term for human wholeness, along with other key covenantal terms such as *tsedeq*, *yashar*, etc., is a central descriptor for what God wants of those who are in covenant with him. This is what God has always been after ... what will satisfy him as far as his human creation is concerned. Old Testament luminaries such as Noah, Abraham, Job, and David are marked as examples of this genuine wholeness. They are not, however, the exceptions, but the guides for how every whole-hearted covenant member is to walk. It is not rule-keeping, and certainly not flawless performance, but being a whole, upright, God-fearing and God-loving human being that is at the center of OT piety.[21]

---

20. "In particular, the word '*saddiq*' appears to be almost synonymous with the word '*tamim*.'" Hartin, *Spirituality of Perfection*, 25.

21. See esp. Edlund, *Das Auge der Einfalt*, 32–35, for this point.

N. T. Wright has put this nicely in his recent *The Day the Revolution Began*. What I call the incorrect perfection view he terms the "works contract," described as follows:

> God told his human creatures to keep a moral code; their continuing life in the Garden of Eden depended on their keeping that code perfectly. Failure would incur the punishment of death. This was then repeated in the case of Israel with a sharpened-up moral code, Mosaic law.[22]

He contrasts this with a view centering on vocation:

> What the Bible offers is not a 'works contract,' but a covenant of *vocation*. The vocation in question is that of being a genuine human being, with genuinely human tasks to perform as part of the Creator's purpose for his world. The main task of this vocation is 'image-bearing,' reflecting the Creator's wise stewardship into the world and reflecting the praises of all creation back to its maker.[23]

What Wright calls the vocation of "being a genuine human being" is precisely what we are arguing *tamim* refers to in Scripture.

Summary

The puzzle of the OT's vanishing perfect people has been solved. Their presence was the result of a particular English translation, the venerable King James Bible. Their disappearance occurred as modern English translators found more appropriate English terms for the Hebrew words and concepts. Noah, Job, Abraham, and the many others were no longer perfect but whole, blameless, intact. They were *tamim*—genuine exemplars of God's intent for his human creatures. Flawed and imperfect, yet oriented from the heart to this God and his ways.

A Note on OT Translations

We have laid at the doorstep of the KJV some of the blame, at least in the anglophone world, for our thinking that the OT requires flawlessly perfect obedience. When we look later at Matt 5:48 ("be perfect"), we

---

22. Wright, *Day the Revolution Began*, 75.
23. Wright, *Day the Revolution Began*, 76.

will suggest that the KJV translators may, in fact, have been intending something more akin to "complete" than "perfect."[24] Nevertheless, readers can see from Table 1 that most modern English OT translations have by-and-large abandoned the word "perfect" in relation to human persons.[25] However, are their alternatives any better?

Table 1: Disappearance of "Perfect" People in the English OT Tradition

OT Figure	KJV	NKJV	NRSV	NIV	ESV	NAS	NJPS	NET	NLT
Noah (Gen 6:9)	*perfect*	*perfect*	blameless	blameless	blameless	blameless	blameless	blameless	blameless
Call to Abraham to "be perfect" (Gen 17:1)	be *perfect*	be blameless	be blameless	be blameless	be blameless	be blameless	be blameless	be blameless	live a blameless life
Call to Israel to "be perfect" (Deut 18:13)	be *perfect*[26]	be blameless	remain completely loyal	be blameless	be blameless	be blameless	be whole-hearted	be blameless	be blameless
Asa (1 Kgs 15:14)	*perfect*	loyal	true	fully committed	wholly true	wholly devoted	whole-hearted	whole-heartedly devoted	completely faithful
200,000 Israelite warriors (1 Chr 12:38)	*perfect* heart	loyal heart	full intent	fully determined	full intent	*perfect* heart	whole heart	by acclamation	single purpose
Job (Job 1:1)	*perfect*[27]	blameless	blameless	blameless	blameless	blameless	blameless	pure	blameless

Clearly, with only a very few exceptions, English OT translators consider "perfect" a less-than-ideal translation in reference to persons.[28]

24. See ch. 6 below.

25. Of course, in reference to God, English "perfect" is still widespread. Interestingly, the OT appears not to actually refer to God's own person as *tam*, but only to his ways, his actions. "This God—his way is perfect (*tamim*)" (Ps 18:30). One could possibly translate the Hebrew "God is perfect in his way," as reference to God himself as perfect. The OT does refer *indirectly* to God as *tam*: see the name *Yotam* ("Yahweh is perfect," Judg 9:5; 2 Kgs 15:32); so Sabourin, "Why Is God Called 'Perfect,'" 266–68. Nevertheless, the fact remains that such language, "God is perfect," is unusual in the OT. By the first century, however, Jews have begun to use *tam* for God himself. See below on Philo and Matt 5:48b, "as your Father in heaven is *teleios*."

26 The CEB continues the KJV "perfect" tradition.

27 The HCSB continues somewhat the KJV tradition: "a man of perfect integrity."

28. As noted before, they do still refer to an animal for sacrifice as "perfect" (Lev 22:21).

The chief alternative is "blameless." The intent of this change is difficult to discern. The *Oxford English Dictionary* defines it as, "Giving no cause for blame; undeserving of reproach; faultless, guiltless." This could, on the one hand, imply little difference from sinless perfection; i.e., can be charged with no single deviation. But one suspects that this idea of laying blame or reproach on someone refers more to their overall reputation. That is, such a person may have flaws and commit sins, but cannot be charged with serious blame before God or society. They are not deserving of major reproach. Their reputation remains whole. Whatever the precise intent of these translators, however, neither is "blameless" a perfect rendering of *tamim*, *shalem*, etc.

Other alternatives such as "loyal," "true," "pure," "fully committed," "wholehearted," and "completely faithful" seek to get at other aspects of this rich covenantal description of the person who walks as desired by God. Terms such as "whole," "complete," "intact," and "integrity" could be added, but the fact is, apart from the rich biblical-covenantal story, no single English word conveys the depth of the call to be *tamim*.

Chapter 3

Probing the Boundaries of Human Wholeness

> Life is not a spelling bee where no matter how many words you have gotten right, if you make one mistake you are disqualified. Life is more like a baseball season, where even the best team loses one-third of its games and even the worst team has its days of brilliance.[1]

Thus far we have examined OT texts that describe various individuals and groups as *tamim* or *shalem*. Such descriptive texts portraying covenantally integrated or perfect (KJV) people were surprisingly prevalent. To these we can now add prescriptive texts, which speak of *God's demand* for this blamelessness, maturity, wholehearted loyalty.

> When Abram was ninety-nine years old, the LORD appeared to Abram, and said to him, "I am God Almighty; walk before me, and be blameless (*tamim*)." (Gen 17:1, "perfect," KJV)

> You must remain completely loyal (*tamim*) to the LORD your God. (Deut 18:13, "perfect," KJV)

> For the eyes of the LORD range throughout the entire earth, to strengthen those whose heart is true (*shalem*) to him. (2 Chr 16:9a, "perfect," KJV)

---

1. Kushner, *How Good Do We Have to Be?*, 181.

Not only did the OT describe individuals as *tamim* and God as demanding the same, but such individuals could even assert their own blamelessness and appeal to their wholeness in prayer to God.

> The LORD rewarded me according to my righteousness; according to the cleanness of my hands he recompensed me. For I have kept the ways of the LORD, and have not wickedly departed from my God. For all his ordinances were before me, and his statutes I did not put away from me. I was blameless (*tamim*) before him, and I kept myself from guilt. (Ps 18:20–23)

> Remember now, O LORD, I implore you, how I have walked before you in faithfulness with a whole (*shalem*) heart, and have done what is good in your sight. (2 Kgs 20:3, "perfect," KJV)

> I am blameless (*tam*); I do not know myself; I loathe my life. It is all one; therefore I say, he destroys both the blameless (*tam*) and the wicked. (Job 9:21–22)

Christian readers, missing the covenantal context, too often hear such statements as boasting or as self-righteousness. But these were not deluded claims to sinlessness; these folks were quite aware that they can and do fall prey to sin. Rather, these are their expressions of allegiance to the gracious covenantal relationship God has placed them in. They "have not wickedly departed from" God and his ways. They "have walked before [God] in faithfulness." The claim to be *tamim* or to have a *shalem* heart amounts to, "I have sought to be faithful to your covenant, to conduct my life according to your ways."

Covenantal View: Only Two Options

There were in the covenantal mind only two options: you were one of the righteous or one of the wicked. One either walked in covenant with God or turned one's back on him. Being in covenant with God was a bit like being married: you either were or you weren't. The first Psalm lays out these two ways.

> Happy are those who do not follow the advice of the wicked, or take the path that sinners tread, or sit in the seat of scoffers; but their delight is in the law of the LORD, and on his law they meditate day and night. They are like trees planted by streams of water, which yield their fruit in its season, and their leaves do not wither. In all that they do, they prosper. The wicked are

> not so, but are like chaff that the wind drives away. Therefore the wicked will not stand in the judgment, nor sinners in the congregation of the righteous; for the LORD watches over the way of the righteous, but the way of the wicked will perish.

The alternative to a *tamim* life, to a pattern of god-fearing and righteous behavior, is illustrated by Solomon in the late stages of his reign. Although he appeared to have been a wise and godly king in 1 Kgs 1–10, chapter 11:1–13 portrays David's son as no longer walking with God.[2]

> For when Solomon was old, his wives turned away his heart after other gods; and his heart was not true (*shalem*) to the LORD his God, as was the heart of his father David. For Solomon followed Astarte the goddess of the Sidonians, and Milcom the abomination of the Ammonites. So Solomon did what was evil in the sight of the LORD, and did not completely follow the LORD, as his father David had done. (1 Kgs 11:4–6)

This last line would be better translated "did not follow him unreservedly" (NAB).[3] The point is that Solomon's obedience, in stark contrast to that of his father David, was not full and wholehearted. He was, instead, an evildoer at this final stage.

Of course, the reality for most of our lives is that we are not 100 percent righteous or 100 percent wicked. We are a mixed bag of good and bad actions, admirable and less-than-admirable intentions. So, how do we, or how does God, judge whether someone fits in the "righteous" or the "wicked" category, since these are the only two options? The traditional perfection model generally worked with a more mathematical scheme, a demand for 100 percent conformity. If all of one's outward actions and inward intentions were good, obedient, righteous all of the time, then one could be designated a righteous person. Such supposedly were the rare and exceptional perfect people in the OT.

---

2. See Knoppers, "Dynastic Oracle," 159–72. For a different view of chs. 1–10 ("scathing critique" utilizing ironic echoes of Deuteronomy), but with little difference in the resultant portrait of an apostate Solomon, see Hays, "Has the Narrator Come," 149–74.

3. The Hebrew construction used here for "follow unreservedly after" (*mille' 'khari*) is found numerous times to describe the faithful scout Caleb versus the other spies and the people who "despised" Yahweh (Num 14:22–24; also 32:11, 12; Deut 1:36; Josh 14:8, 9, 14). Like the latter, Solomon's failure to "follow unreservedly" means he did not follow the Lord's ways, rather than implying he did follow in a partial way.

Rather than an accounting-based scheme, the Bible favors a relational or covenantal framework. David and Solomon are good case studies, since the lives of both were clearly a mixed bag of good and bad, yet one was considered righteous, a "man after God's own heart" (1 Sam 13:14; Acts 13:22), and the other, at least according to 1 Kgs 11,[4] ultimately an apostate, although for much of his life a wise and admirable ruler. David lived his life as a whole in accord with the relationship to Yahweh. This was the path toward which his heart consistently inclined. His sins, as grievous as they were, constituted acts out-of-character as demonstrated by David's repentance from them. Solomon, on the other hand, seemed to start well ("Solomon loved the LORD, walking in the statutes of his father David," 1 Kgs 3:3a), although questions were regularly raised as to the depth of his commitment to Yahweh ("only, he sacrificed and offered incense at the high places," 1 Kgs 3:3b; also 10:26–29). However, Solomon's life ended on quite a different path (11:1–13). His heart turned to other gods and "was not true to the Lord." He abandoned the covenant relationship with Yahweh (11:11).[5] The difference between the two was their *continuing pattern* of behavior, their path of life. When taken as a whole, even when acknowledging temporary and serious departures, David's life proceeded on the Lord's path. Solomon's life as a whole, particularly his late and apparently never-changed abandonment of the Lord, trod a different path. It is not a single misstep that shatters one's perfection or righteousness—that can be repaired via turning back to the Lord and accessing forgiveness through the covenantal provisions—rather, it is a fundamental, life-defining turning from God to other gods, such as Solomon's idolatry. It is the repudiation of faith and of the fear of the Lord.

Humanly Attainable?

If David and many others in the OT era walked with God, does this mean that a God-pleasing life of obedience, biblical wholeness, or perfection, is actually attainable? And closely connected, how did they do this? Was

---

4. Admittedly, the parallel account in 1 Chr 28:1—2 Chr 9:31 omits Solomon's apostasy and portrays him as a righteous king.

5. The case of the historical Solomon is not quite so clear. As we noted, the apostate Solomon of 1 Kgs 11 does not appear in the Chronicles version. Christian tradition is equally uncertain, with Catholic teaching placing him in hell, while Dante's *Divine Comedy* finds him in heaven. See Brueggemann, *Solomon*.

this something they achieved by sheer (i.e., unaided) human ability and willpower? The answer to the first question should be clear enough from our survey in the previous chapter of perfect people in the OT. There we discovered quite a few biblical examples of people who did, in fact, achieve God's desire for human wholeness (*tamim*). They followed the will of God with integrity and were faithful to the relational covenant he had made with them. The simple fact is that God's instructions for his people's lives, his Torah or Law, was from the start intended to be something within their grasp, something doable. "Surely, this commandment that I am commanding you today is not too hard for you" (Deut 30:11).[6] Torah seems to think that even weak human beings can love, serve, and obey the Lord with wholeheartedness, with undivided loyalty, that they can be what God created them to be. The Psalms are full of such assertions.[7]

> Vindicate me, O LORD, for *I have walked in my integrity*, and *I have trusted in the LORD without wavering*. Prove me, O LORD, and try me; test my heart and mind. For your steadfast love is before my eyes, and *I walk in faithfulness to you*. *I do not sit with the worthless, nor do I consort with hypocrites; I hate the company of evildoers, and will not sit with the wicked. I wash my hands in innocence*, and go around your altar, O LORD, singing aloud a song of thanksgiving, and telling all your wondrous deeds. O LORD, I love the house in which you dwell, and the place where your glory abides. Do not sweep me away with sinners, nor my life with the bloodthirsty, those in whose hands are evil devices, and whose right hands are full of bribes. *But as for me, I walk in my integrity*; redeem me, and be gracious to me. My foot stands on level ground; in the great congregation I will bless the LORD. (Ps 26)

> The LORD rewarded me *according to my righteousness*; *according to the cleanness of my hands* he recompensed me. For *I have kept the ways of the LORD, and have not wickedly departed from my God. For all his ordinances were before me, and his statutes I did not put away from me. I was blameless before him, and I kept myself from guilt.* Therefore the LORD has recompensed me according to my righteousness, according to the cleanness of my hands in his sight. (Ps 18:20–24)

6. "Yahweh's commands remain doable." Lundbom, *Deuteronomy*, 823.

7. An outstanding treatment of such confessions of innocence and perfection in the Psalms in line with our thesis is LaRondelle, *Perfection and Perfectionism*, 137–58.

Of course, the OT is quite realistic about the tendency of Israel to go astray, to sin and to disobey. It certainly does not expect that children of Abraham will live sinless lives, nor are these assertions in the Psalms and elsewhere claims to such. What God and his Torah do expect is for the covenant partner to adhere faithfully to him . . . to "walk in integrity," to "trust without wavering," to "keep the ways of the Lord," and to avoid the ways of hypocrites and evildoers. The Psalmist is claiming to have adhered to the Lord and his ways. This is not a self-righteous boast intended to earn God's favor, but an expression of confident faith in Yahweh's covenantal favor. It is the weaker partner taking a stand on Yahweh's offer to bless the one who loves him and walks in his ways. "And I have sought to do this," says the weaker partner.

By What Power?

But was this covenant faithfulness, this wholehearted adherence, something they achieved by their own unaided human ability and willpower? That certainly does not seem to be the way they viewed matters.

> This God is my strong refuge and has made my way blameless (*tamim*). (2 Sam 22:33, ESV)

> Grant to Solomon my son a whole (*shalem*) heart that he may keep your commandments, your testimonies, and your statutes. (1 Chr 29:19, ESV)

> . . . God who equipped me with strength and made my way blameless (*tamim*). (Ps 18:32, ESV)

They recognized that their ability to make such choices and to follow the right path must ultimately be traced to God's own working within them. If asked, "Was this God or you?" they would surely have answered "yes."

The 100 Percent Obedience Issue Once Again

One of the key questions driving this study is: Does the OT, the Torah, the Sinaitic covenant, demand 100 percent conformity to its laws in order to be considered righteous? And, related to this question: Does it see such acceptable obedience as attainable? This study argues for a "no" answer to the first question (100 percent required?) and "yes" to the second (attainable?). The flaws and sins of those termed blameless (*tamim*) and righteous have been encountered at every turn (Noah, Job, David, etc.), yet they are still called blameless and righteous.

Before leaving these questions, it may be helpful to hear and interact with the work of Andrew Das, who has mounted perhaps the strongest argument for the opposite position, i.e., perfect obedience *was* required and, understandably, *was not* humanly attainable. He notes that quite a few OT texts demand obedience to "*all* these commandments," not just to some or most. Wouldn't this point to a more complete or perfect obedience, he asks? Exactly such a demand for error-free, perfect obedience, he finds in Deut 27–30, esp. 27:26, which Paul cites in Gal 3:10.[8]

> Cursed be anyone who does not uphold the words of this law by observing them. (Deut 27:26)

> For all who rely on the works of the law are under a curse; for it is written, "Cursed is everyone who does not observe and obey all the things written in the book of the law." (Gal 3:10)

According to Das, Paul has more than simply the single quoted verse in mind since the apostle adds "in the book of" and changes "the words" to "the things written." To understand Paul's point, we must interpret Deut 27:26 within the flow of its broader context in chapters 27–30. To set the contextual stage, Das notes the pessimistic beginning of the book— Moses reminds the people of their rebellious nature (1:9–46). Then, just before the lengthy central section, the detailed legal code (11:31—26:15), Moses reminds them of the golden calf incident at the giving of the Law (9:1—10:1). Thus, the covenant laws come with the anticipation that Israel will be unwilling and unable to keep them. This pessimistic mood over the whole is heightened when Mount Ebal, the mountain of curse (27:13), not a neutral or positive site, is designated for the later erection of a stone altar of remembrance (27:1–8). The threats of curse there (sixty-six verses) far outweigh the hope of blessing (fourteen verses) in chapters 27–28. Thus, for Das, the assumption lurking just under the surface throughout Deuteronomy is a negative one, namely that God's people are unable to obey all that is written, and this is exactly Paul's implied premise in Gal 3:10.[9] After this lengthy stage-setting, Das then comes to the "rigorous" character of the obedience demanded. Even secret and less egregious sins (e.g., moving a boundary marker) can "jeopardize the

---

8. Das, "Galatians 3:10," 203–23, esp. 205–12; also Das, *Paul, the Law, and the Covenant*. See also the earlier treatment by Deissler, "Perfection," 658–63.

9. Das, "Galatians 3:10," 209–10.

community's relationship to God," which demonstrates "the Law must be obeyed *in its entirety* and not just in public or heinous matters."[10] Then, finally, he comes to the significance of "all." After noting how Deuteronomy regularly speaks of obedience to "all the commandments," he concludes, "This repeated emphasis on doing 'all' that God commands poses a problem for those who deny the Deuteronomic command to obey God's Law *perfectly*."[11] Lastly, he rejects Sanders's rejoinder that this "all" points to *comprehensive* (entire versus selective) rather than perfect or *exhaustive* (every command without failure) obedience.[12]

Das has mounted the most sustained argument that Deuteronomy as a whole, and 27:26 in particular, demands perfect obedience, exhaustive and without failure, and that it is fundamentally pessimistic regarding human nature and such obedience. The following critique takes his points in order.

1. The literary context of Deut 27–30 assumes a pessimistic stance toward Israel's (humanity's) ability to keep Torah.

Das is formally correct that Deut 27, both its context and its content, is pessimistic as to Israel's future keeping of God's covenant commands. As others note, "Deuteronomy 27 expects Israel to fail and disobey. It is pessimistic at this level."[13] Acknowledging a *historical* pessimism (Israel *will not* obey) is not, however, the same as asserting an *anthropological*

---

10. Das, "Galatians 3:10," 210, original italics.

11. Das, "Galatians 3:10," 211, original italics.

12. The rationale given for this rejection is not clear (211–12). He seems to be objecting to Sanders's point that merciful atonement was provided in covenantal nomism for sinning that fell short of fundamental repudiation of God and his ways, and that this implies less-than-perfect obedience is acceptable ("God's mercy to the basically righteous but not always obedient members of Israel," Sanders, *Paul and Palestinian Judaism*, 422). Das's rejection of this stance is clarified elsewhere; in spite of such forgiveness and mercy, "the people's sins were never ignored but always had to be reconciled with God's will through a process of atonement and repentance. God's demands were never set aside. Indeed, it is perfection of conduct that remains the ideal." Das, *Paul, the Law, and the Covenant*, 15.

13. Barker, "Theology of Deuteronomy 27," 280; see 280–94. The larger question, however, of Deuteronomy's overall pessimism or optimism regarding Israel's prospects for obedience remains, in fact, unresolved. On the optimistic side: McBride, "Polity of the Covenant People," 229–44; and Mayes, "On Describing the Purpose," 13–33. On the pessimistic side: Stulman, "Encroachment in Deuteronomy," 613–32, and Stulman, "Sex and Familial Crimes," 47–63. For a readable overview (from the more pessimistic side), see Millar, "Ethics and Human Nature," 161–80.

pessimism (Israel *cannot* obey). *Why* is Deuteronomy pessimistic about Israel's future obedience? Das, after nicely sketching the historical pessimism in Deuteronomy, makes a leap to anthropological pessimism. "Deuteronomy 27–30 . . . offers a pessimistic appraisal *of native human ability to observe the Law*."[14] Das does not justify this leap, but probably considers it self-evident along with the long-standing tradition that imports a theological explanation: "the law primarily and chiefly brings a curse upon man *because of the sinfulness of his nature*."[15] The closest Deuteronomy comes, however, to providing a rationale is the mention of Israel's "stubbornness" (9:27).[16] However, this simply describes Israel's observable behavior and attitude; it does not seek to explain what lies behind this hardness. There is no need to import a more-developed doctrine of human sinfulness to explain the passage; its pessimism comes from the historical pattern of Israel's behavior.[17]

2. Even secret and less egregious transgressions can "jeopardize the community's relationship to God," which demonstrates "the Law must be obeyed *in its entirety* and not just in public or heinous matters."[18]

Again, Das is correct that these curses come due to actions that normally remain hidden from public view; but, again, wrong as to the reason. Rather than implying even a single small and hidden infraction brings the curse, such hidden sins are highlighted "to remind Israel that Yahweh sees and knows what happens in secret. The criminal who escapes the wrath of the community will not escape the wrath of God. The repeated demand that all the people shall say, 'Amen!' had the effect that all wrongdoers are obliged to pronounce their own curse."[19] As Barker

---

14. Das, "Galatians 3:10," 205, emphasis added.

15. Delitzsch and Keil, *Pentateuch*, 3:432, italics added. Cited in Barker, "Theology of Deuteronomy 27," 284.

16. The MT uses a rare nominal form derived from the verbal stem meaning "be hard," and used repeatedly to refer to Israel's stiff neck or hard spirit, i.e., her stubbornness vis-à-vis God (Exod 32:9; Deut 10:16; Judg 2:19; 2 Kgs 17:14; Neh 9:16).

17. Nor did the later rabbis feel the need to develop a doctrine of original sin. Moore, *Judaism*, 1:474–78.

18. Das, "Galatians 3:10," 210, italics original.

19. Wright, *Deuteronomy*, 277, emphasis original.

notes, "The curses thus function to warn those who think they could safely violate the covenant in private."[20]

3. Reference to obeying "*all* the commandments" means exhaustive (perfect) obedience.

Indeed, reference to keeping or obeying "all" the commands is widespread throughout the OT.[21] Careful examination, however, reveals that this phrasing (*all* the commands) means nothing different than "keeping/obeying the commands" without addition of the "all"[22] and is also identical in meaning to keeping/obeying the *covenant*[23] or obeying *God*.[24] The equivalent meaning of these phrases may be seen clearly in Deut 27:26—28:1.

> "Cursed be anyone who does not uphold the words of this law by observing them." All the people shall say, "Amen!" If you will only obey the LORD your God, by diligently observing all his commandments that I am commanding you today, the LORD your God will set you high above all the nations of the earth.

The first line is the basis of Paul's quotation in Gal 3 and speaks of upholding and observing the words of this law without "all" (though Paul's LXX quote does add it). The second and third lines pick up the identical thought but now expressed as "obey the Lord your God" and "observing *all* his commandments." No difference in scope is perceptible between these differing ways of expressing what is expected of the people in relation to God's law/commands/voice. The addition of "all" in 28:1 does *not* indicate a more rigorous obedience than the simple command without "all."

---

20. Barker, "Theology of Deuteronomy 27," 289.

21. See Gen 6:22; Exod 15:26; Lev 4:22; 26:14, 15; Num 15:22, 40; Deut 5:31; 12:28; Josh 1:7; 1 Kgs 9:4; 2 Kgs 18:12; 2 Chr 7:17.

22. See, for example, Exod 15:26 where Moses tells the people they must "give heed to [God's] commandments and keep all his statutes" without intending any difference in scope by the addition of "all" in the second phrase.

23. 2 Kgs 18:12, for example, explains "because they did not obey the voice of the LORD their God but transgressed his covenant" with reference to "all that Moses the servant of the LORD had commanded." Similarly Lev 26:15 where "spurn my statutes" and "not observe all my commandments" equals "break my covenant."

24. Lev 26:14, for example, parallels "if you will not obey me [God]" with "[if you] and do not observe all these commandments."

It may be instructive to bring in the related phrasing, "this entire command."

> Then the LORD commanded us to <u>observe all these statutes</u>, to fear the LORD our God, for our lasting good, so as to keep us alive, as is now the case. If we diligently <u>observe this entire commandment</u> before the LORD our God, as he has commanded us, we will be in the right. (Deut 6:24–25)

This second underlined phrase refers to the multitude of Torah statutes as "this entire commandment," as though it were a singular whole rather than a multitude. Just like the covenant, the commandments, though many, are a package deal. Selective obedience—I'll take these but not those—is not an option; true obedience must be comprehensive of the whole will of God, not merely part of it. If there is any nuance added through the appending of "all," it will be found in highlighting the demand for comprehensive (versus selective) obedience, but it is clearly no more "rigorous" (e.g., 100 percent versus partial or slightly less-than-perfect obedience) than what is expressed by the synonymous phrasing without "all."

Thus, it turns out that Sanders and most Jewish interpreters have been correct all along: Torah does not demand flawless obedience in order to be considered righteous, blameless, or holy.

What Level of Obedience if Not 100 Percent?

But if such blamelessness and righteousness can tolerate some sinning, how much sinning are we talking about? Unfortunately, to even put the question this way (how much? what number or percentage?) risks sidetracking us into overly mathematical ways of thinking. The fact is, the OT does not give us such a number or percentage. When it considers people to be blameless, to have kept the commandments, it is not putting every act and thought individually under a microscope, as it were, looking atomistically for a single word or deed out of place. Instead, it views a human life holistically, as a single whole. One's life is a "path," a "way." What is the trend of that life? In spite of fits and starts, where was it heading? How is this person relating to God and others? When viewed as a whole, would we, or would God, describe this life with "loves and follows God and his ways"? This holistic perspective means that single deviations, individual acts of sin, do not necessarily change the overall judgment. If these acts are out-of-character, the truly blameless person will eventually realize this and change their ways. On the other hand, a single transgression can indeed lead to judgment and destruction, *if* that single act is indicative of a lifestyle, an evil heart, a whole pattern headed in the wrong direction. This is why one reads such dire warnings against any single sin and transgression; rather than an act out-of-character, such a deed may be the pointer to a wicked heart and life.[25]

So, to the question, "How much obedience is enough?" the Bible refuses to give a measurable or mathematical answer, as though 95 percent is a good score, but 90 percent doesn't cut the mustard. The holy, whole, righteous person walks with God . . . their heart is pledged in allegiance to love and honor him in all their ways. Right living is a relationship. And this relationship does not demand perfect conformity from the partner made of frail clay.

This all may strike some as a far too lax view of sin. Does the OT really "tolerate" such a modicum of sinning in the lives of the righteous? Doesn't such a view open the door to some form of cheap grace that says, "It's not such a big deal if I disobey." Clearly, if we are considering how we should and will behave (i.e., future, planned behavior), there is no toleration whatsoever. To intend anything other than wholehearted commitment (*tamim*) to God and his ways is to consciously turn away from him. This is the sign of a heart that is not whole, that does not genuinely love the divine partner.

The reality, however, is that we frail creatures of dust do, in fact, go astray . . . and not always infrequently or insignificantly. Does the OT "tolerate" this? Again, if speaking of one's intent looking forward, the answer is "no." But, when looking back upon accomplished transgression, the OT points the sinner to repentance, forgiveness, and atonement. God "tolerates" us, and relates to us with compassionate understanding of our frail nature. Are there, some may object, no consequences? Of course, just as in any relationship. But to explore this would take us too far astray at the moment.[26]

---

25. On this holistic view of one's life and deeds, see Yinger, *Paul, Judaism, and Judgment*, 284; and Rössler, *Gesetz und Geschichte*, 87, 100–105.

26. The results of sinning in the OT can stretch from divine forgiving and forgetting, to painful discipline, and even to death.

Probing the Boundaries of Human Wholeness

Christian Theological Queries

Christian theologians will almost surely want to pose at least two important challenges at this stage in our investigation. First, if the OT considers righteousness before God to be attainable by sinful, fallen human beings, what has happened to the doctrine of human depravity, of Adam's fall into sinfulness? How can I assert that a fair number of these OT saints were righteous and *tamim*, when plenty of passages seem to claim the opposite: "no one living is righteous before you" (Ps 143:2)? And, second, if such (saving) righteousness was attainable under the Mosaic covenant, doesn't that make the coming of Christ unnecessary? Why would he need to come to save sinners if those sinners had a perfectly viable way of salvation already laid out for them in Torah?

What About Human Depravity?

So, first, what about human sinfulness? The OT is wonderfully candid about its flawed heroes. For example, the "man after God's own heart," David, turns out to be capable of premeditated murder and abuse of power for sexual gratification (2 Sam 11). David would appear to have no illusions about the depth of his wickedness in this regard.[27]

> Wash me thoroughly from my iniquity, and cleanse me from my sin. For I know my transgressions, and my sin is ever before me. Against you, you alone, have I sinned, and done what is evil in your sight, so that you are justified in your sentence and blameless when you pass judgment. Indeed, I was born guilty, a sinner when my mother conceived me. (Ps 51:2–5)

Yet, he can say not too long after this horrific behavior:

> The LORD rewarded me according to my righteousness; according to the cleanness of my hands he recompensed me. For I have kept the ways of the LORD, and have not wickedly departed from my God. For all his ordinances were before me, and from his statutes I did not turn aside. I was blameless before him, and I kept myself from guilt. Therefore the LORD has recompensed me according to my righteousness, according to my cleanness in his sight. (2 Sam 22:21–25)

---

27. The traditional ascription of Ps 51 reads: "A Psalm of David, when the prophet Nathan came to him, after he had gone in to Bathsheba."

This same odd juxtaposition occurs throughout the OT. The seemingly unavoidable wickedness of human beings, including Jews, is echoed everywhere, beginning with Adam and Eve, continuing through all humanity at Noah's time, and highlighted especially in Israel who is repeatedly "stick-necked" and rebellious against the Lord. Add to these the many explicit statements about human sinfulness, and it is crystal clear . . . humans are creatures who sin: "no one living is righteous before you" (Ps 143:2b).[28] Yet, as we noticed in the previous chapter, many of these same folks were called (and saw themselves as) *tsaddiq* (righteous) or *tam* (innocent). These juxtapositions are jarring, to say the least.

Some might see here a hopeless contradiction, but Henry McKeating surely got things right when he explained the tension as follows:

> Statements that God's salvation is only for the righteous may be found side by side in the same psalms with confessions of sin and requests for forgiveness. . . . The sins of such a psalmist are the sins of a believer. The fact that he has failed in particular instances is not inconsistent with his general desire to please God. His are not defiant sins, "sins with a high hand." They are not signs of a contempt of God. . . . They are sins *within* that covenant, or lapses from obedience by a man whose ultimate will is to maintain that covenant. Such a man may know that he is a sinner, and yet appeal to his integrity and uprightness.[29]

> Occasionally a writer is so conscious of his dependence on the grace of God that . . . he will assert that no man *can* be righteous before God, no one can deserve salvation. . . . In comparison with God [Ps 143:1], even the faithful member of the holy people is not pure (see also Ps 130:3; and Ps 51).[30]

This last point seems to move beyond the simple affirmation that everyone *does* sin, to the assertion that no one is *capable* of doing anything else. However, McKeating adds that these sorts of Psalm-statements

> are rare, not in their acknowledgement of sin but in their preoccupation with it. Other psalmists, though equally conscious of the ubiquity of sin, are determined to be cheerful about it [e.g., Ps 65:2–3]. . . . This is not to minimize the seriousness of sin, but to recognize, humbly and thankfully, that though offences will indeed come . . . God does willingly forgive them. Man's sin

---

28. See also Ps 14:3; 25:7; 51:6–7; 130:3; Job 4:17; 9:2; 15:14; 25:4; etc.
29. McKeating, "Divine Forgiveness," 73.
30. McKeating, "Divine Forgiveness," 76.

is inevitable because he is weak. But because God understands this He is the readier to forgive (see Ps 78:38–39; Ps 103:4 [we are but dust]).[31]

But what has happened to the doctrine of human depravity, that Adam's sin led to a change in the very nature of human beings, such that we are no longer capable of righteousness, but are by nature sinners? Since this doctrine is primarily an issue of Christian (not Jewish) theology,[32] we will deal with it further when studying Paul later, esp. Rom 5 ("just as sin came into the world through one man"). For our purposes in this chapter we can simply note that the story of Adam and Eve's sin in the garden plays little role in subsequent OT thinking. Gen 3 is not picked up and reflected upon. The story is certainly about disobedience to God ("don't eat") and its consequences ("you shall die"), and it sets the stage for the reenactment of similar relationship-shattering rebellion by Noah's generation, Israel, etc. But as John Toews notes in *The Story of Original Sin*,

> There is no hint that Adam's moral condition is fundamentally changed by his act of disobedience or that his essential human or genetic nature was essentially altered. The changes effected by the punishment for Adam and Eve's mistrust and disobedience are entirely physical, the pains and struggles of human life.... [T]he story does not speak of a "fall." ... The interpretation of Genesis 3 as a fall reflects a much later Christian understanding which has been read back into the text.[33]

Christian readers may be surprised, but OT scholars of various theological stripes are now pretty much agreed that Gen 3 did not intend to teach an ontological "fall" of humanity in the garden.[34] The moral

---

31. McKeating, "Divine Forgiveness," 77.

32. Although quite diverse, mainstream Jewish tradition is reflected in 2 *Bar* 54:15, 19: "For, although Adam sinned first and has brought death upon all who were not in his own time, yet each of them who has been born from him has prepared for himself the coming torment.... Adam is, therefore, not the cause, except only for himself, but each of us has become our own Adam."

33. Toews, *Story of Original Sin*, 13.

34. Besides Toews (above), see esp. Westermann, *Genesis*, 1:276–78; Brueggemann, *Genesis*, 41 ["Nothing could be more remote from the narrative itself."]; and Arnold, *Genesis*, 62 ["Although philosophical and theological treatments routinely refer to this passage as 'the fall' of humankind, the Hebrew word for 'fall' (*npl*) is not used here. Nor is this concept used anywhere in Israel's Scriptures to relate this passage to humanity's fall from a state of grace infecting all subsequent humans."]. The Orthodox tradition favored human freedom over Augustine's version of corrupted human nature. For a

nature of humanity is not portrayed there as suffering some essential corruption or change. This is not the story of the origin of human sinful nature. Instead, it is the story of the first disobedience. This sets the stage for the subsequent human history, and particularly Israel's history, which both mirror Adam's disobedience.[35] With notable exceptions (Noah, Abraham, etc.) humanity and Israel consistently go astray. They are indeed, sinners, but are such by choice, not by constitution.

What About Christ's Cross?

A second question that Christian theologians are sure to raise runs as follows: if such righteousness was attainable under the Mosaic covenant, wouldn't that make the coming of Christ unnecessary? Why would he need to come to save sinners if those sinners had a perfectly viable way of salvation, of being acceptably righteous before God, already laid out for them in Torah?[36] The fuller examination of the reason for Christ's coming and sacrifice will have to await the later chapters dealing with the NT.

Here it is enough to state that in the OT the ability to live a righteous life does not obviate the need for continued sacrifice and atonement. At the very least, human weakness will require repeated atonement for sin. And more to the point of messiah's necessity, Israel's repeated failure would lead the prophets to expect that God would do something new in the future to rectify this waywardness. The NT sees this atoning necessity fulfilled in Christ.

---

recent defense of original sin, see the essays in Madueme and Reeves, *Adam, the Fall, and Original Sin*.

35. "The Adam story mirrors Israel's story from exodus to exile. . . . He is proto-Israel—a preview of coming attractions." See Enns, *Evolution of Adam*, ch. 4, "Israel and Primordial Time."

36. As Augustine noted, "The good news that Jesus saves had as its corollary that all without exception *need* saving, which means that human sinfulness must be viewed as a congenital state and not just as a condition we acquire through our own individual actions subsequent to birth." McFarland, "Original Sin," 306. A strong impetus for Augustine's doctrine was the fact that the church baptized infants whose sin needing to be cleansed must have been inherent rather than acquired.

Chapter 4

Expanding the Foundation: Wholeness in Jewish Tradition

God knows better than to expect perfection from us.[1]

The Hebrew Scriptures formed the foundation for all subsequent Jewish theologizing about human wholeness, but we dare not think that Jewish reflection on this topic stopped at that foundational point. During the centuries leading up to the Common Era, often referred to as the Second Temple period,[2] influences such as continuing exile and diaspora as well as powerful Hellenistic encroachment led to significant developments in Jewish thought.[3] It was, for instance, during this period that belief in resurrection gained a strong foothold. Some have argued that it was particularly during this intertestamental period of Jewish reflection that views regarding the necessity of flawless obedience hardened among some Jewish groups; and this supposedly led to the views of Jewish groups like the Pharisees who were opposed by Jesus and then Paul. Thus, we will be particularly concerned in this chapter to see if and how Jewish language and thought regarding (perfect) obedience and human wholeness developed.

---

1. Kushner, *How Good Do We Have to Be?*, 10.
2. So called since it covers roughly the period during which the rebuilt Jewish temple stood; i.e., sixth century BCE to first century CE.
3. Nickelsburg, *Ancient Judaism*.

Does the LXX Change the Picture?

Our look at Jewish foundations has focused thus far on the sacred texts composed in the Hebrew language. However, beginning with Alexander's conquest of the Persian Empire and Palestine, Greek language and philosophy became a growing influence on Jewish thinking. During the third to first centuries BCE, Jews translated the Hebrew Bible into Greek, commonly referred to as the Septuagint (LXX).[4] A major task of this section is to ascertain whether this translation of Hebrew terms into Greek resulted in any changes to the conception of perfection or human wholeness we have been studying. This will be of particular importance when we move to wholeness in the NT, since the latter was not only influenced centrally by the OT, but its authors were steeped in the language of the LXX.

The LXX translators employed an assortment of Greek words to render texts using *t-m-m*, *sh-l-m* and the other related Hebrew terms. The widespread use of *t-m-m* for the cultic requirement that sacrificial animals be unblemished is in nearly every instance translated with Greek *amōmos* (without defect or fault; Exod 29:1; Lev 1:3; Num 6:14; etc.).[5] This same Greek word is also used more than a dozen times to translate *t-m-m* and cognates when related to persons and their ways (e.g., 2 Sam 22:24; Ps 15:2; 18:23; Prov 20:7). On several occasions in reference to persons, especially in the book of Job, *amemptos* (blameless, without reproach) appears instead of *amōmos* as the translation of *t-m-m* (e.g., Gen 17:1; Job 1:1). In addition, quite a number of further terms show up as translations of *t-m-m*.[6] And, finally, *teleios* (complete, perfect) is used for *t-m-m* on a few particularly notable occasions, such as Noah's

---

4. Named after the tradition of its alleged marvelous simultaneous translation by seventy scholars. For convenience we use "LXX" to refer to the version of this Greek OT found in MSS Alexandrinus, Vatincanus, and Sinaiticus, and conveniently reproduced in Rahlfs, *Septuaginta*. For further information, see Silva and Jobes, *Invitation to the Septuagint*.

5. The one exception is Exod 12:5, which uses *teleios*. The predominant use of *amōmos* for this cultic requirement is surprising, since its use in this connection was "alien to class[ical] Gk.," which normally used it to refer to someone's irreproachable character (Hauck, "*Amōmos*," 4:830). The choice of *amōmos* by the LXX translators would appear to stem from the similarity of sound to Hebrew *mum* (unblemished) which was used in relation to sacrificial requirements (cf. Lev 22:20–21). See Du Plessis, *Teleios*, 94–95.

6. A partial selection includes *katharos* (pure, Gen 20:5), *hosiotēs* (holiness, 1 Kgs 9:4), *akakia* (innocence, Ps 26[LXX: 25]: 1), and *haplōs* (simply, Prov 10:9).

completeness (Gen 6:9) and God's call to Israel to be whole (Deut 18:13; also 2 Sam 22:26). Thus, there is no single Greek term used to render *t-m-m* in reference to persons, and the choice depended perhaps largely on context or on the preference of different translators.

In passages relevant to our study, the other main Hebrew word, *sh-l-m*, is used primarily, as we noted, in connection with one's heart: "Your hearts must be fully committed to the LORD our God" (1 Kgs 8:61). Most often in these instances the LXX translators chose *teleios* (1 Kgs 8:61; 11:4; 1 Chr 28:9; etc.), but sometimes reached for other terms such as *plērēs* (full, 2 Kgs 20:3), *alēthinos* (true, Isa 38:3), etc. These appear to be synonymous with the ever-recurring "with *all* one's heart" in the sense of a "whole" heart.[7]

But do these varying Greek terms for human wholeness or wholeheartedness introduce subtle differences to the meaning of this concept? While there is rarely true synonymity of terms between two languages, in these cases the overlap is substantial. Thus, just as *t-m-m* pictured that which is whole and complete and fulfills its intended purpose and shape, so *teleios* refers to something or someone who is finished and whole and "has attained the goal (*telos*)."[8] Greek *amemptos* and *amōmos* (blameless, without reproach) put the emphasis on how such a complete walk is viewed by others and by God, while *haplous/haplotēs* (simple, single-minded) highlights undivided character, and *alēthinos* picks up the "genuine[ness]" of that which is *t-m-m* or *sh-l-m*.

From this data we learn two things of importance for our study. First, the Greek translation of the OT does not appear to have changed the meaning and thought of the Hebrew original in terms of our subject. The senses of completeness, totality, maturity, unblemished, and irreproachable important to the Hebrew context are also found when translated into Greek. There is no movement toward a sense of flawlessly perfect obedience or "moral immaculacy."[9] As Du Plessis concludes, the LXX continues "one fundamental motif, that of entirety and wholeness in a divine relationship."[10] This is not to say that the Greek terms are exact

---

7. Most often LXX *holos*, Deut 4:29; 1 Sam 12:24; etc.

8. Hartin, *Spirituality of Perfection*, 22. On *telos* as the foundation for the meaning of *teleios*, see esp. Du Plessis, *Teleios*, 36–73.

9. The determinative study with which our results are in agreement remains Du Plessis, *Teleios*, 94–103, quotation p. 196.

10. Du Plessis, *Teleios*, 98.

mirrors of the semantic content of the Hebrew terms,[11] but the overlapping ranges of meaning are such that there occurs no perceptible shift in meaning when the Hebrew texts are rendered in Greek.

And, second, there is a wide variety of Greek terminology available, with no single word dominating, and several words (*amōmos, amemptos, teleios*, among others) being used in largely overlapping or synonymous ways. Thus, later Jewish authors who wish to speak/write in Greek about a person's completeness, integrity, wholeness, perfection, would not necessarily gravitate to a single Greek word, but could choose from a range of terms with overlapping meaning.[12]

The Dead Sea Scrolls and Perfection

Another important window into Jewish thought about human wholeness during this intertestamental era comes from the DSS produced largely in Hebrew from the third century BCE to the first century CE.[13] Perhaps no other body of Jewish literature latched on to perfection as do the scrolls from Qumran.[14] Sanders opens his discussion of the scrolls with the paradox that has become commonplace among scholars when commenting on this literature, namely "between urging the members to walk perfectly, on the one hand, and saying, on the other, that man is worthless and that perfection of way comes only from God."[15] Repeatedly the scrolls refer to members as "men of perfect holiness" and those "of perfect way" or require of them a probationary entry period "for two

---

11. So, for example, Du Plessis notes that Greek *teleios* involves seeing or accurately perceiving the ideal, the perfect, whereas Jewish tradition was hesitant to pick up the notion of seeing the invisible God; Du Plessis, *Teleios*, 102–3. Klein suggests the LXX generally avoided *teleios* for *tamim* because the former included the thought of moral progress ("allmählich[e] Entwicklung zur Vollkommenheit"), while the latter did not. Klein, *Ein vollkommenes Werk*, 58. While this may be accurate in reference to the usage for sacrificial animals, it is less so in reference to persons.

12. As Du Plessis notes, the "compound idea is more important than singular terminological comparison"; Du Plessis, *Teleios*, 94.

13. A good introduction to the scrolls is VanderKam, *Dead Sea Scrolls Today*.

14. Among the many treatments of this topic, see Rigaux, "Révélation des mystères," 237–62; Deasley, "Idea of Perfection"; Walters, *Perfection in New Testament Theology*, 42–65; and Deasley, *Shape of Qumran Theology*, 210–54.

15. Sanders, *Paul and Palestinian Judaism*, 287–88; and for his entire discussion of perfection and the DSS, 287–98.

full years in perfect behavior."¹⁶ Thus, more than other Jewish sects, the self-understanding and behavioral norms of the Dead Sea community were wrapped up inextricably with their commitment to this perfection or human wholeness. Yet, equally prominent are confessions of sinfulness such as the following.

> What is flesh compared to this?
> What creature of clay can do wonders?
> He is in sin from his maternal womb,
> and in guilty iniquity right to old age.
> But I know that justice does not belong to man
> nor the perfect [*tom*] path to the son of man. (1QH XII, 29–30)

What exactly was this understanding of perfection which seemed to hold both that it was attainable and that sinful humans could not achieve it? Sanders critiques a number of proposed ways of resolution.¹⁷ Perhaps, for instance, there were differing, contradictory views in the sectarian community.¹⁸ This fails, however, since both sides of this tension appear in the same writings. Or, perhaps literary genre explains the difference. "The hymn-prayers naturally emphasize the inability of man and his worthlessness *before God*, while 1QS 1–9 and CD emphasize what he must do to remain a member of the covenant in good standing."¹⁹ This is, however, at best a partial solution, since both notes can be struck in the same hymn (e.g., 1QH IX, 27, 36). Sanders then seeks a theological resolution.

> The requirement of legal perfection is set within a context of gratuity. A man is purified of transgression and has his "way" established only by the grace of God, but he is expected to maintain legal perfection.... [T]he statements that one's perfection of way is the work of God serve to bridge the gap between the confession of man's iniquity and inability and the requirement to walk perfectly.²⁰

---

16. CD B XX, 2, 5, 7; 1QHa IX, 36; 1QS VIII, 10. These and many other such "perfect" references typically use some form of the stem *t-m-m*. Translation and numbering system of DSS texts follow García Martínez, *The Dead Sea Scrolls Translated*.

17. Sanders, *Paul and Palestinian Judaism*, 291–92.

18. Black suggests at least two "philosophies" in Qumran, a "legalistic puritanism or perfectionism" and a prophetic position grounded in grace or divine help. Black, *Scrolls and Christian Origins*, 124–26.

19. Sanders, *Paul and Palestinian Judaism*, 292.

20. Sanders, *Paul and Palestinian Judaism*, 293.

Problematically, throughout his discussion Sanders presumes perfection "is clearly defined as not transgressing at all," i.e., sinless or flawless behavior.[21] It is this reliance seemingly on an English-based understanding of perfection that creates a confusing tension with the acknowledgment of transgressions among the supposedly perfect, and that leads him to mitigate this expectation through grace and atonement. Thus, ultimately for Sanders the scrolls do not actually demand truly perfect obedience, even though he thinks they seem to speak this way. Hence he can enlist the scrolls to support his argument that no forms of Judaism required perfect obedience (with one exception, 4 Ezra). As we will see in a moment, I think Sanders is correct that the Qumran documents did not demand perfection, but wrong in the way he gets there.

Andrew Das and Perfection in the Scrolls

Before heading there, however, we should hear from those who argue that the scrolls do, indeed, demand this impossibly high standard of flawless obedience. We will follow the argument of Andrew Das, since he is responding explicitly to Sanders.[22] Das largely echoes Sanders that a whole host of texts appear to demand perfect or "strict and absolute" obedience. Following Braun, he gives emphasis to the heavy use of "all" in many of these texts ("obey *all* these commands"), and thus holds that the sectarians "*intensified* the requirement of obedience" vis-à-vis the OT.[23] He rejects, however, Sanders's contention that atonement provided a mitigation of this rigid and unrealistic demand. First, he notes rightly that some transgressions, especially intentional ones, could not be thus mitigated, but resulted in automatic expulsion from the community.[24] And, second, in direct opposition to Sanders's mitigation, for Das the

---

21. Sanders, *Paul and Palestinian Judaism*, 288, with ref. to 1QS III, 9–11; 1QH XIV, 17. He speaks similarly of it as "legal perfection" (292), "legalism" (293) and "legalistic works-righteousness" (291), "legally perfect" (297), and adds that a sect-member "obeys the law to the most minute detail" (296).

22. Das, *Paul, the Law, and the Covenant*, 17–23. Others who find perfect obedience demanded in the DSS include: Black, *Scrolls and Christian Origins*, 118–24; Walters, *Perfection in New Testament Theology*, 42–65; and Condra, *Salvation for the Righteous Revealed*. Black attributes this unrealistic expectation "to the unreal world of apocalyptic fantasy in which the sect lived" (122), while Braun alleges inconsistency.

23. Das, *Paul, the Law, and the Covenant*, 23; emphasis original.

24. On intentional and unintentional sins, see Anderson, "Intentional and Unintentional Sin," 49–64.

provision of atonement instead "confirms" the sect's convictions about perfection. Das does not spell this last point out as fully as one might like, but his reasoning seems to be, "Each sin had to be atoned for in some way for the individual to be restored to a proper status as an individual of 'perfect righteousness.'"[25] But note how he appears to have switched the terms of the argument. When asserting the sect's demand for perfection, he speaks of actual behavior ("each sin"); but when considering restored perfection via atonement, he means an ascribed status. As to actual behavior, they are clearly no longer perfect. Whatever his logic, Das has admitted that the sect did not actually demand perfect obedience, sinless performance, even if they did require some sort of righteous status.[26]

The one thing nearly all these interpreters agree on is that the scrolls *sound like* they demand and expect perfection of community members. But this observation is already skewed by overreliance on the English gloss "perfection." For, in fact, the scrolls speak nowhere of perfection as understood through this English term. Instead, they speak in all these places of those who are *tamim*, wholeheartedly, consistently, fully devoted to the God of Israel and the new covenant as promulgated by the Teacher and laid out in the scrolls.[27] In light of the Hebrew vocabulary chosen in the scrolls as well as the OT tradition reviewed in the previous chapter, there need be no expectation of an unrealistic sinlessness when they refer to themselves as a "house of *tamim*." As the ancient OT worthies were sound, complete, wholeheartedly loyal to Yahweh, so the sectarians as

---

25. Das, *Paul, the Law, and the Covenant*, 20. This reading receives confirmation when in a later section dealing with rabbinic literature he takes issue with Sanders' contention that the allowance for sacrifice and repentance show that perfection was not expected. "In fact, the reverse is true. The entire system . . . was designed to rectify the situation caused by disobedience of any of God's laws and commands. The very existence of this system shows that the rabbis saw God's law as demanding perfect obedience. Failure in any respect had to be rectified" (37). But this is very strange; gaining forgiveness for imperfection is not the same as obeying perfectly. If forgiveness thus restores "perfection," why do Das and others argue that "perfection" is impossible in Gal 3:10? And what exactly is a perfection, an unerring sinlessness that has been broken? The sort of perfection that Das wants ultimately to argue for (á la Gal 3:10) is one that may never be broken; a single misstep means no more perfection!

26. Oddly, and apparently without realizing it, Das ends up agreeing with Sanders that in the DSS God provided the imperfectly obedient with a means of covenantal status maintenance. This is pretty much what Sanders's "covenantal nomism" was all about.

27. Hartin, *Spirituality of Perfection*, 27–29, hints in this direction, but misses the fact that *tamim* was already an ethical concept, not only a cultic one, in the OT (27).

the new covenant Israel at the end of days, and in the strength of God's Spirit and grace, fulfill this call of Israel's God to "walk before me, and be *tamim*" (Gen 17:1). And, on the flip-side, there is no tension, to speak nothing of contradiction, with their confession of weakness and inability apart from the enabling grace and Spirit of God.

> As for me, in God is my judgment;
> in his hand is the *soundness of my path
> with the uprightness of my heart;
> and with his just acts he cancels my sin. (1QS XI, 2–3)

> For to man (does not belong) his path,
> nor to a human being the steadying of his step;
> since judgment belongs to God,
> and from his hand is the *soundness of the path. (1QS XI, 10–11)[28]

Thus, the teaching of the scrolls regarding obedience and human wholeness can be naturally interpreted as a continuation of the OT foundation. However, according to Du Plessis, alongside this continuity with OT tradition, the community also brought adjustments to the understanding of this wholeness, which may prove significant as we move forward.[29]

1) *Tamim* is now a sectarian concept, only the members of the Dead Sea community, and not larger Israel, are *tamimim*.

2) There is a select group of *tamimim* within the larger community of *tamimim*, "a higher and esoteric grade."

3) This wholeness is now more closely aligned with knowing than in the OT, particularly knowledge of the mysteries revealed to the sect; thus, novices can grow in wholeness through studying Torah and perceiving these eschatological mysteries.[30]

---

28. * I have replaced "perfection" (Martinez) in both places with "soundness" (Hebrew *tōm*).

29. Du Plessis, *Teleios*, 105–7.

30. Or, as Deasley states, "While all were perfect some were more perfect than others." Deasley, *Shape of Qumran Theology*, 213.

Other Second Temple Voices

Of course, the Qumran community was a relatively small sect, living in isolation near the Dead Sea; perhaps its views and those represented in the LXX were atypical of other Jews of the period. Perhaps the perfectionistic strand in Jewish theology alleged by some had its origins in another strand of Jewish thought.[31] In what follows we will examine carefully a host of Second Temple writings to ascertain what they thought about human perfection or wholeness. In this we will cover particularly those texts that have been used to argue for a "perfect obedience" stream of Jewish thought.[32]

Fourth Ezra (2 Esdras)[33]

Fourth Ezra is Sanders's famous "exception" to the otherwise universal Jewish pattern of covenantal nomism, the one text he thought clearly taught the necessity of flawless law-keeping.[34] We will focus on one passage in this text that seems to explicitly affirm such perfectionism and will use this as a gateway into 4 Ezra's teaching on this subject.

> Now this is the order of those who have kept the ways of the Most High, when they shall be separated from their mortal body. During the time that they lived in it, they laboriously served the Most High, and withstood danger every hour, that they might keep the Law of the Lawgiver perfectly. (7:88–89)[35]

This passage comes in the third vision covering the final judgment (6:35—9:25), including the post-judgment state of both the righteous

---

31. Walters will suggest, for instance, that Paul's perfect law-keeping doctrine stemmed from such a Jewish minority opinion found in 4 Ezra as well as in the DSS. Walters, *Perfection in New Testament Theology*, 81.

32. See one such list of potential perfection texts in Charlesworth, "Prayer of Manasseh," 629 n. 652.

33. Although probably composed after the destruction of Jerusalem, perhaps during the reign of Domitian (81–96 CE), it witnesses to a strand of Jewish thinking that overlaps with the NT; Stone, *Fourth Ezra*, 9–10.

34. "In 4 Ezra one sees how Judaism works when it actually does become a religion of individual self-righteousness. . . . All that is left is legalistic perfectionism." Sanders, *Paul and Palestinian Judaism*, 409. On this term "covenantal nomism," see above, p. 12 n. 4.

35. Translation from Metzger, "Fourth Book of Ezra," 1:516–59 n. 540.

and the wicked (7:26-131).³⁶ Throughout 4 Ezra, including this section, the author is exceedingly pessimistic about human behavior. "For who among the living is there that has not sinned, or who among men that has not transgressed your covenant?" (7:46; also 7:68; 8:35; etc.) This leads to a corresponding pessimism as to the fate of the mass of humanity. "Many have been created, but few will be saved" (8:3). In fact, the "many" turn out to be "almost all who have been created" (7:48; also 7:138-40). Ezra turns out to be one of the very few whose obedience qualifies them to enter the blessed future. However, he regularly seeks to identify himself with the mass of sinners whom he pities (e.g., 8:4-36). The angel, however, rebukes him for this identification with sinners (8:46-47), even though such humility is otherwise praiseworthy (8:48).³⁷ To these observations on 4 Ezra few would make objections.

Interpretations diverge, however, over the presence of perfectionistic thought. Alongside the explicit "keep the Law of the Lawgiver perfectly" (7:89), those who argue for perfectionistic legalism in 4 Ezra find it implicitly and "consistently maintained" throughout.³⁸ They point to the markedly rigorous character of the demanded obedience and to the fact that in 4 Ezra only "a few" seem capable of such obedience (i.e., an obedience beyond simple covenantal faithfulness). The possibility of repentance after disobedience is barely mentioned. They note, in addition, that the pattern of covenantal nomism only works when divine mercy and atonement are applied to cover the sins of the righteous but imperfect people. In 4 Ezra, however, mercy is not obtained by this means, but is denied to all but "perfectly" obedient Jews. Thus, all that remains to save is an obedience so complete that no mercy or atonement is required. As Longenecker summarizes, divine mercy is "available only to those

---

36. A crucial portion of this section (7:36-140) was missing from the Latin MSS used for earlier translations, but has since been recovered. On this see Metzger, "'Lost' Section of II Esdras," 153-56.

37. This reflects the same phenomenon we witnessed in the OT where those who are whole and righteous, nevertheless, admit their unworthiness before God.

38. Sanders, *Paul and Palestinian Judaism*, 409-18, citation 416. For "perfectionism" arguments see Das, *Paul, the Law, and the Covenant*, 45-53; Walters, *Perfection in New Testament Theology*, 66-72; and Longenecker, *2 Esdras*. In this last-noted 1995 book Longenecker modified his earlier position of "covenantal abrogation" in favor of "covenantal redefinition," which amounts to covenantal nomism for the exceptional few only.

Expanding the Foundation: Wholeness in Jewish Tradition

who merit his favour by their works in accordance with the law (that is, grace is available to those who have no need of it!)."³⁹

This is, however, a serious misreading of 4 Ezra, and particularly of the teaching on wholehearted obedience. Following Barclay and others, I will explain here how understanding "perfect" law-keeping in 7:89 in the ways Jewish tradition to this point had consistently understood it (complete, integral, whole) puts the largely correct observations in the perfectionistic reading summarized above in quite a new light.⁴⁰

If we resist being misled by English translation, 7:89 ("that they might keep the Law of the Lawgiver perfectly") does nothing more than use traditional language to speak of "the righteous" (7:99) who "have kept the ways of the Most High" (7:88). It asserts straightforwardly that they keep or observe Torah completely and wholeheartedly, though certainly not flawlessly.⁴¹ They exercise "great effort" (7:92) in resisting evil and holding to the path of life; in biblical terms they love and serve⁴² God with all their heart, soul, mind, and strength. They "have trusted the covenants of the Most High" (7:83). This depiction is part of an extended description of those who "kept [or adhered to]⁴³ the ways of the Most High" (7:88–99), and which stands in contrast to the group who has "scorned," "not kept," and "despised" God and his ways (7:76–87).⁴⁴ This contrast makes clear enough that we are not dealing with one rare and unusual group, the flawless law-keepers, versus the remainder who commit sin, even if only a single transgression. Instead, it is the traditional contrast between those who adhere to God and those who scorn his ways.

---

39. Longenecker, *Eschatology and the Covenant*, 271. Some earlier arguments for perfection in 4 Ezra, including those of Sanders, sought to limit the actual viewpoint to statements by one of the characters, usually the angel Uriel. For critique of this approach, see Barclay, *Paul and the Gift*, 281–83.

40. Barclay, "Constructing a Dialogue," 3–22; Barclay, *Paul and the Gift*, 280–308; deSilva, "Grace, the Law and Justification," 25–49; Bauckham, "Apocalypses," 161–75; Moo, "Few Who Obtain Mercy," 98–113.

41. The Latin text (*perfecte*), translated from a Greek translation of a lost Hebrew original (*tamim*?), suggests the same fullness or completeness as seen in the Hebrew tradition.

42. 7:98: him whom they have served in life.

43. Myers: adhered to.

44. For this consistent contrast in 4 Ezra and other Jewish apocalyptic literature between those who "keep Torah (perfectly)" and those who despise or scorn it, see Rössler, *Gesetz und Geschichte*, 77–88.

God and Human Wholeness

But what about the numerous pointers to the rarity of such righteous persons?

> And now I see that the world to come will bring *delight to few, but torments to many*. For an evil heart has grown up in us, which has alienated us from God, and has brought us into corruption and the ways of death, and has shown us *the paths of perdition and removed us far from life—and that not just a few of us but almost all who have been created*. (7:47–48; also 7:138–40 ["not one ten-thousandth of mankind"]; 8:1–3, 35, 41; 9:20–22)

There is no denying 4 Ezra is more pessimistic than many Jewish traditions as to the numerical size of the faithful remnant. This reflects, on the one hand, an emphasis we find elsewhere; namely, compared to the multitudes of the nations, we, the righteous, are few. But, even more importantly to 4 Ezra, the righteous remnant within Israel is very small. This concept of a small remnant of faithful Jews, in contrast to the many who were unfaithful, had been part of Israel's theological tradition for centuries. However, with the destruction of Jerusalem in 70 CE, an event central to 4 Ezra's perspective, this concept gained in importance. How painfully few must be the righteous in Israel, if God were unwilling to spare the nation on their account.[45] Perhaps more importantly for the author of 4 Ezra, the rarity of genuine obedience and its disastrous consequences should act as a supreme motivation for the recipients of this apocalypse, urging them to vigorous and laborious attention to Torah. Thus, this notion of rarity arises not from some particularly rigorous or perfectionistic attitude, but from the historical situation[46] and from the persuasive aims of the author.[47]

---

45. On the "survivors" or "remnant" in 4 Ezra's thought, see Stone, *Fourth Ezra*, 148–49. This historical contingency also answers Sanders's rationale for finding perfection rather than the loyalty of covenantal nomism in this text. "*Loyalty is not impossible for well nigh all, but perfect obedience is.*" Sanders, *Paul and Palestinian Judaism*, 416. In fact, however, Jerusalem's destruction was taken as a judgment on the disobedience of well nigh all Israel.

46. "The pessimism of the book springs not so much from its lofty standards as from historical experience." Collins, *Apocalyptic Imagination*, 169.

47. In fact, this notion of comparative scarcity of genuine obedience is not meant as a sort of scientific calculation, a soteriological math, so to speak. It serves, as said, historical and rhetorical aims. In many contexts it falls out of view altogether and the author envisions a "multitude" of righteous persons (13:12, 39; etc.).

This also helps explain the downplaying of mercy and repentance in 4 Ezra. Many statements do seem to envision a merciless judgment without the possibility of repentance.

> And the Most High shall be revealed upon the seat of judgment, and compassion shall pass away, and patience shall be withdrawn. (7:33)[48]

However, as Barclay has shown convincingly, this "no mercy" tone, though only gradually accepted by Ezra, is repeatedly asserted by another character, Uriel, and refers consistently to the conditions of the future world.[49] At that time, including at the judgment which opens that world, strict justice will prevail.

> The day of judgment is decisive and displays to all the seal of truth. Just as now a father does not send his son, or a son his father, or a master his servant, or a friend his dearest friend, to be ill or sleep or eat or be healed in his stead, so no one shall ever pray for another on that day, neither shall anyone lay a burden on another; for then everyone shall bear his own righteousness or unrighteousness. (7:104–5)

Mercy and the possibility of repentance, on the other hand, are urged repeatedly by Ezra.

> [The Most High] is called giver, because if he did not give out of his goodness, so that those who have committed iniquities might be relieved of them, not one ten-thousandth of mankind could have life; and judge, because if he did not pardon those who were created by his word and blot out the multitude of their sins, there would probably be left only very few of the innumerable multitude. (7:138–40)

Uriel's response does not deny the operation of divine mercy for the many, but makes it clear that such mercy is limited to the present world.

> The Most High made this world for the sake of many, but the world to come for the sake of few. (8:1)

---

48. When Ezra asks if he may intercede for those who have sinned (7:102–3), the angel's answer concludes with, "Therefore, no one will then be able to have mercy on him who has been condemned in the judgment" (7:115); and Ezra's repeated pleas for mercy are turned aside (7:132—8:62).

49. See esp. Barclay's analysis of the crucial third section; Barclay, *Paul and the Gift*, 288–300.

The same dialectic applies to repentance—opportunity during the present age, but none at judgment or in the future world (7:82; 9:10–12).

To reiterate, perfection (or even near-perfection) is nowhere in view in 4 Ezra. This is clear for the present age when mercy and repentance function. But it is equally true even when denying mercy at the judgment and future world; the author does not envision flawless obedience as required for a positive verdict. It is still covenantal righteousness, "the way of which Moses . . . spoke" (7:129), which is operative.

Jubilees

As a mid-second-century BCE form of rewritten Bible, *Jubilees* is closely tied to OT precedents both in its story-line (largely a retelling of much of Genesis) and language. Exemplary behavior is tied to Torah-commandments and the covenant between God and Israel (23:16), and terms like righteous, upright, faithful, etc. are used with overlapping semantic content. An emphasis on keeping "all the commands" occurs just as in the OT (1:23–24; 20:7; etc.).

Also very reminiscent of the OT, the language of wholeness or perfection is used at many points in *Jubilees* in reference to ancient worthies.

- Noah: "On account of his righteousness in which he was perfected, his life on earth was more excellent than (any of) the sons of men except Enoch." (10:17)[50]
- "Abraham was perfect in all of his actions with the Lord and was pleasing through righteousness all of the days of his life." (23:10)
- Jacob "is upright in his way and he is a perfect man. And he is faithful." (27:17)
- Jacob is Isaac's "perfect and upright son, because he has no evil but only goodness." (35:12)
- Rachel "was perfect and upright in all of her ways." (36:23)[51]

Thus, we would expect the perfection language in *Jubilees* to largely echo the *tamim*-tradition from the OT. This is confirmed in the two instances

---

50. Translation of *Jubilees* taken from Wintermute, "Jubilees," 1:35–142.

51. The vast majority of references in the OT and Jewish literature to humans as *tamim* have males either explicitly (e.g., Gen 17:1) or implicitly in view. This is one of the rare cases where a female is called *tamim*.

where we have an extant Hebrew text.⁵² *Jubilees* even quotes Gen 17:1 in 15:4 ("Be pleasing before me and be perfect.") making the tie-in with the OT concept of human wholeness (*tamim*) particularly clear.⁵³ Hence, when Noah is described as a perfect man who "did not transgress anything which was ordained for him" (5:19), as in the OT this marks him not as sinless, but as one who is whole (*tamim*) and integral, rather than being a divided or two-faced person.⁵⁴

Das, however, uses the perfection texts we have noted to argue that *Jubilees* expects nothing less than flawless obedience.⁵⁵ He acknowledges that righteous people in *Jubilees* were imperfect, and that the covenant provided means for the maintenance of their righteousness (e.g., atonement, forgiveness; = covenantal nomism). But the presence of texts referring to some individuals as "perfect" convinces Das that "the ideal remains strict and perfect obedience of the law."⁵⁶ Thus, an unreconciled tension is said to run throughout *Jubilees* between a gracious covenantalism on one side and a stringent perfectionism on the other. As seen elsewhere in Das's study, his readiness to simply adopt the nuance of sinlessness inherent in the English translation "perfect," without exploring the Hebrew and OT milieu, vitiates the argument.⁵⁷

Second Baruch

Much like 4 Ezra, the Jewish apocalypse 2 Baruch also responds to the catastrophe of 70 CE,⁵⁸ and in light of that disastrous judgment upon Israel's faithlessness urges renewed and rigorous obedience to Torah.

---

52. 4Q223–24 (4QpapJubilees^h) has *tamim* at 35:12 and 36:23. See VanderKam and Milik, "Jubilees," 102, 114.

53. The description of Jacob as a "perfect man" (27:17) echoes Heb *tam ish* of Gen 25:27. See Kugel, *Walk through Jubilees*, 138 n. 252.

54. VanderKam suggests a priestly overtone in the reference to Noah's perfection; he "adhered flawlessly to the Lord's will as it was expressed in laws of cult and purity." VanderKam, "Righteousness of Noah," 23.

55. Das, *Paul, the Law, and the Covenant*, 13–17.

56. Das, *Paul, the Law, and the Covenant*, 16.

57. Somewhat confusingly, although holding firmly to a non-perfectionistic covenantal nomism for *Jubilees*, Sanders appears to agree as to the particularly rigorous nature of the expected obedience ("perfect obedience is specified"). Sanders, *Paul and Palestinian Judaism*, 381.

58. Usually dated around 100 CE (Klijn, Gurtner).

Although earlier considered an example of typical Jewish legalism,[59] more recent study confirms its covenantal character.[60] The righteous in Israel are clearly not sinless, since they, too, need divine mercy and cleansing (77:6–7; 78:7; 84:10; 85:15).

Das brings two arguments to enlist 2 Baruch as a witness to perfectionistic Judaism. First, he thinks that "nomism begins to take precedence over covenant," such that "mercy is contingent upon obedience."[61] However, he misreads how divine grace coexists with a strict demand for human obedience in Jewish soteriology. For Das, conditional statements (if you obey) imply a downplaying of election and mercy. But, just as in Paul, Jews could wholeheartedly affirm that all is of grace while simultaneously holding that one must walk worthy of that calling in order to enjoy its benefits. Second, he calls 21:11 as a witness to perfectionism. "In 21:11 the many who have sinned only *once* are contrasted with 'many others' who 'have proved themselves to be righteous,'"[62] i.e., sinless. Unfortunately, Das's reliance on Klijn's English translation has led him astray. Gurtner's translation of this verse defuses the entire issue: "And if in time many have sinned, still not a few others have been righteous."[63] Thus, there is no reference to Jews who sinned only once or even not at all, but only to two clearly-defined groups, sinners and the righteous.[64]

Psalms of Solomon

Although the specific language of perfection or wholeness is not used in PssSol, we mention it due to its clear witness to the continuing Jewish

---

59. See, for example, Charles, *Apocalypse of Baruch*, lxix–lxx, lxxxi–lxxxiv; and Harnisch, *Verhängnis und Verheissung*, 213, 225–26.

60. See Bauckham, "Apocalypses," 175–82, who notes 2 Baruch is more inclusive (even some Gentiles) and less pessimistic (not only a tiny remnant is obedient) than 4 Ezra.

61. Das, *Paul, the Law, and the Covenant*, 54, 55; cf. esp. 48:22; also 14:57.

62. Das, *Paul, the Law, and the Covenant*, 56, original emphasis. Klijn's translation reads: "And while many have sinned once, many others have proved themselves to be righteous."

63. Gurtner, *Second Baruch*, 55.

64. Others have suggested 2 Bar 9:1 as a testimony to sinlessness. "And I, Baruch, came with Jeremiah, whose heart was found to be pure from sins." While possible that Baruch here attributes actual sinlessness to Jeremiah, the language of one's "heart being found pure" suggests, instead, that this refers to Jeremiah's fundamental inner attitude which has been cleansed.

belief that the righteous were not perfect, did not have to be sinless. Two groups are contrasted in these psalms. On the one hand is the "sinner," who "adds sin upon sin in his life; he falls—his fall is serious—and he will not get up. The destruction of the sinner is forever" (3:10–11). These are the wicked who do not praise God (3:1), whose heart is far from the Lord and who break his law (4:1) and who "live in hypocrisy" (4:6). On the other hand are the righteous and devout who fear God (2:33), truly love him (6:6), "live in the righteousness of his commandments" (14:2), and constantly seek to remove unintentional sins (3:7). As in the OT and elsewhere in Jewish sources, the righteous do sin,[65] which leads Winninge to label them "the sinfully righteous."[66] Such sins of the righteous differ, however, from the wicked acts of sinners since they do not reflect the individual's heart. Because the righteous love God, they seek cleansing and forgiveness from repeated, accidental, or unknown sins through repentance, confession, and fasting (3:8; 9:6; 10:1; 13:10), whereas the wicked hide their sins, desiring from the heart to continue in them.[67] The idea that acceptable obedience to Torah required perfect compliance simply does not fit in this world of thought.

Prayer of Manasseh

> You, therefore, O Lord, God of the righteous ones,
> did not appoint grace[68] for the righteous ones,
> such as Abraham, and Isaac and Jacob,
> those who did not sin against you;
> but you appointed grace for me, (I) who am a sinner. (v. 8)

---

65. The messiah, on the other hand, may be viewed as sinless (17:36, "free [*katharos*] from sin"). However, Trafton wonders about the possible connection to Ps 51:2 and David's desire to be "cleansed" or "pure" from his sin with Bathsheba; i.e., this may not be an assertion of sinlessness at all, but that messiah will reflect the cleansed Davidic king (rather than the adulterer). Trafton, "What Would David Do?," 172.

66. Winninge, *Sinners and the Righteous*, 131–34.

67. For an overview of soteriology in PssSol, see Atkinson, "Enduring the Lord's Discipline," 151–55; and Falk, "Psalms and Prayers," 35–51. For similar conclusions as to sin and righteousness in the PssSol, see Büchler, *Types of Jewish-Palestinian Piety*, 128–95; and Winninge, *Sinners and the Righteous*, 131–34. For an older, largely discredited, view of the PssSol as representing pharisaic works-righteousness, see Braun, "Vom Erbarmen Gottes," 1–54.

68. Both here and in line 5, Codex A has "repentance [*metanoia*]" in place of "grace." Cp. v. 7 where "repentance" has been appointed for sinners.

This text seems to speak of the patriarchs as sinless ("who did not sin against you") over against all others who do sin.[69] The former needed no grace (or repentance or forgiveness) since they were righteous (sinless?). While such an interpretation cannot be excluded, this notion of sinlessness is so out of line with common Jewish understanding that one is prompted to seek an alternate interpretation.

The one ostensibly praying here is King Manasseh, a notorious idolater whose apostasy led Judah to ruin (2 Kgs 21:1–18). The parallel account in 2 Chr 33:11–17 speaks of his later repentance and of his humble prayer that was recorded "in the Annals of the Kings of Israel" (v. 18), but was not recorded in 2 Chronicles. Our text claims to provide that prayer.[70] Thus, the "sinner" praying is not the common Israelite, whose general faithfulness includes some sinning; this "sinner" is a notorious apostate. He speaks of "sins multiplied more than the sand of the sea" (v. 9a) and of provoking God's fury because he "set up idols and multiplied defilement" (v. 10). In contrast stand the patriarchs "who did not sin against you," i.e., did not do what Manasseh did . . . rebel and live in idolatry. Thus, they are portrayed not necessarily as sinless, but as having refrained from apostasy like Manasseh's.

One element in the prayer causes some difficulty for either interpretation, namely that God "did not appoint grace [or repentance] for the righteous ones." Even the (supposedly sinless) patriarchs were thought to need covenantal lovingkindness (unless this testifies to a works-righteousness which "earns"). This text may, however, not be speaking of God's *chesed* at all, his covenantal lovingkindness, but of repentance, and particularly of that fundamental turning from sin we might refer to as conversion.[71] Thus, one might read vv. 7b–8 as follows (my freer rendering): "You, O Lord . . . appointed conversion (heartfelt sorrow for one's evil ways) as the salvation for sinners (like Manasseh). You, therefore, O Lord . . . did not appoint this grace for the righteous ones, like the patriarchs, who did not sin in this way against you."

---

69. See Falk, "Psalms and Prayers," 14–15.

70. Dated somewhere between 200 BCE and 50 CE; Charlesworth, "Prayer of Manasseh," 627.

71. See verse 7b where Charlesworth suggests "conversion, penitence" as an alternate meaning of the Syriac, "Prayer of Manasseh," 636 n. a2.

Testament of Abraham[72]

> For behold, Abraham has not sinned and he has no mercy on sinners. (v. 10:13b)

The text seems to attribute sinlessness to Abraham. Two considerations make that conclusion, however, less certain. First, Abraham refers to himself as "a sinner and your completely worthless servant" (9:3). Second, in ch. 10 Abraham is being compared with egregious sinners (theft and sexual immorality) "who pass their lives in sin" (10:13a). Thus, rather than asserting that Abraham had never sinned in any fashion, this text may simply confirm that he has not sinned in any of these more egregious and habitual ways.

Testament of Issachar

As testimony to a Jewish belief in perfection, some point to the Testament of Issachar.

> I am a hundred and twenty-two years old, and I am not aware of having committed a sin unto death.
> I have not had intercourse with any woman other than my wife, nor was I promiscuous by lustful look.
> I did not drink wine to the point of losing self-control. I was not passionately eager for any desirable possession of my neighbor.
> There was no deceit in my heart; no lie passed through my lips.
> I joined in lamentation with every oppressed human being, and shared my bread with the poor.
> I did not eat alone; I did not transgress boundaries;
> I acted in piety and truth all my days. The Lord I loved with all my strength; likewise, I loved every human being as I love my children. (7:1–6)

Issachar here denies having committed during his long life "a sin unto death," which refers to "a grave, unpardonable sin."[73] He then lists a variety of such mortal transgressions he has not practiced. It is to this he

---

72. Dated ca. 100 CE; Sanders, "Testament of Abraham," 874–75.

73. Jonge and Hollander, *Testaments of the Twelve Patriarchs*, 250, with reference to Num 18:22 (LXX): lit. "death-bringing sin"; Num 15:30–31, deliberate sin "with a high hand"; 1QS 8.22—9.2; Jub 21.22; 26.34; 33.13, 18; and 1 John 5:16.

refers when claiming he has not sinned. Rather than a denial of having committed any single transgression, Issachar appeals to his life pattern, which is summed up in the final line ("I acted in piety and truth all my days. The Lord I loved with all my strength").[74]

A Few Additional Texts

Several of the perfection-texts alleged by others can be quickly dispatched.

Tobit 3:14

> You know, O Master, that I am innocent of any defilement with a man.

This is hardly a claim to moral perfection, but a simple assertion by Sarah that she is free of grosser sexual sin.

Apocalypse of Sedrach 15[75]

There is nothing in this chapter that asserts sinlessness, but some may find it implied in the statement that "sinners are not saved" (15:3). However, this clause is suspect textually, and a perfectionistic implication is directly contradicted by 15:1-2, which notes that God alone is "without sin" and calls "not the righteous but sinners."

Life of Adam and Eve 18:1[76]

> And Eve said to Adam, "You live on, my lord. Life is granted to you, since you have done neither the first nor the second error, but I have been cheated and deceived, for I have not kept the command of God."

There is no assertion of Adam's sinlessness here. Rather, Eve, who was deceived twice by the devil (see LAE 10 for the second deception

---

74. For similar protestations of innocence in the Psalms, see Ps 24:3-4; 26:1-12. Kwakkel, *According to My Righteousness*.
75. Dated between 150-500 CE; Agourides, "Apocalypse of Sedrach," 606.
76. Dated 200 BCE-100 CE; Johnson, "Life of Adam and Eve," 252.

subsequent to the eating of the forbidden fruit), says Adam committed neither of these particular acts of disobedience.

> *Testament of Zebulun 1:4*
>
> I am not aware, my children, that I have sinned in all my days, except in my mind. Nor do I recall having committed a transgression, except what I did to Joseph in ignorance, because in a compact with my brothers I kept from telling my father what had been done, although I wept much in secret.

The speaker claims to have avoided all bodily transgressions except one, which was "in ignorance." He is, on the other hand, aware of sins in the "mind," that is in thought or disposition.[77]

> *Testament of Levi 10:2*
>
> See, I am free of responsibility for your impiety or for any transgression which you may commit until the consummation of the ages . . . in leading Israel astray and in fomenting in it great evils against the Lord.

A surface reading might assume that sinlessness is expected by the concern for "any transgression which you may commit." However, the text speaks of a type of impiety that would result in "leading Israel astray and in fomenting in it great evils against the Lord." That is, this is concerned with a more fundamental apostasy.

The remainder of this chapter will deal with two further bodies of Jewish literature that typically play a significant role in our reconstruction of early Jewish theology, and, thus, of our understanding of Jewish thoughts on perfection or human wholeness. These are Philo, the first-century Hellenistic Jewish philosopher, and the early Jewish rabbis whose sayings are collected and commented on in the Talmud.

---

77. On this important concept of mind or disposition in the Testaments, see Jonge and Hollander, *Testaments of the Twelve Patriarchs*, esp. 330 (on TGad 335). For an alternate perspective, see Kee, "Ethical Dimensions," 259–70, who argues that the ethical vision of the Testaments is more Stoic than Jewish covenantal, in which case a sin in the "mind" would probably refer to an even more serious lack of virtue.

Philo

With hundreds of uses of the Greek adjective and verb *teleios/teleiō*, perfection is clearly a major emphasis for Philo.[78] His indebtedness not only to Jewish Scripture but equally to Platonic, and especially Stoic, philosophy is widely acknowledged,[79] which suggests that his understanding of perfection will show influences of both, but may not be an exact representation of either. Thus, in the more Jewish vein, human completeness can only come through God's grace,[80] and such wholeness will come through following the divine commandments.[81] Yet, the very nature of his *teleios*-concept is thoroughly Stoic. It is "complete emancipation from the power of the passions"[82] and ultimately consists in the vision of the Ideal, of God.[83]

Philo considers only a few exceptional Jewish patriarchs to have been completed or perfect persons in the Stoic sense of complete emancipation from passions. Thus, preeminently Moses, "being perfect, has no inadequate or lowly ideas, nor is he willing to remain in a state in which the passions have even a moderate influence; but he, by his exceeding power, does utterly extirpate the whole of the passions, root and branch."[84] Of course, even for these exceptional cases such perfection is only possible by God's grace. For the remainder of humankind, God has given the commandments of Torah that they might progress toward the state of completion, and those who in this way make progress, even though not having thoroughly reached their goal, still obtain the divine reward.[85]

---

78. Carlston, "Vocabulary of Perfection," 133–60, esp. 133–47. Carlston provides an exhaustive catalog of all uses in Philo's corpus of the *teleios* word-group.

79. See, for example, Williamson, *Jews in the Hellenistic World*; and Dihle, "Das Streben nach Vollkommenheit," 260–66.

80. "Perfection is found in no created thing, but . . . does appear in them at times owing to the grace of the great Cause of all things" (*De Plantatione*, 93; cited in Hartin, *Spirituality of Perfection*, 31 n. 48).

81. *De Specialibus Legibus*, IV.140.

82. Philo, *Legum Allegoriae* III, 131; from Yonge, *Works of Philo*.

83. "And what can be more perfect among all the virtues than the sight of the living God" (*De Ebrietate*, 83; cited in Hartin, *Spirituality of Perfection*, 30 n. 44). See also Du Plessis, *Teleios*, who says Philo's "whole scheme of belief is concentrated on this harmonious unification of virtue and wisdom in the pure perception of God" (116).

84. *Legum Allegoriae* III.134. Also *Ebr.* 94 ("the most perfect Moses").

85. Williamson, *Jews in the Hellenistic World*, 206–7.

Expanding the Foundation: Wholeness in Jewish Tradition

Pleasing God according to Torah, as far as Philo is concerned, does not require flawless obedience.[86]

Philo is important for our study since he shows clearly the blending of OT and Greek philosophical ideas that was taking place during this period in Jewish thought. Thus, *teleios* now refers both to growth in virtue, knowledge, and wisdom, as well as to the Greek ideal of the vision of god (perception) as key.[87] Although we will see hints of this same combination in the NT, it is particularly in the post-apostolic and medieval periods that this combination will take the understanding of Christian spirituality in new directions.

Entering the World of the Rabbis

Our access to the thought-world of the early Jewish rabbinic movement must be through the Mishnah (ca. 200 CE) and Talmud (completed ca. 600 CE). Since these were not put into writing until after the first century CE, we cannot simply assume that their statements represent earlier thinking as previous generations of scholars were wont to do.[88] Nevertheless, this literature is important to our study as a further indication of the development of Jewish thought during and after the first century.

Solomon Schechter illustrates a widespread rabbinic attitude toward keeping the commandments.

> Another consequence of this fatherly relation [i.e., of God with Israel] is that Israel feels a certain ease and delight in the

---

86. Andrew Das points to these exceptional people in Philo as proof that "perfect obedience of the Mosaic law is the ideal." However, while a more complete obedience may well remain the "ideal," even Das admits that it was not "required" in Philo in order to obtain the reward. "When an individual fails in that [perfect] obedience, there remains a larger system that involves mercy and forgiveness." Das, *Paul, the Law, and the Covenant*, 23–31, citation 24.

87. Du Plessis, *Teleios*, 115–18. As Völker summarizes: "For Philo perfection is nothing other than the pinnacle of human life. Here the vision of God is bound together with the highest ethical achievement; one's entire existence becomes service to God and to one's brothers. This all is felt to be a gift of God and is an imitation of God." Völker, *Fortschritt und Vollendung*, 263.

88. Some readers will be familiar with the helpful collection of rabbinic texts in the Strack-Billerbeck commentary on the New Testament. These texts are often used uncritically to provide Jewish background to NT texts, when, in fact, many of the alleged parallels and contrasts may only have arisen later. A useful introduction to the world of the rabbis and their literature is Stemberger, *Introduction*.

> fulfilment of the Law which to slaves is burdensome and perplexing. For "the son who serves his father serves him with joy, saying, 'Even if I do not entirely succeed (in carrying out his commandments), yet, as a loving father, he will not be angry with me'; whilst the Gentile slave is always afraid lest he may commit some fault, and therefore serves God in a condition of anxiety and confusion."[89]

Rather than seeing the Law as stipulations of a rigorous taskmaster expecting nothing less than perfection, the rabbis viewed Torah as the instructions of a father and attended to their fulfillment with "ease and delight." Even failure to "entirely succeed" could not dim this loving fatherly relation.

Thus, the great majority of those studying the rabbinic writings in the past several decades would agree with Sanders that "human perfection was not considered realistically achievable by the Rabbis, nor was it required."[90] As Philip Alexander notes, for example, "there appears to be no implication that in order to reap the ultimate rewards it is necessary to fulfill the whole Torah perfectly. The righteous person is not necessarily perfect. . . . Perfectionism of the sort that seems to affect some early Christian writers is not a feature of the Mishnah."[91]

This is not to deny that there are passages that seem to promote some sort of perfectionistic thinking. But, as anyone familiar with this literature quickly learns, statements from the rabbis are not always what they may appear on a surface reading. For instance, numerous texts speak of three groups: the perfectly righteous, the perfectly wicked, and those in between.[92] At face value, this seems to assume there are some "perfectly righteous" individuals. However, as Loewe comments: "I doubt whether the Rabbis really believed that any human being was 'perfectly' righteous or 'perfectly' wicked. Just like other hypothetical cases that we

---

89. Schechter, *Aspects of Rabbinic Theology*, 55, citing *Tanḥ.* 19, בנ.

90. Sanders, *Paul and Palestinian Judaism*, 137; also Sanders, "On the Question," 103–26.

91. Alexander, "Torah and Salvation," 261–301, citation 284. There was, of course, a great deal of reflection on perfection in rabbinic and in medieval Judaism, but this dealt more with the attainment of human happiness, the ultimate human good, than with our topic of moral-legal perfectionism. See esp. Tirosh-Samuelson, *Happiness in Premodern Judaism*, ch. 3, "The Happy Life of Torah in Rabbinic Judaism" (101–42).

92. Found, for example, in tractate *Kiddushin* 40b of the Babylonian Talmud.

Expanding the Foundation: Wholeness in Jewish Tradition

have had before, this was an exercise in logic, all rhetorical arguments and possibilities being taken into account."[93]

Particularly interesting in these writings are the repeated reminders of single acts of sin that exclude the sinner from the Age to Come. If a single act of disobedience brings eternal loss, this would seem at first glance to imply a requirement of perfect obedience.

> And these are they that have no share in the world to come: he that says that there is no resurrection of the dead prescribed in the Law; and [he that says] that the Law is not from Heaven, and an Epicurean. R[abbi] Akiba says: Also he that reads the heretical books, or that utters charms over a wound and say, *I will put none of the diseases upon thee which I have put upon the Egyptians: for I am the Lord that healeth thee* (Ex. 15.26). Abba Saul says: Also he that pronounces the Name with its proper letters.[94]

The point, however, is not that any single transgression of the sort named spoils one's otherwise perfect law-keeping, but that any one of these sins can amount to breaking covenant with God. Each one, whether denial of central Torah teaching (e.g., resurrection) or uttering healing spells, may reveal a heart no longer submitted to Yahweh and his ways. In fact, even a seemingly small or innocent transgression such as using a verse from the Song of Solomon for secular entertainment can damn. For it, too, may be the first step on the road to casting off the yoke of the Law.[95]

Andrew Das disagrees with this portrayal of rabbinic thought on perfection.[96] His only actual positive evidence as far as I can see is found in *b.Sanh.* 81a: "When R. Gamaliel read this verse he wept, saying, 'Only he who does all these things shall live, but not merely one of them!'" Das perceives here an emphasis on perfect obedience, on doing "all these things" in contrast to "merely one of them" or even some (but not all) of them.

This section of the tractate is discussing Ezek 18:5–9, which details a series of separate righteous actions: not eating upon the mountains,

---

93. Montefiore and Loewe, *Rabbinic Anthology*, 603.

94. Sanhedrin 10.1; p. Peah 16b, as cited in Sanders, *Paul and Palestinian Judaism*, 134.

95. Sanders, *Paul and Palestinian Judaism*, 128–47.

96. "The rabbis *did* at times assert that God's justice requires perfect obedience." Das, *Paul, the Law, and the Covenant*, 36; his whole argument for this point is found on 32–37.

not defiling a neighbor's wife, etc. The question raised is whether a person who violates two commands suffers two penalties or only one, and whether this would be the more severe penalty or only the penalty for the first infraction?[97] After detailing rabbinic positions the text then comes to Ezek 18:9, which reads, "He is just, he shall surely live."

> When R. Gamaliel read this verse he wept, saying, "Only he who does all these things shall live, but not merely one of them!" Thereupon R. Akiba said to him, "If so, *Defile not yourselves in all these things*.[98]—is the prohibition against *all* [combined] only, but not against one?" [Surely not!] But it means, *in one* of these things; so here too, for doing one of these things [shall he live].

The debate appears to be over the meaning of "all" in "all these things." Should we read such texts cumulatively? (i.e., Only the one who does $x + y + z$ is affected.) Or should we read the text seriatim? (i.e., The one who does x, or y, or z is affected?) Gamaliel takes the former position, while Akiba the latter. In any case, contra Das, the debate is not over how many commandments a person must keep in order to be considered righteous.

Thus, to conclude this brief exploration of rabbinic literature, we agree with Campbell's findings.

> Of course, it does not take a specialist in Judaism to realize immediately that this description [demand of perfect obedience] cannot be found within Judaism in such terms. *The particular definition of Judaism prescribed by Justification theory is simply not found in the extant Jewish sources.* Indeed, hardly a jot or tittle in the entire Old Testament, the Dead Sea Scrolls, the Apocrypha and Pseudepigrapha, other Jewish corpora such as the writings of Philo and Josephus, or the extant rabbinic writings arguably supplies explicit evidence for this particular soteriology. So, put bluntly, *that this account of Judaism is absent from the Jewish sources roughly contemporary to Paul is self-evident.*[99]

---

97. *Sanhedrin*, 81a.

98. Lev 18:24.

99. Campbell, *Deliverance of God*, 113, italics original. He acknowledges Uriel's position in 4 Ezra as a possible exception (seemingly perfect obedience required but nowhere found), but notes it "is trenchantly opposed by Ezra" (957 n. 34).

Chapter 5

Perfection in Hellenistic Tradition

> "Morality" in the ancient sense is a specifically traditioned
> way to live a full human life.[1]

Although the topic of this book is perfection in biblical and theological tradition, we cannot avoid a closer look at perfection in Hellenistic tradition. There are at least two reasons for this. First, biblical reflection on human wholeness utilized the Greek language. This is clear for the NT documents that were written in Greek, but is likewise true for the OT, which was known widely among early Christians and educated Jews, especially in the diaspora, in its Greek translation, the LXX. The second reason will become particularly relevant when studying the developments of perfection in the patristic and medieval periods when elements of Greek philosophy guided many leading Christian thinkers. Thus, while by no means a full-scale study of perfection in Hellenistic tradition, this brief section should provide insight into what Greek-speakers understood when using this language of perfection, and into their perspectives on the nature, end, and ultimate perfection of the human.[2]

In an earlier chapter we looked briefly at the Greek terms used to translate perfection texts from the Hebrew OT. There we noted that these Greek translation terms corresponded fairly well with what the Hebrew terms intended to communicate. Here, however, we will delve a bit more

---

1. Rowe, *One True Life*, 193.
2. A readable introduction to the subject is Passmore, *Perfectibility of Man*, 29–95.

deeply into the way Hellenistic tradition itself spoke and thought about perfection.

The Greek adjective *teleios* occurs widely in classical Greek and has "the meaning of attaining completeness in the sense that one has attained the goal (*telos*)."[3] This completeness or wholeness can be applied to various spheres. Cultically a sacrificial animal is to be *teleios*, "blameless" or "without blemish" (par. *amōmos, amemptos*) in the sense of completing all cultic requirements. Animals and persons are *teleios* in the sense of "full-grown" or "mature," i.e., those who have reached the goal of their nature. One's skills are *teleios* when all aspects of the skill have been mastered; thus, a "perfect [or accomplished] Sophist" is one who "can spin fine discourses,"[4] i.e., who has mastered the skills that are to characterize a true Sophist. And, of course, the gods are *teleios*, "indicating that these gods had accomplished everything that they set out to do," i.e., had reached their *telos*.[5]

The frequent English translation, "perfect," is actually misleading for these contexts, since a strong ethical or moral element is normally implied by the English term. When we say "no one's perfect," we are most commonly thinking "everyone makes mistakes," "everyone sins," "everyone falls short of some exhaustive and absolute standard of being or performance." This ethical connotation is, however, precisely what is normally missing in the use of Greek *teleios*.[6] As Delling notes, "the word is not primarily ethical; it is purely formal."[7] A quote from Aristotle captures well this formal sense.

> *Teleios* is that which constitutes an aggregate from which no component part is absent. . . . A physician, for example, is *teleios* and flutist is *teleios* when in consistency with the requisite aptitudes of their respective crafts, they are lacking in nothing. In metaphorical sense, we also speak of sycophants and thieves as perfect by calling such depreciative qualities good. And virtue

---

3. Hartin, *Spirituality of Perfection*, 22. On *telos* as the foundation for the meaning of *teleios*, see esp. Du Plessis, *Teleios*, 36–73.

4. Hartin, *Spirituality of Perfection*, 68, citing Plato, *Cratylus*, 403e.

5. In another sense, of course, namely morals, the gods were far from perfect. Passmore, *Perfectibility of Man*, 29–57.

6. Until very late, perfection "was a concept on a human scale and pertained to the skills, deeds, and productions of people, of the physician and the flutist, without a theological or even a moral meaning. These developed only in the 17th century." Tatarkiewicz, *On Perfection*, 17.

7. Delling, "*telos*, etc.," 68.

is a certain perfection, and each thing is then perfect when in accordance with the species of its proper excellence of virtue no part of the natural magnitude is deficient.[8]

Thus, buildings, horses, carpenters, and philosophers can be perfect in this formal sense of *teleios*, while hardly being perfect in the moral-ethical sense. This confusing of the proper formal sense of *teleios* with the more common ethical sense of English perfect has bedeviled most Christian discussions of perfection. One of the chief aims of this book is to try and untangle this mess.

What, then, did this all mean when the Hellenistic world reflected on human perfection? Did they think such perfection, such attainment of the goal or purpose (*telos*) of human existence, was humanly possible? And what did that look like? We will take Plato's views for one window into this Hellenistic perspective.[9] What we might call ultimate reality, or Truth, exists for Plato not in this visible, material world, but in the unseen world of Ideas or Forms. What we see and experience are but shadows of this reality. Thus, the beauty of a flower in this material world is but the dim reflection of true Beauty in the unseen. Or, the love experienced in a true friendship is the shadow of that true Love that is not seen or material. To grasp this knowledge, to see and to know this true unseen reality, is the philosopher's quest. Thus, for much of Greek philosophy, human perfection is connected primarily with the attainment of knowledge. The perfect man for Plato "is he who has attained φρόνησις, 'firm and true views,' insight and philosophical knowledge."[10] The material world, including the human body, is at best a veil that dims our perception of this unseen reality, and is for some philosophers an outright hindrance or evil. Thus, for most, progress toward the ultimate good involves turning away from focus on this world, from human passions, desires, and distractions, and contemplating the world of unseen realities. True perfection requires philosophy.

> The way to perfection, then, was to concentrate only on the actions of the soul: that is, thinking. By thinking the soul disengages itself from the body and attains to the vision of its own,

---

8. Aristotle, *Metaph*. IV.16.1021b. 12ff. Cited in Du Plessis, *Teleios*, 74.

9. While Aristotle, Zeno, Parmenides, and other Greek philosophers differed in significant ways from Plato, I have tried to limit the brief sketch above to that which would generally be agreeable to most. See, for example, Kirk, *Vision of God*, 23–38; LaRondelle, *Perfection and Perfectionism*, 11–20.

10. Delling, "*telos, etc.*," 69.

divine being, which is the remembrance, *anamnesis*, of its preexistent divinity.[11]

This all, then, has ramifications for the purpose and conduct of human life. The key question in ethics for much of the Hellenistic tradition was not "what is the right thing to do in this situation?" or "what is justice?" etc. Rather, "What should my life be like?"[12] That is, it was concerned with one's life as a whole rather than focused upon individual ethical decisions. And this "How should I live?" question requires that I grasp the end (*telos*) of my life as a whole. I must figure out "why" (or "for what") I live before I can answer "how" I should live in order to attain that end. For the ancients, from Aristotle to the Stoics and Epicureans, the answer was happiness (*eudaimonia*), or what might be better termed *the good human life*. This is certainly not a life filled with as much sensual enjoyment as possible, but a full and satisfying life; a life lived according to reason, transcending the rule of our animal passions, and aimed at an ever-growing apprehension of unseen Reality.[13] Although the philosophers could sometimes use the language of "knowing god" for apprehending this unseen Reality, such theistic language was not the norm.[14] It would be Philo, the Hellenistic Jewish philosopher, who would mediate a theistic form of this Greek *eudaimonia* tradition for the developing Christian tradition.[15]

When we come to consider the patristic writings on perfection, the development of Plato's thoughts in what is termed Middle Platonism will become relevant. As Allen and Springsted summarize,

> The Middle Platonists viewed the human soul as belonging to another realm but as now fallen into the sense world. The object of life is to purify the soul by philosophy so we may return to a disembodied life in which we enjoy the vision of true reality.[16]

---

11. LaRondelle, *Perfection and Perfectionism*, 12, with reference to Plato's *Phaedo* 72 e ff.; and *Phaedrus* 247 c ff.

12. Annas, *Morality of Happiness*, 27.

13. For this tradition of *eudaimonia*, see David, Boniwell, and Ayers, *Oxford Handbook of Happiness*, esp. the essay by Pawelski, "Introduction to Philosophical Approaches to Happiness," 284–300.

14. Kirk, *Vision of God*, 23–38.

15. Kirk, *Vision of God*, 38–46.

16. Allen and Springsted, *Philosophy for Understanding Theology*, 47.

We will see that the ascetic impulse in monasticism as well as some of the meditative and intellectual aspects of the higher life draw inspiration from this Middle Platonist stream.

We might gain some clarity on all this by contrasting it with the view of human wholeness (*tamim*) we discovered in mainstream Jewish tradition. There we saw that Jews conceived of the aim and perfecting of human life as something lived on earth and *coram deo* (before God). The whole or complete human life had to do with wholehearted living for the Lord *in this creation*. It had to do with one's *behavior in the body*—one should live in upright fashion according to God's instructions. The end (*telos*) of a good human life is found in the divinely ordained relating of God and creatures of flesh, not in the transcendence of creatureliness.

Part Two

The New Testament and Wholeness-Perfection

Chapter 6

Jesus and Perfection

> We will be happy when we are what God wants us to be—people of goodness, kindness, mercy, and forgiveness; people who come to life in loving and serving others.[1]

Jesus Preaches Human Wholeness for Israel (Matt 5:48)

We come now to the text that has played a dominant role in past discussions of perfection. "Be perfect, therefore, as your heavenly Father is perfect" (Matt 5:48). What could be more natural for English-speakers when reading this translation than to think Jesus is calling for sinless perfection, for a level of obedience and holiness akin to God himself ("as your heavenly Father"). This seems, as well, to make good sense of his comparison with the Pharisees. Although their obedience to God's demands was considered particularly stringent among Jews at this time, the righteousness Jesus is demanding "exceeds" even that (Matt 5:20). In fact, even the breaking of "one of the least of these commandments" (5:19) somehow impinges on this righteousness, understood traditionally as flawless perfection in behavior.

The chief difficulty with this interpretation is probably felt immediately by everyone hearing it. We instinctively reply, "Nobody's perfect, Jesus!" What is he doing in calling us to an impossible task?[2] Interpreters

---

1. Wadell, *Happiness*, 2.
2. Although focused more on Paul's writings, a small group of scholars has argued for actual sinless perfection as a possibility, and, thus, as a realistic expectation of

who think Jesus did mean flawlessness here have provided a variety of responses to this obvious difficulty.[3]

- Jesus is setting forth an *ideal* toward which disciples should strive; what mattered was not so much whether they actually reached the ideal (i.e., Jesus didn't actually demand or expect that they would "be perfect"), but whether their hearts were intent on this aim, to love God and neighbor.

- This verse is not actually a summons to action, but instead holds up a *mirror* to reveal our sinfulness. It serves to show how far short we fall.[4]

- Since this is humanly unattainable, the verse is an *implicit invitation* to receive the perfection/righteousness of Christ himself (imputation), rather than trying to establish our own. We can be perfect if we accept Christ's perfection on our behalf in faith.[5]

- Matthew 5–7 is an *interim ethic*, emergency regulations for the brief period until the final consummation of all things, but never intended as a realistic way of life in this world.[6]

Another group of interpreters, finding these explanations inadequate, has suggested that Jesus meant something other than flawless obedience by this call to perfection, something that is realistic and humanly attainable.

- The Roman Catholic tradition developed an understanding of "be perfect" as "evangelical counsels." This "perfection" referred to the particularly rigorous demands of chastity, poverty, and obedience, and was addressed not to all Christians, but to those with religious callings, like monks and priests. The laity did not have to be perfect, but had a more relaxed ethic.

Christ: Wernle, *Der Christ*; Windisch, *Taufe und Sünde*; and more recently, Umbach, *In Christus getauft*. For critique of this view, see Yinger, "Review of *In Christus getauft*," 309–11.

3. For a thorough review of the interpretation of the sermon, see Kissinger, *Sermon on the Mount*.

4. See Powell, "Reading Matthew," 27–30.

5. So, for example, Lohse, "'Vollkommen Sein,'" 131–40, esp. 136–38.

6. Schweitzer, *Mystery of the Kingdom of God*, 94–115.

- The Wesleyan movement claimed perfection was actually attainable through entire sanctification, a second experience of grace. However, they nearly always meant an inner intent of perfect love, and not a sinless perfection in deed or character.
- Others, followed in our study, suggest that perfection in Jewish tradition does not actually mean flawlessness in the English-language sense, but something more like wholeness, wholehearted devotion, integrity, completeness.

This brief survey of interpretations raises two questions that I think are fundamental for understanding this text and for our project.

1. Why is Jesus issuing this call to perfection? Which means we will have to determine how 5:48 fits into the larger Sermon on the Mount. If "be perfect" was (or was not) intended as a realistic call to a path of discipleship, how about the rest of the sermon? Why was Jesus preaching this? And, how does 5:48 fit into its context?

2. What exactly did Jesus mean by this particular command to "be perfect"? How does it relate to sinlessness and holiness? Where did Jesus get this idea from?

Chapters 5–7 form the first of five blocks of Jesus's teaching in the gospel of Matthew, each of which ends with the transitional phrase, "Now when Jesus had finished saying these things" (7:28; 11:1; 13:53; 19:1; 26:1). So, it would seem the author wanted us to see this material, traditionally called the Sermon on the Mount, as a cohesive unit.[7] This block presents Matthew's grand vision for the church and Jesus's vision for the people of God he is (re)forming. It opens with the "eschatological blessings that characterize the faithful" (5:3–12, the Beatitudes).[8] Then follows the body of this vision, the life and task of this blessed disciple-group in the world, in three large sections.

---

7. Since it is not crucial to the point we are making here, it is immaterial whether we consider 5:1 and 7:29 the outer limits, or allow the unit to begin at 4:23 and end at 8:1; on this, and the structure of the sermon generally, see Allison, "Structure," 423–45.

8. Allison, "Structure," 429. Thus, these are not "entrance requirements" to get into the kingdom. In fact, they are not primarily ethical demands at all (see esp. 5:11–12), but descriptors of the sorts of people who do/will enjoy the blessings. Of course, the people so described must and will seek to live in this way; thus, there is certainly an ethical implication. See the fuller treatment of Guelich, "Matthean Beatitudes," 415–34.

Summary heading: You are salt and light for this world (5:13–16)[9]

1. The disciples and Torah (5:17–48)
2. The disciples and traditional piety (6:1–18; almsgiving, prayer, fasting)
3. The disciples and social issues (6:19—7:12; relation to worldly goods and to neighbors)

Warnings (7:13–27)
Conclusion to the block (7:28—8:1)

These are the marching orders for Israel living under the rule of God now breaking into this world.

> EXCURSUS: WHO IS JESUS ADDRESSING IN THE SERMON?
>
> In light of the well-known dispute as to whether some of these counsels are meant for all Christians (so Luther) or primarily for those with religious callings (monks, priests, and bishops), a note about the addressees of the sermon is in order.[10] The Jewish "crowds" constitute the initial audience (5:1a) and the reaction of the "crowds" is highlighted at the conclusion (7:28). These are "the Jewish people as distinguished from their leaders."[11] Like Israel as a whole, however, the crowds are an ambivalent character in Matthew's story—sometimes eager to listen, but at other times hostile. Thus, while the crowds are certainly hearers of these teachings, Matthew notes that it is the "disciples" in particular who gather around Jesus on the mountain (5:2b), and some sections are clearly aimed at these "insiders" rather than the crowds (e.g., "you are the salt of the earth," 5:13). Thus, the primary addressees of this message are "disciples," those prepared to adhere to Jesus as teacher and lord. These disciples constitute the eschatological Israel whom John the Baptist and

---

9. Note the implicit polemic: "you" are the salt and light, *not* the scribes or Pharisees, or Jerusalem, the temple, Torah, or other groups in Israel. This explains why Jesus next moves on to true Torah obedience (5:17–48). See the helpful treatment in Hagner, *Matthew 1–13*, 97–102.

10. "But you hear Christ talking here [Matt 5:48] not to bishops, monks, and nuns, but in general to all Christians who are His pupils." Luther, "Sermon on the Mount," 129.

11. Cousland, *Crowds in the Gospel of Matthew*, 22.

> Jesus are calling into existence through repentance and faith. The twelve, for whom Matthew frequently reserves the term "the disciples," are, like the twelve tribes, representative of all Israel.[12] Although the sermon is potentially relevant for a larger Christian audience ("make disciples of all nations," Matt 28:19), its initially intended audience is the Jewish people of God gathering around Jesus.

And because this vision revolves around Israel and the God of Israel, the first thing to be clarified is the role of Torah (= instruction, guidance, law). Will Jesus abolish or fulfill God's Torah ("Do not think that I have come to abolish the law or the prophets," 5:17)? And how do his marching orders compare to those of the widely recognized interpreters of Israel's Torah ("unless your righteousness exceeds that of the scribes and Pharisees," 5:20)? Jesus clarifies by positing six contrasts between his instructions and those of Israel's traditional interpreters. "You have heard that it was said (their interpretation) . . . but I say to you." Each contrast takes up an aspect of Israel's obedience to the law of Moses:

- murder (vv. 21–26)
- adultery (vv. 27–30)
- divorce (vv. 31–32)
- oath-taking (vv. 33–37)
- retaliation (vv. 38–42)
- love of enemies (vv. 43–48)

In each instance Jesus "exceeds" the typical way of looking at these Torah instructions by pressing to their humanizing center, to the way in which the *mizwoth* (commandments) allow mercy and human wholeness to flourish.[13] Thus, "do not murder" leads away from anger and insults to wholesale reconciliation ("come to terms quickly with"). Prohibition of adultery seeks the formation of males' attitudes (how one "looks at a woman") and behavior for the good of women. Non-retaliation speaks of self-sacrifice in the interest of others ("go also the second mile").

12. "Repräsentanten Gesamt-Israels" (Lohfink, "Wem gilt die Bergpredigt?," 280). See also Wilkins, *Concept of Disciple*.

13. I am adopting here the phraseology of Pinchas Lapide, who sees the sermon as Jesus's "messianic program for true humanization—in the sense of becoming worthy bearers of the divine image." Lapide, *Sermon on the Mount*, 23.

God and Human Wholeness

For Jesus, that which is most fundamental to all Torah-obedience is love. "All antitheses of the S[ermon on the]M[ount] are exemplifications of the love-command in Lev 19:18. This means that the love-command directs the interpretation of the Torah commandments. Correctly interpreted, these Torah commandments are 'fulfilled' in the sense that with the love-commandment, the whole Torah is fulfilled."[14] The golden rule encompasses all of the law and the prophets (Matt 7:12). This is the hermeneutical key that helps decide if a particular interpretation of the letter of the law belongs in the kingdom or not. The Pharisees are not technically wrong to protest against healing (= working) on the Sabbath, but they fail to allow love to function as the humanizing center of Torah ("The sabbath was made for humankind, and not humankind for the Sabbath," Mark 2:27). "To enter the kingdom requires a righteousness superior . . . to that of the scribes and Pharisees, *namely, a way of understanding the law different from theirs*. The Antitheses . . . (5:21–48) will make this plain."[15]

Excursus: Jesus's Problem with the Pharisees

Since Jesus speaks here of his teaching as requiring a superior righteousness to that which the Pharisees required, perhaps we should clarify briefly just exactly what the Pharisees' problem was according to Jesus. This is important because the answer one gives to this question will greatly affect how we understand his demand for perfection vis-à-vis the Pharisees' demands ("you have heard . . . but I say"). One traditional answer is that the Pharisees were legalists. If one kept all the rules, one would be in good standing with God . . . you would be righteous. Jesus opposed this rule-keeping mentality, replacing Law with grace. Not surprisingly, the Sermon on the Mount has traditionally been troublesome for this view, since Jesus seems here far too Law-friendly. "Whoever breaks one of the least of these commandments, and teaches others to do the same, will be called least in the kingdom of heaven; but whoever does them and teaches them will be called great in the kingdom of heaven" (Matt 5:19). But not to worry, Jesus is simply pushing the Pharisees' legalism to its logical limits. *If you want to be righteous*

---

14. Betz, *Sermon on the Mount*, 205.

15. Cuvillier, "Torah Observance," 153, italics added. Or as LaCocque states: For Jesus, "The torah itself remains central as long as compassion is primordial." LaCocque, *Jesus the Central Jew*, 107; see also 181 and 186 ("love superceding justice").

based on legalistic Torah-obedience, here's what it would have to look like ... not an evil thought, not an angry word, in fact, not a single sin. ... You would need to be perfect, as perfect, holy, and sinless as God himself!

However, what if legalism wasn't the problem at all?[16] We have argued above that Jesus's fundamental disagreement with the Pharisees was not over Law versus grace. On the importance of God's Torah and obedience to it, they were essentially agreed,[17] as well as on the priority of God's grace for all human effort and blessing.[18] Where they consistently clashed was over the divine intent for Israel embedded in the commandments, that is, over hermeneutics. How is Israel to understand and commit themselves to the revealed will of God? This has to do, in part, (1) with the Pharisees' inability (refusal) to recognize Jesus's God-given authority as the eschatological sent-one ("but I say to you"), and equally (2) with a fundamental disagreement as to the aim of the commandments. As Jesus frames this, "The sabbath was made for [for the sake of][19] humankind, and not humankind for the Sabbath" (Mark 2:27).[20] For Jesus, priority in interpreting the commandments must be given to how they bless and enrich human beings for whose sake they were established, and only secondarily to their casuistic extension. The Pharisees, at least in Jesus's opinion, reverse this hermeneutical order, and are thereby more willing to "tie up heavy burdens, hard to bear, and lay them on the shoulders of others; but they themselves are unwilling to lift a finger to move them" (Matt 23:4; par. Luke 11:46).

It is in light of this hermeneutical disagreement, rather than the problem of legalism, that Jesus concludes the sermon with a pointer to the mercy of God who blesses both the good and the evil with sun and rain (5:43–47). Instead of stopping short with

---

16. Among scholars of ancient Judaism and of the Bible it has now become nearly a given that first-century Jews, including the Pharisees, were *not* legalists. See Sanders, *Paul and Palestinian Judaism*; and for an older Jewish protest, Isaacs, "Is Judaism Legalistic?," 259–68.

17. Hence, Jesus's seemingly odd affirmation of their Torah-teaching authority in Matt 23:2–3: "The scribes and the Pharisees sit on Moses' seat; therefore, do whatever they teach you and follow it."

18. See esp. Sanders, *Paul and Palestinian Judaism*.

19. BDAG, s.v. *dia* + accus., 2a: "the reason why something happens, results, exists."

20. See the same point among some (later) rabbis: "The Torah says, 'profane a Sabbath for human beings, that they may observe many Sabbaths'" (Sabb. 151b; cited in LaCocque, *Jesus the Central Jew*, 71).

the Pharisees' technically correct casuistry, Jesus calls Israel to be whole and complete in loving God and others, *teleios/tamim*, like God himself.

The final antithesis, keeping the "best argument" for "last where it will be remembered,"[21] takes up the love-command of Lev 19:18 ("love your neighbor"). Notable is the addition of "and hate your enemy," which does not occur in this, or any, OT text. The general idea, however, that one loves one's friends and not those who do one ill, was commonplace in the ancient world, including ancient Judaism.[22] The opposite—doing good to one's enemies—was less common, but certainly not unknown. Thus, Seneca recommends, "If you wish to imitate the gods, do good deeds also to the ungrateful: for the sun also goes up upon the evil, and the sea stands open even to pirates."[23]

However, though Jesus was not unique in rejecting retaliation and hatred toward enemies, his call for *love* of enemies was rare to nonexistent elsewhere.[24] Precisely this open-hearted generosity of spirit ("makes his sun rise on the evil and on the good"), this self-giving kindness, most essentially characterizes God the father for Jesus, and for that reason must also characterize those who would claim to be his children ("so that you may be children of your Father in heaven"). "As God is unrestricted in His goodness, so according to v. 48 the disciples of Jesus should be 'total' in their love, bringing even their enemies . . . within its compass, v. 44f."[25]

It is just at this point that Jesus introduces the language which interests us in this book. "Be *teleios*,[26] therefore, as your heavenly Father is *teleios*." As noted in an earlier chapter, this language in both Hebrew and Greek speaks not of some sort of flawlessness, of moral impeccability, but

---

21. Thurston, "Matthew 5:43–48," 170.

22. So, for example, a Delphic maxim: "To friends be kind, against enemies retaliate" (cited in Nolland, *Gospel of Matthew*, 265 n. 256). Or the DSS: "Love the sons of light . . . and hate all the sons of darkness" (1QS 1.9–10). See Reiser, "Love of Enemies," 411–27.

23. *Ben.* 4.26.1. Cited in Nolland, *Gospel of Matthew*, 267.

24. Nolland, *Gospel of Matthew*, 267; further on such comparisons 264–70.

25. Delling, "*telos, etc.*," 74.

26. Although the Greek future (*esesthe teleioi*) could be read as a promise/prediction or an exhortation-wish ("may you be"), the imperative sense is rightly preferred by most interpreters in line with the imperatives opening the 1st, 2nd, 4th and 6th antitheses (vv. 21, 27, 33 and 43). See Nolland, *Gospel of Matthew*, 270–71.

of a fullness and wholeness in which someone or something conforms to its design and purpose. God, of course, is the preeminent exemplar of one who is all that he/she is meant to be ("as your heavenly Father is perfect"). Most importantly for the Jewish view, God is undivided love.

> The LORD, the LORD, a God merciful and gracious, slow to anger, and abounding in steadfast love and faithfulness. (Exod 34:6)

And, thus, Jesus wraps up this section of the sermon[27] with a call to imitate precisely this mercy[28] and lovingkindness that form the key to his Torah-interpretation and that encapsulate true human wholeness.

When Jesus points to God himself ("as your father in heaven is") as the model for human behavior, he is taking up a long-standing *imitatio dei* tradition in Judaism.[29] The central divine character-trait in Judaism was mercy.

> The LORD, the LORD, a God merciful and gracious, slow to anger, and abounding in steadfast love and faithfulness, keeping steadfast love for the thousandth generation, forgiving iniquity and transgression and sin. (Exod 34:6-7)

The creation of human beings in the image of God (Gen 1:26; 5:1; etc.) meant that they were to "image" or reflect their maker, that is to look like him in their character and behavior. They were to be holy as he is holy (Lev 11:45; 19:2; etc.), which meant, above all, to show love and mercy as does God (Lev 19:18, 34; Deut 6:5; 10:12-13, 19; 11:22; etc.).[30] Jesus's

---

27. "The section concludes with a final maxim (v. 48) that sums up the underlying theological doctrine not only for vv. 43-48 but also for all of the antitheses and, indeed, for the S[ermon on the]M[ount] as a whole. The last word of v. 48 ('perfect') seems to connect with the last word of SM/Matt 5:17 ('fulfill'), thus making the entire section on the antitheses (vv. 17-48) a ring composition. The connection implies that 'fulfilling the Torah' in the sense intended by the SM is tantamount to 'perfection.'" Betz, *Sermon on the Mount*, 296.

28. Understood this way, the Lukan version ("Be merciful, just as your Father is merciful," Luke 6:36) is simply an alternate way of saying the very same thing, and can be documented elsewhere in Jewish literature: "As our father is merciful (*raḥman*) in heaven, so be ye merciful on earth" (Pseudo-Jonathan Targum of Lev 22:28; cited in Sabourin, "Why Is God Called 'Perfect,'" 637).

29. This *imitatio* tradition in Judaism has been well-documented and described; see "Von der *imitatio dei* zur Nachfolge Christi," in Schoeps, *Aus frühchristlicher Zeit*, 286-301; "The Imitation of God" in Abrahams, *Studies in Pharisaism*, 138-82; and Schechter, *Aspects of Rabbinic Theology*, 199-218.

30. On this *imitatio* tradition behind Matt 5:48, see the lucid treatment in

wording itself, "be *teleios*, as your father in heaven is *teleios*," may be patterned after this tradition. Just as Jesus himself fully exemplified this divine mercy as the "friend of sinners," so he calls his disciples to follow, or imitate, him, and thus to reflect the divine mercy-image.

This reminder of the Jewish *imitatio* tradition also clears up another misunderstanding of Matt 5:48. Not infrequently one hears something like the following: By perfect Jesus surely means an absolute, flawless, sinless perfection, since he says "as your father in heaven is perfect"; and surely God is perfectly holy, without sin or corruption of being. However, for at least three reasons, it is highly unlikely this is what Jesus means. 1) Jewish tradition rarely used the language of "perfection" to speak of God himself, his being and essence. Instead, they spoke of his "ways" as perfect; i.e., how he acts. Thus, this is unlikely to be a reference to divine essence. 2) The *imitatio* tradition in the OT and in Judaism made reference not to ontology (what God is essentially), but to function, how God acts and is experienced by Israel. 3) The Greek particle (*hōs* [as]) functions here modally (as God acts) rather than ontologically (as God is), which is confirmed by the Lukan version ("as your father is merciful," i.e., shows mercy).[31]

Translating "Be Perfect" in Matt 5:48

One of the earliest known attempts to translate Matt 5:48 into English was Wycliffe's 1384 translation from the Vulgate.

> Therfore be ye parfit, as youre heuenli fadir is parfit.[32]

Wycliffe's *parfit* reflected the Middle English adjective (ca. 1300) that was derived from the identical Old French *parfit* meaning "finished, completed, ready," both of which had relation to Latin *perfectus* meaning "completed, excellent, accomplished, exquisite."[33] He was translating the Vulgate's *perfecti/perfectus* here and not the Greek NT *teleios*. His choice of *parfit*, then, was most likely influenced by two factors. First, his Middle English *parfit* (finished, completed, ready) was a suitable gloss for the

Feldmeier, "'As Your Heavenly Father Is Perfect,'" 431–44.

31. Du Plessis, *Teleios*, 171.
32. From the 1384 edition.
33. Online Etymological Dictionary, http://www.etymonline.com/index.php?term=perfect. Additional details of etymology and development in the *Oxford English Dictionary* article.

Jesus and Perfection

Vulgate's *perfecti/perfectus* (completed, excellent, accomplished, exquisite), both in meaning and in sound. Second, he will likely have had in mind the long tradition of patristic and medieval interpretation of Matt 5:48, which understood this perfection as the elimination of human passions in order to enable godlikeness in knowledge and mystical union.[34] One thinks here of the rationale for monastic discipline to perfect or complete the saint through the mortification of the flesh.

From the fourteenth to sixteenth centuries Middle English *parfit* was in the process of being replaced by the newer spelling *perfect* (spelling still varied during this period).[35] The translations of Tyndale and Coverdale adopted this newer spelling.

> Tyndale (1525): "ye shall therfore be perfecte eve as youre father which is in heauen is perfecte."[36]

> Coverdale (1535): "Ye shall therfore be perfecte, euen as youre father in heaue is perfecte."[37]

Tyndale's writings made clear what he understood by this translation and that it was not any sort of moral or sinless perfection.

> The text saith not, Ye shall be as perfect as God; but perfect after his example. To be perfect, in the scripture, is not to be a monk or a friar, or never to sin. For Christ teacheth not here monks or friars, but his disciples and every Christian man and woman. And to be in this life altogether without sin is impossible. But to be perfect is to have pure doctrine without false opinions, and that thine heart be to follow that learning.[38]

While sinless or morally flawless behavior may well have been a possible, but minor, sense of the developing English word,[39] the meaning of French and Latin antecedents along with the history of interpretation of Matt 5:48 suggest they heard Jesus calling for disciples to be complete and finished exemplars of the kind of person God desired.

---

34. See ch. 11 below and the works by Burgess and Flew referenced there.

35. See *Oxford English Dictionary* 11:535–37. Middle English *parfit* was Latinized into *perfit, perfect*.

36. From the earliest edition (1525), http://www.studylight.org.

37. From the 1535 edition, https://www.studylight.org.

38. Tyndale, *Expositions and Notes*, 71.

39. *Oxford English Dictionary*, 536, B.4.b–c.

Our King James translators followed Tyndale and Coverdale with the gloss *perfect*. It seems unlikely that they intended thereby to convey a new thought—the expectation of sinless perfection or absolute, godlike moral character. We find during this early period of English translation a constant attempt, such as with Tyndale and with Wesley and many others, to clarify that the choice of this word *does not imply* moral flawlessness, even though the word *could* apparently contain this element within its broader range of meaning.

The final step in cementing the place of *perfect* in Matt 5:48 came when the Reformation established the requirement of *perfect obedience* as an integral element in the proper understanding of justification by faith alone. Sinful human beings cannot produce the sinless righteous law-keeping that God demands, but God in his grace offers to credit their account with the perfect and flawless obedience of Christ himself. "Be ye perfect" means that even a single transgression brings the verdict of "sinner," and necessitates that God's grace alone can redeem the sinner. Now this understanding of perfect had a strong theological underpinning.

The power of this particular translational tradition is truly amazing. We noted earlier that nearly all English translations have long-since abandoned the use of English "perfect" when translating OT texts using *tamim, shalem*, etc. They realized that this English gloss does not communicate accurately the sense of the original. NT translators have been a bit slower to respond. Table 2 reveals significant movement away from the gloss "perfect" in English NT translations.

Table 2: "Perfect" Largely Retired in NT Translations

NT text	Greek	ET's still using "perfect"	Other glosses
Luke 6:40	katartismenos	KJV "perfectly trained": NKJV	"fully qualified/trained": NRSV, NIV, NLT, ESV, NAB, NAS, NET, CEV, HCSB "fully prepared": CEB "completed training": GNB
1 Cor 2:6	teleios	KJV	"mature": NRSV, NIV, NLT, ESV, NAB, NAS, NET, CEV, HCSB, CEB, GNB, NKJV
Eph 4:12	katartismon	KJV	"equip": NRSV, NLT, ESV, NAB, NAS, NET, NKJV, CEB "prepare": NIV, GNB "training": HCSB

Jesus and Perfection

2 Tim 3:17	artios	KJV	"proficient": NRSV "thoroughly equipped": NIV, CEB "competent": ESV, NAB "adequate": NAS "dedicated": NET "complete": NKJV, HCSB "fully qualified": GNB
Heb 13:21	katartisai	KJV	"make complete": NRSV, NKJV "equip": NIV, NLT, ESV, NAS, NET, CEB, HCSB "furnish": NAB "make ready": CEV "provide": GNB
Eph 4:13	teleion	KJV, NKJV	"maturity/mature manhood": NRSV, NIV, NLT, ESV, NAB, NAS, NET, CEB, CEV, GNB, HCSB
Gal 3:3	epiteleisthe	KJV, NLT, ESV, NAS, NKJV	"ending": NRSV, NAB "attain your goal": NIV "finish": NET, CEB, GNB "complete": CEV, HCSB
2 Cor 13:9	katartisin	KJV, NRSV, NIV, GNB	"mature": NLT "restoration": ESV "improvement": NAB "made complete": NAS, NKJV, CEB "fully qualified": NET "do even better": CEV
2 Cor 13:11	katartizesthe	KJV, NIV, GNB	"put things in order": NRSV, CEB "grow to maturity": NLT "aim for restoration": ESV "mend your ways": NAB "be made complete": NAS, NKJV "set things right": NET
Phil 3:15	teleioi	KJV, NAS, NET (in quotes)	"mature": NRSV, NIV, NLT, ESV, NKJV, CEB, CEV, GNB, HCSB "perfectly mature": NAB
Col 1:28	teleion	KJV, NIV, NLT, NAB, NKJV	"mature": NRSV, ESV, NET, CEB, CEV, GNB, HCSB "complete": NAS
Col 4:12	teleioi	KJV, NLT, NAB, NAS, NKJV	"mature": NRSV, NIV, ESV, NET, CEB, GNB, HCSB
Heb 6:1	teleiotēta	KJV, NRSV, NKJV	"maturity": NIV, NLT, ESV, NAB, NAS, NET, CEB, CEV, HCSB
1 Pet 5:10	katartisei	KJV, NAS, NKJV, GNB	"restore": NRSV, NIV, NLT, ESV, NAB, NET, CEB, HCSB "make complete": CEV

Table 3, however, highlights six NT texts where "perfect" largely refuses to budge.

Table 3: "Perfect" Translation Still Dominant

NT text	Greek	ET's using "perfect"	Other translations
Matt 5:48	*teleios*	NRSV, NIV, NLT, ESV, KJV, NAB, NAS, NET, NKJV, GNB, HCSB	"complete": CEB "always acts like your Father in heaven": CEV
Matt 19:21	*teleios*	NRSV, NIV, NLT, ESV, KJV, NAB, NET, NKJV, GNB, HCSB	"complete": NAS, CEB
Phil 3:12	*teteleiomai*	KJV, NIV, NLT, ESV, NAS, NET, NKJV, CEB, CEV, GNB	"reached the goal": NRSV, "perfect maturity": NAB "fully mature": HCSB
Heb 10:1	*teleiosai*	KJV, NRSV, NIV, ESV, NAB, NAS, NET, NKJV, CEB, GNB, HCSB	"provide perfect cleansing": NLT "free from sin": CEV
Heb 10:14	*teteleioken*	KJV, NRSV, NIV, NLT, ESV, NAB, NAS, NET, NKJV, CEB, GNB, HCSB	"set free from sin": CEV
Jas 3:2	*teleios*	KJV, NRSV, NIV, NLT, ESV, NAB, NAS, NET, NKJV, GNB	"full maturity": CEB "mature": CEV, HCSB

We will deal with the four non-gospel texts in another chapter, but readers can note that translators apparently feel bound to retain "perfect" in translating the two important Matthean texts ("be perfect" and "if you would be perfect"). As we have discussed regarding Matt 5:48, commentators frequently point out that *teleios* here probably means complete rather than perfect. Either translators across the board disagree with commentators at this point, or, more likely in my opinion, the sound of "therefore, be perfect as your heavenly father is perfect" is so firmly rooted in the English Bible tradition that even the best translators cannot bring themselves to choose a different word. Tradition has trumped clear communication.

Matthew 19:21

We can now proceed somewhat more expeditiously with the only other gospel text using *teleios*, Matt 19:21. It adds some additional nuances to our understanding of this wholeness but in large part agrees with what we have already discovered.

Jesus and Perfection

Then someone came to him and said, "Teacher, what good deed must I do to have eternal life?" And he said to him, "Why do you ask me about what is good? There is only one who is good. If you wish to enter into life, keep the commandments." He said to him, "Which ones?" And Jesus said, "You shall not murder; You shall not commit adultery; You shall not steal; You shall not bear false witness; Honor your father and mother; also, You shall love your neighbor as yourself." The young man said to him, "I have kept all these; what do I still lack?" Jesus said to him, "If you wish to be perfect, go, sell your possessions, and give the money to the poor, and you will have treasure in heaven; then come, follow me." When the young man heard this word, he went away grieving, for he had many possessions. (Matt 19:16–22)

There is general agreement that Matt/Luke have drawn from Mark 10:17–22 for the basic story as well as for the following interchange with the disciples regarding wealth (Mark 10:23–27 par.), and that this core of the narrative is historical.[40] Matthew's account shows numerous significant differences from the Markan forerunner (underlined in the table below), many of which will be commented on below. The most significant for our purposes is Matthew's insertion of *teleios*.

Table 4: Synoptic Comparison, Rich Young Man Story

Matt 19:16–22	Mark 10:17–22	Luke 18:18–23
Then someone came to him and said,	As he was setting out on a journey, a man ran up and knelt before him, and asked him,	A certain ruler asked him,
"Teacher, what good deed must I do to have eternal life?"	"Good Teacher, what must I do to inherit eternal life?"	"Good Teacher, what must I do to inherit eternal life?"
And he said to him, "Why do you ask me about what is good? There is only one who is good.	Jesus said to him, "Why do you call me good? No one is good but God alone.	Jesus said to him, "Why do you call me good? No one is good but God alone.
If you wish to enter into life, keep the commandments." He said to him, "Which ones?"	You know the commandments:	You know the commandments:

---

40. Many consider the ensuing interchange with Peter as to "leaving all" (Mark 10:28–30 par.) to be a later addition, not originally belonging to this particular story. For details, see Davies and Allison, *Critical and Exegetical Commentary*, 3:40–41.

Matt 19:16–22	Mark 10:17–22	Luke 18:18–23
And Jesus said, "You shall not murder; You shall not commit adultery; You shall not steal; You shall not bear false witness; Honor your father and mother; also, <u>You shall love your neighbor as yourself</u>."	'You shall not murder; You shall not commit adultery; You shall not steal; You shall not bear false witness; You shall not defraud; Honor your father and mother."	'You shall not commit adultery; You shall not murder; You shall not steal; You shall not bear false witness; Honor your father and mother."
The young man said to him, "I have kept all these; <u>what do I still lack?</u>"	He said to him, "Teacher, I have kept all these since my youth."	He replied, "I have kept all these since my youth."
Jesus said to him, "<u>If you wish to be perfect</u>, go, sell your possessions, and give the money to the poor, and you will have treasure in heaven; then come, follow me."	Jesus, looking at him, loved him and said, "You lack one thing; go, sell what you own, and give the money to the poor, and you will have treasure in heaven; then come, follow me."	When Jesus heard this, he said to him, "There is still one thing lacking. Sell all that you own and distribute the money to the poor, and you will have treasure in heaven; then come, follow me."
When the young man heard this word, he went away grieving, for he had many possessions.	When he heard this, he was shocked and went away grieving, for he had many possessions.	But when he heard this, he became sad; for he was very rich.

Just prior to the narrative of Jesus's approach to Jerusalem (20:17), and following a block of teaching on matters related to the community and discipleship (18:1—19:1a), Matthew narrates a series of teaching interactions between Jesus and various groups that took place in "Judea beyond the Jordan" (19:1). The structure and content of 19:1–30 mirror fairly closely those in Mark (10:1–31).[41]

- 19:3–12: question/test by Pharisees over divorce law, with brief response to disciples
- 19:13–15: disciples question Jesus receiving little children
- 19:16–30: question/interaction with wealthy young man re: wealth and entering kingdom (vv. 16–22), with response to disciples (vv. 23–30)
- 20:1–16: parable of laborers in the vineyard

The first three pericopes deal broadly with what could be termed household matters in the life of disciples (divorce, children, and wealth)[42] as

---

41. Matthew inserts a saying about eunuchs (19:10–12).
42. See Carter, *Households and Discipleship*; and endorsed by Davies and Allison,

three different groups (Pharisees, disciples, young inquirer) put questions to Jesus's teaching and actions. The pericope in question has obvious ties to the Sermon on the Mount.[43]

To begin the story, the young man asks, "Teacher, what good deed must I do to have eternal life?" Matthew, or his oral tradition, has made several adjustments to the Markan account. First, he has eliminated the young man's address to Jesus as "good teacher."[44] This allows Matthew, second, to avoid the seeming denial of Jesus's goodness in the Markan account ("Why do you call me good? No one is good but God alone" Mark 10:18). Third, Matthew brings this omitted "good" into the man's question itself ("What good deed must I do?" Matt 19:16). The insertion of "good" could imply *a particular good deed* (so NRSV) or *additional good thing/action* (NIV), or, more likely, *a more abstract question*, "What good must I do?"[45] This is essentially the same question as that posed in Mark's gospel ("What must I do?" Mark 10:17). As Jesus's answering citation of Torah-commandments will confirm (vv. 18–19), the man is asking about proper Torah obedience.[46] He seeks to learn from Jesus what is required to obtain eternal life, which is synonymous with entering into life (v. 17b) or the kingdom of heaven/God (v. 23b). Jesus's initial answer is what one would expect of a Jewish teacher, "keep the commandments" (v. 17b), followed by a listing of several of the ten commandments and the Levitical command to love one's neighbor.

In the context of observant Judaism, there is no reason to suspect the man of hubris or hypocrisy when he replies, "I have kept all these" (v. 20b).[47] All of this—keeping Torah as the path of life—would have been

---

Critical and Exegetical Commentary, 3:2.

43. In addition to the use of *teleios* (5:48), there is discussion of divorce (5:31–32) and reference to the love command of Lev 19:18 (5:43–48).

44. So the Alexandrian MS tradition (B, ℵ, D, L, Θ, etc.); the majority of MSS read "good teacher" in harmony with Mark/Luke.

45. See Nolland, *Gospel of Matthew*, 789 n. 786. In any case, this should not be seen as evidence of "Jewish legalism."

46. See Luck, "Die Frage nach dem Guten," 282–97. Also Luz, *Matthew 8–20*, 511.

47. The Markan note that Jesus "loved him" after this response (Mark 10:21) argues against the man's supposed hypocrisy. Paul, too, considered himself blameless in keeping the commandments (Phil 3:6b), and Luke could speak of Paul as one who observed the law (Acts 21:24). See also Sir 15:15: "If you choose, you can keep the commandments." Among ancient interpreters, Chrysostom and Basil accepted the man's claim of obedience, while Jerome, Hilary, Luther, and Calvin disputed it. Hagner is correct that the man "could hardly have been successful in obeying the commandments *as*

common to Jesus as well as his opponents, but the young man is aware that Jesus finds this common position deficient. This had been precisely the point of the earlier antitheses ("you have heard . . . but I say"). Thus, the young man presses further, "what do I still lack?" (v. 20c).

Now, in Jesus's answer to the question of what a law-observant Jew still lacks, comes the crucial point for our study. "If you wish to be *teleios*, go, sell your possessions, and give the money to the poor, and you will have treasure in heaven; then come, follow me" (v. 21b). A long tradition of interpretation sees in this phrase ("if you wish to be perfect") a second, higher plane of salvation or discipleship, beyond the mere obtaining of eternal life. As we will detail in a subsequent chapter, this developed later into the monastic "counsels of perfection." While the common believer could attain eternal life through the normal means of obedience and sacraments, it was only those willing to wholly mortify the flesh through the vows of poverty, chastity, and obedience who could attain to this higher perfection, often associated with the beatific vision.[48]

This interpretation founders, however, on a simple observation. When the man states he has kept the commandments, i.e., the traditional path to life, Jesus does not say something like, "Yes, that will be good enough for eternal life, but let me show you an even higher level of heavenly attainment." Instead, the young man is still asking what he "lacks," i.e., for the obtaining of precisely that life which has been seeking, and which he knows Jesus has been preaching. Jesus's "if you wish to be complete [*teleios*]" implies that the traditional path of obedience is now insufficient for inheriting the life of the age to come. In addition, Jesus's answer ("sell all, give to the poor, follow me") is precisely the way he announces everywhere and to all for entry to the rule of God, the life of the age to come, not for a second stage of spirituality. And, finally, the young man's concluding response ("he went away grieving") is hardly what a reader would expect if the man's obedience were sufficient for eternal life, just not for the higher attainments.

---

interpreted by Jesus in the Sermon on the Mount," but that somewhat different point is precisely what will be taken up in the next interchange about what he lacks to be *teleios*.

48. Harrington sees a two-level teaching in this passage; however, he sees not two levels of Christian discipleship (religious vs. laity), but a higher way for Jewish disciples of Jesus ("perfection") versus the traditional path of keeping commands for life for other Jews. Harrington, "Rich Young Man," 1425–32. This suggestion, however, misses the correct relationship between obtaining eternal life and perfection (see above).

Jesus and Perfection

Again, as we have seen in so many other instances, the English translation "perfect" sets us on a wrong path. *Teleios* refers not to some superior stage of salvation or spiritual development. Nor does it propose a goal unattainable by mortals. Rather, it is another way of referring to the righteous, to those who are complete and whole as God envisioned, to those who keep the commandments, who fear and please God from the heart, like Abraham and Job. As Carter phrases, to be perfect in this text is to "have a will identified with God's will,"[49] and that can come now only by following Jesus and his teaching wholeheartedly.[50]

This brings us to Jesus's call to this wealthy Jewish man, which combines both an economic element ("sell possessions and give to the poor") and the more common "come, follow me." The latter element is precisely what the man lacks, even with his traditional Jewish obedience to Torah. The new age, the rule of God breaking in with the preaching of Jesus, now demands that one listen to the eschatological herald. As Carter concludes: "What has been lacking for the man, therefore, is his commitment to the rule of God encountered in Jesus."[51]

But what of the call to renunciation of possessions? Is this a universal call to personal impoverishment for the sake of others; i.e., one cannot be a true disciple without such voluntary poverty?[52] Is it intended only for those called to the itinerant lifestyle of Jesus and the twelve?[53] Is it a unique call to this particular wealthy man? We do not have time for a thorough unpacking of this theme of wealth and the gospel, nor is it crucial to our investigation, so a few comments here on the relation between this call to renunciation and human wholeness (*teleios*) will have to suffice.[54] The immediately ensuing saying about the difficulty of the "rich entering the kingdom" (vv. 23–27) suggests that attitudes to wealth were

---

49. Carter, *Households and Discipleship*, 122.

50. The same language was taken up with very similar meaning by the Qumran community ("house of perfection") in reference to themselves as the only group in the last days to hold fast to the God of Israel. Davies, *Setting of the Sermon*, 209–15.

51. Carter, *Households and Discipleship*, 122.

52. "So therefore, none of you can become my disciple if you do not give up all your possessions" (Luke 14:33).

53. During Jesus's earthly ministry, it would appear there were at least two modes of following: 1) itinerancy, as exemplified by Jesus and the twelve, for which renunciation of possessions, family, etc. was the norm; and 2) settled followers (e.g., Lazarus, Mary, and Martha) of whom such radical renunciation was not required. See Theissen, *Sociology of Early Palestinian Christianity*, 9–23.

54. For a helpful overview of the topic, see Hays, "Rich and Poor," 800–810.

considered integral to discipleship. Such calls to renunciation of wealth for the sake of the poor can be found throughout the gospel tradition (e.g., Luke 5:11, 28). However, it does not appear possible to document a consistent and universal call to poverty.[55] What is clear, however, is that money, and the disciple's relation to it, was not neutral, but dangerous.

> Jesus thought of money like fire: a useful thing in its proper place, but in abundance ever more likely to leap its bounds and to consume its erstwhile master.[56]

Much as in Judaism, human wholeness for Jesus cannot be divorced from how we live in the world and how we relate to it and to others. Like the heavenly father, the disciple of Jesus will use this world's goods for the sake of the kingdom and for blessing others. No other attachment may be higher than the attachment to God, and now to God's messianic agent, Jesus. To be whole, *teleios*, meant the crucifixion of this attachment for this rich young man as for anyone who would follow Jesus and participate in God's rule.

---

55. See, for example, the many examples of non-poor disciples; e.g., Lazarus, Mary, and Martha; wealthy women supporters of Jesus; early Acts church; Corinthian house-church leaders; etc.

56. Hays, "Rich and Poor," 804.

Chapter 7

Finding Perfection in Gal 3:10, or Maybe Not?

Man suffers but believes in happiness, he falls but believes in perfection.[1]

Although Matt 5:48 has played the driving role in much general Christian reflection on "perfection," for the Reformation tradition Paul came to play an equally important role. In particular, Luther's understanding of Pauline justification by faith apart from works required the assumption of perfect law-keeping in order to work.[2] The cross of Christ shines brightly in Luther's thinking as the one-and-only path to righteousness and salvation for sinners, for all human beings without exception. Why must that be so? Because all have failed to keep God's law ... no one, except Christ, has or can keep the law because the standard is flawless, 100 percent obedience to all commands all the time.[3]

For this crucial plank in his argument, Luther found a stout partner in Gal 3:10–14. Before turning to it in detail, a reminder as to just how crucial this bit of his argument is. First, without this premise of perfect law-keeping, the Reformation's understanding of justification might seem to be endangered. To many this can only mean a return to Roman Catholic synergism (thus the heat generated by this topic). Second, the Pauline doctrine of sin and of humanity's sinfulness may have to be reconceived.

---

1. French saying attributed to Guizot in Tatarkiewicz, *On Perfection*, 20.
2. Campbell, *Deliverance of God*, 112–14.
3. See Luther's Smaller Catechism cited earlier, ch. 1.

If the law is not impossible to keep (i.e., something less than perfection is required), why does Paul think all are sinners (e.g., Rom 3)? Have we misunderstood him on this important topic? And third, is the cross of Christ thus rendered less than absolutely necessary? If the law was not an impossibly high bar, and some, even if very few, may indeed have reached it, would they no longer need the cross? Does this presume an alternative to the cross for some? Are there indeed some "doers of the law who will be justified" (Rom 2:13)? As the reader will discern, this topic of perfection is far from being merely academic or esoteric but drives right to the heart of Protestant identity.

Since Luther (and most who have followed him) found his chief ally in Gal 3:10, that is where we now turn in order to determine whether this text does, in fact, presume the doctrine of perfect law-keeping.

> For all who rely on the works of the law are under a curse; for it is written, "Cursed is everyone who does not observe and obey all the things written in the book of the law." Now it is evident that no one is justified before God by the law; for "The one who is righteous will live by faith." But the law does not rest on faith; on the contrary, "Whoever does the works of the law will live by them." Christ redeemed us from the curse of the law by becoming a curse for us—for it is written, "Cursed is everyone who hangs on a tree"—in order that in Christ Jesus the blessing of Abraham might come to the Gentiles, so that we might receive the promise of the Spirit through faith. (Gal 3:10–14)

Although this text does not use the term *teleios* or cognates, the requirement of perfect law-keeping is understood by many to be *necessarily implied* by the logic of Paul's argument.[4] A long history of Pauline interpretation reads Gal 3:10 in light of the following syllogism.[5]

Major premise	The law curses those who do not keep it perfectly ("Cursed is everyone who does not observe and obey all the things written").

---

4. For this view see esp. Schreiner, "Paul and Perfect Obedience," 245–78; and for the rejection of this view, Cranford, "Possibility of Perfect Obedience," 242–58.

5. Guy Waters considers this "perhaps the oldest and most longstanding" interpretation of Gal 3:10, and cites John Calvin for this early view; Waters, *End of Deuteronomy*, 93 n. 64.

Finding Perfection in Gal 3:10, or Maybe Not?

Minor premise (implied)	No one keeps (or can keep) the law perfectly.
Conclusion	Therefore, "all who rely on" keeping the law are under a curse.

This is the interpretation adopted by Reformation leaders and which still finds supporters, though they now find themselves in a diminishing minority.[6] As detailed in the chapter on perfection in Jewish tradition, the "Sanders revolution" has rightly caused most interpreters to abandon this position, since its assumed human inability to keep Torah now appears un-Jewish.[7] This would mean Paul's argument was a risky innovation that would carry little rhetorical weight with his opponents.[8]

However, if failure to keep the law perfectly is not the reason for the curse, what is a better explanation? To get at this for our purposes, there are only a few issues that need to be clarified.

1. Who exactly are those Paul has in view when he speaks of "all who rely on the works of the law"? Are they "legalists" who depend on some level of obedience to be accounted righteous?

2. What is the point of Paul's citation of Deut 27:26 ("Cursed is everyone who does not observe and obey all the things written in the book of the law")? Does he assume that anything less than flawless obedience ("obey all the things written") brings a curse?

3. Why is Paul bringing all this up at this point in his argument?

---

6. A partial list includes: Mussner, *Der Galaterbrief*; Hübner, *Law in Paul's Thought*; Schreiner, "Is Perfect Obedience," 151–60; Longenecker, *Galatians*; Smith, *What Must I Do*; Das, "Galatians 3:10," 203–23. For an overview of interpretations of Gal 3:10, see Scott, "'For as Many as Are of Works,'" 188–94.

7. Although Matlock himself ultimately favors the "human inability" reading of Gal 3:10, see his helpful engagement with recent interpretations, most of which deny the "unfulfillability" thesis: Matlock, "Helping Paul's Argument Work?," 154–79.

8. See esp. Cranford, "Possibility of Perfect Obedience," 242–58. Interestingly, Sanders retained the view that Paul, himself, in contrast to his Jewish tradition, upheld the requirement of perfect legal conformity. Sanders, "On the Question," 105.

Who Are the "Works of Law" Group?

First then, who exactly are those Paul has in view when he speaks of "all who rely on the works of the law"? What is it about them or about their behavior that brings upon them a curse? Unfortunately, those readers limited to English will immediately be led astray by quite a few of our modern translations. The people in view in the verse are said to be those who "rely on" or "depend on" observing or keeping the works required by the law.[9] That is, their problem is imagining they can keep the law sufficiently to merit justification. But because they can't, i.e., can't keep it *perfectly*, they fall under the curse of the law. As we have seen in the chapter on Jewish tradition, neither the OT nor Jewish tradition suggest any of this line of thinking, which makes it unlikely that Paul would have made such an un-Jewish argument at this crucial point.[10]

Readers of the Greek NT can see quickly that English translations have introduced an interpretive paraphrase. The Greek text reads *hosoi gar ex ergōn nomou*, which can be rendered "for as many as are of the works of the Law" (NAS, KJV). This may at first seem difficult to understand, which explains why so many translations reach for an interpretive paraphrase. However, this is actually not as tricky as it at first appears. The language of a person or group being "of" someone or something is a commonly used means of group identification in Greek, and is often found in Paul's letters, including Galatians. He earlier referred to Peter fearing *tous ek peritomēs* ("those who are of circumcision," Gal 2:12; cf. also Rom 4:12; Col 4:11; Tit 1:10; Acts 11:2) meaning those *identified by* circumcision, that is, Jews. Israelites are *hoi ex Israēl* (Rom 9:6), those who are of, or belong to, Israel. And Jews can be called *hoi ek nomou* (Rom 4:14; cf. also v. 16), those identified by their connection with Torah. All of these combinations with *ek/ex* identify a particular group or party by its major identifying mark ("the circumcision party," "the law party").[11]

---

9. ESV, NAB, NIV, NLT, NRSV.

10. As Hays puts this point, "This is such a ridiculous caricature of Judaism ... that it could hardly have been taken seriously as a persuasive argument in Paul's time. If Paul had made such claims, the rival Missionaries could easily have refuted him by pointing out that the Law makes ample provision for forgiveness of transgressions through repentance, through the sacrificial system, and through the solemn annual celebration of the Day of Atonement." Hays, "Letter to the Galatians," 257.

11. Paul does this most explicitly in 1 Corinthians where he refers to various factions as "those who are of Paul ... of Apollos ... of Cephas ... of Christ" (1 Cor 1:12; but using the simple genitive, rather than the preposition *ek*). On this "partisan" use of

Finding Perfection in Gal 3:10, or Maybe Not?

This is what Paul means when he refers to "those who are of works of law."[12] They are the law-observance party, those whose primary identity is found in their adherence to Jewish Torah and the behaviors it mandates for Jews.[13] It does not imply an attitude of legalistic reliance upon their own performance, as many of our translations suggest. Instead, in this context Paul is simply contrasting a law-observance party ("Judaizers" in older parlance) with a new group whose primary identity is found in their faith in Messiah Jesus. These latter are *hoi ek pisteōs* (Gal 3:7, 9; lit. those who are of faith), the faith (or faithfulness) party. Thus, on the one side are "those of [the] faith," Christ-followers, whose central religious identity is found in their relationship with Jesus Messiah. On the other side are all those who find their religious identity (their relationship to God) most centrally defined by their relationship to Jewish Torah and the lifestyle it mandates. They are "those of law-works."

Why Are the "Works of Law" Group Under a Curse?

Second, what is the point of Paul's citation of Deut 27:26 ("Cursed is everyone who does not observe and obey all the things written in the book of the law")? Why is this law-party under a curse? Is Paul emphasizing the "all" in a way that implies perfect law-keeping? That is, are these law-party folks under a curse because they have failed to do *all* the commandments of Torah without exception or failure, they have failed to *perfectly* obey?

Many have noted that Paul's quotation does not match exactly any of our known versions of this verse.[14]

---

the preposition *ek*, see Garlington, "Paul's 'Partisan εκ,'" 567–89.

12. How one takes the phrase ("works of law") is equally as important as how one interprets the preposition. Instead of a legalistic reliance upon one's own performance, "works of law" refers to how Jews were identified in the ancient world. They were the people identified by those behaviors mandated in Torah, such as circumcision, Sabbath-keeping, food regulations, etc. For more detailed treatment, see my earlier study, Yinger, *Paul, Judaism, and Judgment*, 169–75, and Yinger, *New Perspective on Paul*, 20–23, 48–50.

13. Martyn translates "those whose identity is derived from observance of the Law." Martyn, *Galatians*, 307. Among the many studies coming to a similar conclusion, see Young, "Who's Cursed," esp. 80–81; and Zoccali, "What's the Problem with the Law?" 388 ("those who derive their identity from the ordinances of Torah").

14. See, for example, Stanley, *Paul and the Language of Scripture*, 238–43.

God and Human Wholeness

Paul: Cursed is everyone who does not continue in all things which are written in the book of the law, to do them. (NKJV)

MT: Cursed be anyone who does not uphold the words of this law by observing them. (NRSV)

LXX: Cursed is everyone who does not continue in all the words of this law to do them. (author's trans.)

The main difference for our purposes is the addition of "all [*pasin*]" in the LXX, which appears to be followed here by Paul. Richard Longenecker, along with many other exegetes, takes this added "all" to be the point Paul wishes to stress.[15] This, however, misses the point of Deut 27:26 in its original context, and it misses the reason for Paul's citation in light of Jewish tradition.[16] Chapter 27 of Deuteronomy outlines the warning to be given to Israel when they finally enter the promised land. At that time, as the people are crossing the Jordan, the Levites are to recite various covenant stipulations and to remind the nation of the curse that will come to them for not following these directives (vv. 15–25). The chapter concludes with the summarizing statement, "Cursed be anyone who does not uphold the words of this law by observing them. All the people shall say, 'Amen'!" (v. 26). This ending forms a fitting bookend to the chapter, mirroring its opening line: "Then Moses and the elders of Israel charged all the people as follows: Keep the entire commandment ['*th kal hamitsvah*] that I am commanding you today" (v. 1). Thus, the point of the chapter originally was to reinforce the traditional covenantal arrangement with the nation at the beginning of their new situation in the land. If they adhere to (continue in, affirm) Yahweh's covenant, they will experience the Abrahamic blessings; but if they depart from Yahweh's ways, they will experience the curses of the covenant.

This warning was later taken up by the prophets when accusing Israel of national rebellion.[17]

---

15. So Longenecker, *Galatians*, 117–18, with a list of others taking this position. These exegetes often point to Gal 5:3 ("Once again I testify to every man who lets himself be circumcised that he is obliged to obey *the entire law [holon ton nomon poiēsai]*") as corroborating evidence for Paul's interest in stressing the "all." However, in this latter verse Paul is not stressing "all [*pas*]" as in 3:10, but the "whole [*holos*]" of the law, i.e., including circumcision rather than a partial selection of commands.

16. See the earlier treatment of Deut 27:26 (29–33).

17. On Paul's adoption of this prophetic tradition, see Sprinkle, *Paul and Judaism Revisited*, 82–86; and Grindheim, "Apostate Turned Prophet," 545–65, esp. 558–61.

Finding Perfection in Gal 3:10, or Maybe Not?

> Hear the words of this covenant, and speak to the people of Judah and the inhabitants of Jerusalem. You shall say to them, Thus says the LORD, the God of Israel: Cursed be anyone who does not heed the words of this covenant, which I commanded your ancestors when I brought them out of the land of Egypt, from the iron-smelter, saying, Listen to my voice, and do all that I command you. So shall you be my people, and I will be your God, that I may perform the oath that I swore to your ancestors, to give them a land flowing with milk and honey, as at this day. (Jer 11:2–5)

The problem in the prophets' day, as in Paul's, was not that some of the people obeyed 99 percent of the commandments, but failed an assumed standard of 100 percent perfection. Rather, it was the covenantal problem of fundamental loyalty or disloyalty to their God. Would they keep his ways, his "whole command," or not? Would they "establish," "ratify," and "carry out" the covenant relationship laid upon them?[18] As Don Garlington states matters, "The Judaizers are not under the curse because they have failed to keep the law 'perfectly,' but because they have proven defective in the central matter: fidelity to the God of Israel."[19]

But this last point (the opponents are defective in fidelity to God) raises an equally controverted and crucial question: What is the basis or rationale for Paul's charge? If Paul is simply asserting, "You have failed to be faithful to our God and his covenant," his argument will fail, since the opponents can simply disagree and respond, "No, we haven't." Does Paul have some convincing rationale for his assertion that those counting on Jewish covenant identity have been unfaithful to God and are under the covenant curses (Gal 3:10)?

---

18. Many of our English translations make it difficult to discern this covenantal context in Paul's quotation, instead suggesting that a certain level of human performance is in view: "observe and obey all the things written" (NRSV; also NLT), "continue to do everything written" (NIV), "persevere in doing all the things" (NAB), "keep on doing everything" (NET). The Hebrew original called the nation to uphold, affirm, carry out the covenantal arrangement with its stipulations (*yaqim*, hiphil, see BDB, ad loc.). The LXX's *emmenei* (remain, persevere in) is a faithful rendering of this sense of living out covenant loyalty. While this clearly involved "doing" the commands, the point is not a certain level of performance but the fundamental loyalty of the heart lived out in behavior.

19. Garlington, "Role Reversal," 109. Barclay's conclusion is similar: "Paul's logic does not assume that blessing would require individuals to be perfect in Torah-observance, but simply that Israel's history proved her collective and persistent incapacity to be obedient." Barclay, *Paul and the Gift*, 405–6 n. 439.

Paul's apparent failure here to make the rationale explicit—something noted by most commentators—has led to numerous suggestions. 1) The most common, and the traditional Protestant explanation, is that Paul assumes Torah demands of an individual perfect obedience. Thus, it should be obvious to Paul's listeners that they are law-breakers, whether great ones as in apostasy or small sinners as in a single transgression. As many have noted, however, Jewish tradition did not agree with this perfect law-keeping thesis, and Paul's opponents would have simply rejected his argument. Because this perfection thesis has been rejected by most interpreters, others seek for alternate explanations. 2) According to Scott and Wright, first-century Jews generally recognized that their nation was not experiencing the blessings of the covenant.[20] They did not "possess" the promised land, for one thing. Some of them still lived in it (though most were scattered), but they did not rule over it; the Romans were the true possessors of the promised land. In an extended sense, the curse of exile was still in effect. So, when Paul says the people of the Mosaic covenant ("of the works of Torah") are under a curse, this refers to the visible fact that they suffer under exilic conditions. Though plausible, this rationale is certainly not explicit. 3) Dunn, differing from both the previous suggestions, favors ethnocentricity as Paul's unstated rationale in this text. This refers to Israel's attitude of favored nation status which led too often to exclusion of Gentiles, whereas the Abrahamic promise was meant specifically to *include* Gentiles. This attitude and resulting behavior constituted a failure to keep the covenant.[21] Again, while plausible, such an ethnocentric attitude is not explicit as the problem. 4) A fourth possibility looks to Israel's refusal, and the refusal of Paul's opponents, to acknowledge that Jesus's coming has inaugurated the climactic eschatological era. Their refusal to acknowledge such a new covenantal era, in which no longer Torah-zeal but Christ-faith identifies the righteous of the covenant, brings the curse. This eschatological unbelief constitutes failure to uphold the covenant.[22] For our purposes in this book, it is not necessary to decide this issue, other than to note the implausibility of the perfection thesis, and the presence of equally plausible alternatives. Thus, Gal 3:10 does not contain an assumption of perfect law-keeping.

---

20. Wright, *Climax of the Covenant*, 137–56; Scott, "'For as Many as Are of Works."
21. See Dunn, *Commentary on the Epistle*, 172–74.
22. Garlington, "Role Reversal," 85–121; and see now esp. Zoccali, "What's the Problem with the Law?" 377–415, esp. 399.

Finding Perfection in Gal 3:10, or Maybe Not?

Paul's Reasoning in Gal 3:10

Now to the third question raised at the beginning of this chapter, why is Paul bringing all this up at this point in his argument? Is it to quash the false hopes of some in Galatia who think they will be able to keep Torah sufficiently for salvation (so the traditional reading), or does he have some other aim? The paragraph opens with "for as many as are of works of law are under a curse" (3:10; author's translation). The problem he now addresses has something to do with a group (the Torah-works party) who, so Paul wishes to assert, are "under a curse." The opening *gar* ("for") shows that this important assertion is a continuation of an argument he has already started . . . so we will have to pick up that argument.

After Paul's initial recitation of the history as to how his circumcision-free gospel for Gentiles is God-given and in agreement with the gospel preached by the other apostles (1:11—2:10), he then launches into the main topic of the letter, "a person is justified not by the works of the law but through faith in Jesus Christ" (2:16).[23] As Paul notes (2:11–14), the central problematic in this phrase lay at the heart of an earlier disagreement between himself and Peter . . . did Gentile Jesus-followers need "to live like Jews" (2:14b) in order to be justified? That is, did they need to adopt Torah-works such as food laws (the issue earlier in Antioch), sabbath-keeping, etc., in order to be considered a member of the righteous ones, the elect, the people of God?[24] Peter's behavior in separating himself

---

23. This is widely considered the main proposition of the argument. For an early and influential statement of this view, see Betz, *Galatians*, 15, 114. Also, since I here and elsewhere tend to translate *pistis Christou* with "faith *in* Christ" rather than "faith *of* Christ," a brief word on this debate is in order. The Greek phrase, without context, is capable of either translation. Traditionally it has been understood as a reference to the believer's act of trusting Christ ("faith *in* Christ"). In past decades, however, many scholars have argued that it often in Paul's letters refers to Christ's own *pistis*, his faithfulness to God even to the point of death on a cross. This is the "faith *of* Christ." If Gal 2:16 is read this latter way, it states that justification comes not through "works of law" but through what Christ has done, through his faithful life and death, rather than stating it comes through the believer's faith in Christ. Proponents of both positions generally accept that Paul holds theologically to both of these. Justification finds its source in Christ's faithfulness and its instrument in the believer's faith. The difference comes down to which idea is preeminent in particular Pauline verses. In the case of Gal 2:16, Paul's use of "believe in Christ [*pisteuein + eis*]" immediately following in parallel to this phrase tips the scale for me toward "faith *in* Christ" as the better translation. On the whole, see the debate over *pistis Christou* between Hays and Dunn in Hays, *Faith of Jesus Christ*, 249–71 (Dunn: faith in Christ), 272–97 (Hays: faith of Christ).

24. Debate continues over whether "justify/justification" refer to the meeting of a

from table fellowship implied, as far as Paul was concerned, that such Gentiles needed to adopt Jewish identity and behavior. Paul's subsequent argument (3:1—5:12) seeks to prove they do not.

The first point in his proof (3:1–5) draws upon the Galatians' own experience. As they look back on their own initial reception of the gospel and of the Spirit, did God work among them "by the works of the law, or by the hearing of faith?" (3:5b, NKJV). That is, did they have to adopt Jewish identity first (keep Torah-works), or was faith in messiah the only condition? The question is rhetorical, since both Paul and the Galatians know that the pressure to adopt Jewish identity only came later. This point is followed quickly by a Scripture proof (3:6–9). Abraham himself foreshadowed this entry "by faith" since he was considered righteous by faith (citing Gen 15:6).[25]

Next comes our text under consideration. Paul has just argued from the Abrahamic narrative in Scripture that the children of Abraham were always meant to include both Jews and non-Jews ("all the Gentiles will be blessed in you"), with inclusion open to both equally through faith ("those who believe are blessed with Abraham"). This is in perfect agreement with his main proposition that righteous standing comes through allegiance to messiah (faith) rather than through Jewish identity (2:16). But, this carries a negative corollary: Jewish identity, i.e., adherence to Torah-works, is not the crucial identifier.

Following this first argument from Scripture comes a second (3:15–18). Although many details of this paragraph remain disputed, the main point is explicit. "My point is this: the law, which came four hundred thirty years later, does not annul a covenant previously ratified by God, so as to nullify the promise" (v. 17). That is, God's later Torah covenant at Sinai with Israel cannot nullify the earlier covenant promise to Abraham to bless all nations through his seed.[26] Paul notes particularly that

---

forensic-legal standard or to covenantal inclusion. The former fits well with the traditional perfection thesis (has one kept the legal standard *perfectly*), while the latter is reflected in my reading above ("be considered a member of the righteous ones"). Those interested in pursuing this issue could read the debate between John Piper (forensic view) and N. T. Wright (covenantal view): Piper, *Future of Justification*; and Wright, *Justification*.

25. In another letter, Paul will expand on this point, pointing out that Abraham's circumcision (Gen 17), one of those Torah-works that identify him as Jewish, only came later *after* he had already been considered righteous by faith (Gen 15); see Rom 4:9–12.

26. Referring to any or all of the following promises to Abraham: Gen 12:1–3;

Finding Perfection in Gal 3:10, or Maybe Not?

this earlier promise was to a singular "seed," which is Christ, rather than to many as at Sinai (v. 16). Thus, receiving God's blessing, belonging to Abraham's seed, cannot be limited to those defined by Torah, since the giving of Torah to the many at Sinai came much later than the original promise to the one.

So, to our earlier question, Why is Paul bringing all this up at this point in his argument? Answer: He is seeking to prove his thesis that Gentiles do not need to adopt Jewish identity and lifestyle in order to be part of the people of God (Gal 2:16). They are now considered members of the righteous ("justified") via faith in messiah rather than via Jewish identity ("works of law"). Gal 3:10–14 constitutes his scriptural proof of this particular point. The argument at this stage has no need to, nor interest in, showing that everyone is a sinner due to failure vis-à-vis a supposed bar of perfection.

Was Luther All Wrong?

Since we opened this chapter by challenging Luther's interpretation of Gal 3:10, it is only fair that we return to him in closing. I have argued that he was wrong to assume perfect law-keeping as an element of this verse. This does not, however, in my opinion mean we ought to chuck Luther and the Reformation out the window.[27] In many ways they got the thrust of Paul's argument right. Paul's opponents, the Torah-works party, thought allegiance to messiah wasn't quite enough for Gentiles; they needed to add Jewishness to the mix for God to be satisfied. Luther transposed this to his own day. He felt Catholic leadership was telling simple Christian people faith in Jesus wasn't quite enough for God to be satisfied; they needed to add particular works of obedience such as penance, indulgences, etc. Luther was right to protest this in the name of *solus Christus* (Christ alone). He was wrong in thinking Paul simply had an early version of Catholic works-righteousness in his different historical context.

13:14–18; 17:1–14; 22:16–19.

27. See Dunn's repudiation of a similar charge; Dunn, *New Perspective on Paul*, 18–23 ("Anti-Lutheran?").

Chapter 8

Human *Teleios* Throughout the Pauline Letters

> If there is such a thing as human perfection, it seems to emerge precisely from how we handle the imperfection that is everywhere, especially our own. What a clever place for God to hide holiness, so that only the humble and earnest will find it! A "perfect" person ends up being one who can consciously forgive and include imperfection rather than one who thinks he or she is totally above and beyond imperfection. It becomes sort of obvious once you say it out loud. In fact, I would say that *the demand for the perfect is the greatest enemy of the good.* Perfection is a mathematical or divine concept, goodness is a beautiful human concept that includes us all.[1]

Even if Gal 3:10 does not imply perfect law-keeping, the Pauline letters[2] elsewhere use *teleios* eight times, often translated "perfect" in our English versions.[3] What exactly did the apostle have in mind? Perhaps hidden somewhere among them is a new insight regarding perfection.

---

1. Rohr, *Falling Upward*, xxii–xxiii.

2. In academic NT scholarship, seven letters are widely considered authentically from Paul (Romans, 1–2 Corinthians, Galatians, Philippians, 1 Thessalonians, Philemon) with one additional currently a toss-up (Colossians). The authorship of the other five (2 Thessalonians, Ephesians, 1–2 Timothy, Titus) remains under serious dispute. My conclusions will rely on these "authentic" letters with occasional glances at "disputed" texts.

3. In addition, the noun *teleiotētos* (perfection, completeness) occurs once (Col 3:14) and verbal forms relevant to our study twice (Gal 3:3; Phil 3:12).

Human *Teleios* Throughout the Pauline Letters

Several passages in Paul's Corinthian correspondence have possible relevance for our topic, all of which use forms of the adjective *teleios* (perfect, complete, mature) or the verb *teleioō* (to complete, to perfect). These are,

- 1 Cor 2:6 ("among the *teleioi* we speak wisdom")
- 1 Cor 13:10 ("but when *to teleion* comes, the partial will come to an end")
- 1 Cor 14:20 ("in thinking be *teleioi*")
- 2 Cor 12:9 (God's power is "made perfect" [*teleitai*] in weakness)

Two of these we can omit from consideration, since they are not referring to any supposed perfection of human beings with this *teleios* language.[4]

1 Corinthians 2:6 ("Among the *Teleioi* We Speak Wisdom")

Here Paul refers to a group as the *teleioi*. Two questions must be answered for this text. First, who are the members of this group? In particular, are they all believers in Christ, or, as later Christian tradition would argue, are these a more spiritual, more holy, subgroup among believers (e.g., clergy, ascetics, mystics)? And, second, what exactly does Paul mean when he refers to them as *teleioi*? Does this possibly entail sinlessness as would seem to be implied by the KJV translation perfect?

Commentators are divided as to whether the *teleioi* are all believers or an advanced subgroup.[5] Supporters of the latter point especially to 3:1–4 where Paul speaks to the whole congregation as not spiritual (*pneumatikoi*), as people of the flesh and infants. Since the *teleioi* and the *pneumatikoi* ("spiritual ones") appear to be synonymous (cf. 2:13b), the *teleioi* must be a subgroup of the larger, mostly immature and unspiritual, congregation. Such commentators note additionally that *teleios* was

---

4. For 1 Cor 13:10, see the brief comments later in this chapter. Second Corinthians 12:9 speaks not of human beings, but of Christ's "power" coming to full flower ("made complete") in human weakness.

5. See Grindheim, "Wisdom for the Perfect," 702 nn. 749–50, for a listing of commentators on differing sides.

technical language of the ancient mystery religions referring to initiates into hidden knowledge, i.e., an elect subgroup of human beings.[6]

Decisive in my opinion, however, for the former viewpoint (*teleioi* = all believers in Corinth) is the flow of Paul's argument surrounding this statement.[7] His discussion of wisdom began at 1:18, where he argued that the message of the cross is the antithesis of human wisdom ("God's foolishness is wiser than human wisdom," 1:25). This is the seemingly foolish message the Corinthians have received for their own salvation, "so that your faith might rest not on human wisdom but on the power of God" (2:5). But Paul is not willing to evacuate the gospel of all claim to wisdom. "Yet among the *teleioi* we do speak wisdom, though it is not a wisdom of this age or of the rulers of this age, who are doomed to perish" (2:6). It is this divine wisdom of the cross, the gospel itself, which has been revealed to "those who love him" (2:9), to "us" (2:10; believers). This group has received the Spirit of God (2:12) and is taught by the Spirit (2:13). Believers are "spiritual ones [*pneumatikoi*]" (2:13) versus the "soulish person [*psychikos anthrōpos*]" (2:14) who judges the gospel to be foolishness, i.e., unbelievers. In 3:1–4 Paul does not reverse this (as the other interpretive viewpoint argued above), but challenges the congregation. By their divisive behavior ("I am of Paul, I am of Apollos") they are *looking and acting like* unspiritual, fleshly, merely human persons. This cannot, and must not, be, if they are indeed as Paul himself is convinced (cf. 1:1–9), God's field and temple (3:5–17) who belong to Christ (3:21–23). Thus, Paul uses *teleioi* as a designation for all believers, much like "saints," even if their current behavior as "unspiritual" seems to be calling that into question (3:1–4).

But what exactly is Paul saying about these believers in Corinth when he refers to them as *teleioi*? With one exception, standard English translations render this as "the mature" rather than "the perfect."[8] Our previous lexical investigations demonstrated that "whole, mature, complete" are better glosses for *teleios* than "perfect." Paul is not setting flawed, sinful persons over against those who are flawless and perfect, but is contrasting those who are spiritually immature, infants fed with milk (3:1–2), versus mature adults. The latter understand the gospel of Christ

---

6. So Conzelmann, *1 Corinthians*, 60–61.

7. In addition to the commentaries by Fee, Thiselton, Schrage, Collins, et al., see Grindheim, "Wisdom for the Perfect," 704–5.

8. NRSV, NIV, NLT, ESV, NAB, NAS, NET, NKJV. The KJV is the exception ("among them that are perfect").

crucified, "which enables the self to *live responsibly and wisely for others and for the good of the whole community.*"⁹ This is the very wholeness we have posited for *tamim* and *teleios* in Jewish and Christian tradition elsewhere. Paul stands in this Jewish line along with Jesus. Like Jesus, he is convinced a community characterized by self-giving love, a "be perfect" community, is realistic and to be expected, even if some are still looking less than complete.

1 Corinthians 14:20 ("In Thinking Be *Teleioi*")

In 1 Cor 14:20, Paul again refers to the Corinthians as *teleioi*. However, in this case it is their cognitive activity, their thinking,¹⁰ which is so designated, not directly their behavior. As seen in 2:6 above, the contrast is not between flawed and perfect individuals, but between mature versus childish ones. "Brothers and sisters, do not be children in your thinking; rather, be infants in evil, but in thinking be adults."

Philippians 3:12–16 ("Not That I Have Already . . . Reached the Goal")

Moving on to the letter to the Philippians, we read,

> Not that I have already obtained this or have already reached the goal [*teteleiōmai*]; but I press on to make it my own, because Christ Jesus has made me his own. Beloved, I do not consider that I have made it my own; but this one thing I do: forgetting what lies behind and straining forward to what lies ahead, I press on toward the goal for the prize of the heavenly call of God in Christ Jesus. Let those of us then who are mature [*teleioi*] be of the same mind; and if you think differently about anything, this too God will reveal to you. Only let us hold fast to what we have attained. (Phil 3:12–16)

In a seeming paradox, Paul here refers to himself and the Philippian believers ("those of us")¹¹ as already *teleioi* (v. 15), yet simultaneously says

---

9. Thiselton, *First Epistle to the Corinthians*, 231.

10. On the term, used only this once in the NT (*hapax legomenon*), *tais phresin* ("in matters of the mind"), see Thiselton, *First Epistle to the Corinthians*, 1119–20.

11. The Greek *hosoi* does not imply some are *teleioi*, while others are not, but simply refers to all within a particular category as in Rom 8:14, "as many as (all who = all

he himself has not yet been completed [*teteleiōmai*] (v. 12). Turning first to verse 12, we note that Paul speaks of having "obtained" something and pairs it with the verb *teleioō* (to complete an activity), found only here in his writings.[12] The "obtaining" and the "completing" are not two distinct things, but parallel ways of describing the same. Debate continues over what precisely the first image, the not-yet-obtained goal, is.[13] Numerous commentators still argue that some sort of perfectionism is implied, usually as Paul's response to an alleged opponent's position claiming to offer perfection to adherents.[14] Such views are weakened by their reliance on questionable mirror-reading of the text as well as by Paul's seeming acceptance of their terminology a few verses later ("we who are *teleioi*"). The immediate literary context, on the other hand, suggests this not-yet-obtained goal is the full knowledge of Christ at the resurrection (vv. 10–11), the "prize of the heavenly call of God in Christ Jesus" (v. 14).[15]

Paired with this is the perfect-tense verb form, *teteleiōmai*. Interpreters favoring some sort of perfection reading in the first phrase see in this verb as well a reflection of the opponents' teaching. Such opponents ostensibly promise the obtaining of some state of perfection, whether through mystery-rites, Hellenistic philosophy, or deeper attention to Jewish Torah.[16] However, rather than invoking such speculation about unknown opponents, it seems much simpler to interpret this verb in line with the literary-contextual suggestion made for the first phrase. The most common use of *teleioō* is for completing an activity, bringing

believers) are led by the Spirit, these are the children of God." See esp. Fee, *Paul's Letter*, 355–56 and n. 319.

12. Some MSS have the verb *teleioō* at 2 Cor 12:9, but the preferred reading employs *teleō*. On this verse see above, n. 4.

13. A listing of options can be found in Hawthorne, *Philippians*, 150–51.

14. Older commentators suggested a background in the mystery cults (Beare), while more recent ones favor some combination of Jewish and/or Hellenistic perfection teaching (e.g., O'Brien, Koester).

15. See Fee, *Paul's Letter*, 343–45; O'Brien, *Epistle to the Philippians*, 420–22; and similarly, Arnold, *Christ as the Telos*, 198 ("Christ as the telos of his life"). This view receives confirmation in the section that follows (3:17–21) where Paul contrasts the *telos* of the opponents (destruction) with the eschatological transformation of believers.

16. While this verb, *teleioō*, could be used of initiation into mystery rites or for achieving some state of completion or perfection in Hellenistic and Jewish teaching, these are subsidiary meanings that would need to be suggested to the reader by the context. We have argued above that this context favors the simpler and more dominant meaning of the verb.

something to its anticipated end, to finish or accomplish something.[17] Paul will immediately take up the image of a runner striving for an end-goal [*telos*] in a race (vv. 13–14). That goal, also outlined in vv 10–11 as the full knowledge of Christ at the resurrection, is one Paul has not yet obtained or reached [*teteleiōmai*].

There is, however, a different wholeness that Paul is quite ready to apply to himself and other believers right now. "Let those of us then who are mature [*teleioi*] . . ." (v. 15a). We have seen this sense earlier (1 Cor 2:6). That is, Paul and other believers are complete and mature in Christ, wholeheartedly devoted to God and his ways. There is no need to wrestle with perfection, whether moral, spiritual, or otherwise, since the adjective need not imply such. Nor do we need to take this as an ironic comment;[18] Paul fully expects his converts to live holy, God-honoring lives as they press on toward the eschatological goal.

Galatians 3:3

This goal is referenced once more in Gal 3:3.

> Are you so foolish? Having started with the Spirit, are you now ending with [*epiteleisthe*] the flesh?

Numerous English translations perceive a reference to "perfection" in this text.

- "being made perfect [or perfected] by the flesh" [Douay-Rheims; ESV; KJV; NKJV; NAS]
- "trying to become perfect by your own human effort" [NLT]

Others, however, correctly perceive that a reference to something ending or being completed better suits the parallel with "having started with the Spirit."[19]

---

17. BDAG, ad loc.
18. Contra Hawthorne, *Philippians*, 155–57. For a non-ironic "mature" interpretation similar to ours, see O'Brien, *Epistle to the Philippians*, 433–37, although O'Brien understands v. 12 in terms of the opponents' perfection teaching.
19. For this meaning throughout the NT literature, see BDAG, *epiteleō*. Paul uses the same verbal pairing in Phil 1:6 ["the one who began a good work among you will bring it to completion (*epiteleō*) by the day of Jesus Christ"].

- "ending with the flesh" [NAB; NJB; NRSV; RSV]
- "trying to attain your goal [or finish] by human effort" [NET; NIV]

In the context of Paul's Galatian dispute the meaning is straightforward. They began their Christian walk by simply receiving Paul's message with faith. Their reception of the Spirit at that time, without becoming Jewish via circumcision, testified to God's acceptance of them (3:1–2). However, now they are tempted to complete this path by getting circumcised in their flesh.

Wholeness-Perfection in the Disputed Letters

A number of texts in the disputed Pauline letters speak of a future status of completeness or perfection.[20] Does the Paul of these letters view such perfection as currently impossible and only to be obtained at the Eschaton? Having just seen Paul refer to himself and other believers as already *teleioi*, we now consider several texts that seem to portray the same as a not-yet realized, future, expectation.

Colossians 1:28

> It is he [Christ] whom we proclaim, warning everyone and teaching everyone in all wisdom, so that we may present everyone mature [*teleion*] in Christ.

Paul is here speaking of the goal of his apostolic ministry, which encompasses his suffering, teaching, and preaching (1:24–29). The desired result is "to present everyone mature in Christ." But *when* and *where* does Paul envision such a presentation of mature [perfect] believers? Is this goal only reached beyond death, at the resurrection/judgment?[21] Is this parallel to his conviction that "we will all stand before the judgment seat of God" (Rom 14:10; cf. also 2 Cor 5:10) the moment at which all imperfections are transformed? Or does this presentation of his churches

---

20. If Paul did not author these texts, these words may still have relevance for post-Pauline developments, but can say little about Paul's own stance. For those, like myself, who tie the production of these letters more closely to the historical Paul, the attempt should be made to integrate them into a Pauline view of wholeness-perfection.

21. So Sappington, *Revelation and Redemption*, 187–90; "free from blame or accusation at the last judgment" (189–90).

to God occur *during* Paul's ministry?²² Is it parallel to Epaphras's prayer later in this same letter that the Colossians "may stand mature [*teleios*] and fully assured in everything that God wills" (Col 4:12)?

The verb used here [*paristanō*] means "to cause [someone, something] to be present" (BDAG), and is used of Paul's being presented before a governor (Act 23:33) and Jesus's presentation in the temple (Luke 2:22; see also Acts 1:3; 9:41). It can be used as a technical term in two different settings, either of which could be relevant for this passage.²³ First, priests "present" sacrifices. Paul uses the verb metaphorically in this sense in Rom 12:1, "I appeal to you . . . to present your bodies as a living sacrifice, holy and acceptable to God." The use of the same verb in Col 1:22—"so as to present you holy and blameless and irreproachable before him"—points to this meaning, since "holy and blameless [*hagious* and *amōmous*]" are words commonly used in the LXX in reference to sacrificial animals.²⁴ But, secondly, individuals are "presented" before a judge as was Paul in Acts 23:33. Thus, the third adjective in 1:22—"so as to present you holy and blameless *and irreproachable* [*anenklētous*] before him"—can be used of an innocent party in courtroom proceedings, and is not cultic as are the other two.²⁵

So, is Paul speaking of:

a. an eschatological presentation as perfect sacrifices,

b. an eschatological presentation before the divine courtroom,

c. a presentation of believers in this life as sacrifices, or

d. a presentation of believers in this life as innocent?

Commentators can be found supporting each of these positions.²⁶ My own, admittedly cautious, suggestion leans on the overall tone and

---

22. So Lohse, *Colossians and Philemon*, "is hardly to be understood in a futuristic-eschatological sense, related to the final judgment. Rather, the results of the apostolic work should be visible in the conduct of the community" (78–79 n. 80).

23. For details on these technical uses, see BDAG, 1.d and e.

24. "Seven days shalt thou purify the altar and sanctify it; and the altar shall be most holy, every one that touches the altar shall be hallowed [*hagiasthēsetai*]. And these are the offerings which thou shalt offer upon the altar; two unblemished [*amōmous*] lambs of a year old daily on the altar continually, a constant offering" (Exod 29:37–38, Breton trans.). For further details, see commentaries by Lohse, Dunn, et al.

25. Thus, 1 Cor 1:8, "so that you may be blameless on the day of our Lord Jesus Christ." See further, Grundmann, *anenklētos*, TDNT 1.357.

26. According to Moo, "most commentators" favor the eschatological option; Moo,

thrust of Paul's argument to this point. The opening prayer that they may "lead lives worthy of the Lord" (1:10) and "endure everything with patience" (1:11) shows the letter's concern for the recipients' behavior in this world.[27] Following the Christ-hymn (1:15–20), the same concern continues with reference to their former "evil deeds" (1:21) and the desire that they be "irreproachable" (1:22) and "continue ... steadfast in the faith" (1:23). Instruction in the desired good behavior of his Gentile converts before the watching world forms the subject of his "warning ... and teaching" in 1:28.[28] This tips the scales toward reading "that we may present everyone mature in Christ" as a this-worldly moral appearing of these believers before God and others.[29]

This is not to dismiss entirely that Paul, in his overall theological vision, perceives an eschatological presentation of believers to God (see "a" and "b" above). This seems clear enough from hints in the immediate context[30] as well as reference to the same elsewhere in his letters.[31] However, this cannot be disconnected from their discipleship in this life. Paul's regular expectation is that disciples "be blameless and innocent, children of God without blemish *in the midst of a crooked and perverse generation*" (Phil 2:15), that is, in this life.[32] For Paul, the future judgment will not bring a verdict based on an act of grace somehow disconnected from our works in this life. Rather, such a judgment reckons with "what has been done in the body" (2 Cor 5:10) and renders its verdict "according to each one's deeds" (Rom 2:6).

Letters to the Colossians, 161.

27. I leave aside the intractable problem of identifying the precise nature of presumed opponents who may be urging the behavior Paul is concerned with. See Hagner, *New Testament*, 566–68, for a brief overview.

28. The Greek verb *noutheteō* is not normally used for warnings of future judgment, and, alongside *didaskein* here, refers to pastoral instruction and admonition on how to live and what to avoid. See Behm, *noutheteō*, in *TDNT* 4.1021.

29. "It is not the 'last judgment' which is in focus, but rather the evident daily conduct of the believer." Barth and Blanke, *Colossians*, 267. See also, Cavin, *New Existence*, 173. Compare my earlier preference for an eschatological reading. Yinger, *Paul, Judaism, and Judgment*, 281.

30. In light of the way "hope" is used eschatologically in 1:5 ("the hope laid up for you in heaven"), the mention of "the hope of glory" in 1:27b most likely refers to this future hope, rather than present transformation into the image of his glory.

31. Rom 14:10; 2 Cor 5:10; etc.

32. Note the use also in this text of similar Greek terminology [*amemptoi, akeraioi, amōma*] for his this-worldly moral expectation.

Excursus: Wholeness-Perfection and Judgment According to Works

These last-cited verses point out Paul's firm and repeated belief in a final judgment according to works.[33] He thinks believers in Christ will "stand before the judgment seat of God" (Rom 14:10), their deeds "done in the body" (2 Cor 5:10) will be examined, and these "doers of the law" (Rom 2:13) will be justified. The standard for this judgment will not be flawless obedience (e.g., sinlessness), but a life characterized by faithful devotion to Christ and his ways. God will examine their hearts and behavior to see if they have been *teleios* (NT), *tamim* (OT), wholehearted in following him. Paul gives no indication that he thinks this might be in tension with his equal insistence on justification by faith apart from works of the law. For Paul, as for most Jews, inward allegiance (faith) and outward loyalty (works) were two ways of expressing the same reality. As Jesus put matters, "if you love me, you will keep my commandments" (John 14:15).

Returning now to the text of Col 1:28 ("so that we may present everyone *teleios* in Christ"), can we fill out more precisely this *teleios* (maturity, perfection, completeness) that he expects? Our lexical work earlier in this volume has argued that some kind of flawless perfection is not in view. Instead, Paul here envisions "the complete and undivided way in which a person ... is oriented toward God or toward Christ."[34] Again, like Jesus and Jewish tradition, Paul calls for the *tamim* life, a life of love and wholehearted devotion to God and his ways.

Colossians 4:12

Epaphras, who is one of you, a servant of Christ Jesus, greets you. He is always wrestling in his prayers on your behalf, so that you may stand mature [*teleioi*] and fully assured in everything that God wills.

As the letter ends, Paul sends greetings to the Colossian believers from other coworkers, including Epaphras, who is himself one of the earliest converts and leaders from Colossae (1:7; 4:12). Paul notes Epaphras's

---

33. For details see Yinger, *Paul, Judaism, and Judgment*.
34. Schweizer, *Colossians*, 112. Cited in Moo, *Letters to the Colossians*, 161.

vigorous prayers for the Colossians. The wording of his prayer-concerns echoes concerns Paul has previously noted as his own. Thus, he is

- always (1:3)
- wrestling (1:29)
- in his prayers on your behalf (1:3, 9)
- so that you may stand mature (1:28)
- and fully assured (2:2)
- in everything that God wills (1:9).

The prayer that they may "stand" uses a favorite Pauline metaphor, that of the believers standing firm, like a person or building that is not shaken, does not fall.[35] Although Paul can at times use it for a future standing in judgment (Rom 14:4), he uses it most commonly for believers standing firm in their faith (1 Cor 10:12; 2 Cor 1:24; Eph 6:11, 13; see also 1 Cor 15:1; Rom 5:2). Some commentators see in the passive voice [*stathēte*] a reference to divine enabling (you have been made to stand [by God]),[36] but this is doubtful since "the passive form of this verb has an intransitive sense."[37] Thus, Epaphras prays that the Colossians may hold firmly to Christ in the face of challenges and continue to walk in a worthy manner without falling into sin or error. This aligns with the parallel hope in 1:28.

As to the content of that hope, we have already dealt above at length with *teleios* in 1:28. The most likely sense is that the Colossian believers may continue to be mature, wholly devoted to Christ and his ways, not that they may be sinless. Colossians 1:22–23 provides a good commentary on the content of this wholeness: "holy and blameless and irreproachable before him . . . continu[ing] securely established and steadfast in the faith, without shifting from the hope promised by the gospel."

The final phrase in this text adds an element not found in 1:28. Epaphras's prayers are uttered that the Colossians might be "fully assured in everything that God wills." The phrase is highly reminiscent of Rom 12:2, which we will examine below: so that you may discern what is the will of God—what is good and acceptable and perfect.[38] The last part—"in

---

35. On the whole, see Grundmann, *histēmi*, in *TDNT*, 7.646–53.

36. E.g., O'Brien, *Colossians, Philemon*, 253.

37. Moo, *Letters to the Colossians*, 344; Rom 14:4 (addition of "and the Lord is able to make them stand") confirms this interpretation.

38. See below, 117–18.

everything that God wills"—could conceivably modify the verb (to stand in all the will of God), or either or both of the adverbs (mature and/or fully assured in all the will of God). If connected with the verb or with *teleios*, the phrase points to their behavior, their standing or maturity, as in accord with the will of God. The connection with the final word, *peplērophorēmenoi* (filled completely),[39] is, however, to be preferred in light of Col 1:9. "We have not ceased praying for you and asking that you may be filled [*plērōthēte*] with the knowledge of God's will in all spiritual wisdom and understanding." Just as Paul opens the letter with the wish that they be full with the will of God, and has spoken of them being filled with the fullness (*plērōma*) who is Christ (1:9, 19; 2:9), so he now ends it with this same expectation.

Ephesians 4:13

> The gifts he gave were that some would be apostles, some prophets, some evangelists, some pastors and teachers, to equip the saints for the work of ministry, for building up the body of Christ, *until all of us come* to the unity of the faith and of the knowledge of the Son of God, *to maturity* [*eis andra teleion*, lit. to a complete person], to the measure of the full stature of Christ. We must no longer be children, tossed to and fro and blown about by every wind of doctrine, by people's trickery, by their craftiness in deceitful scheming. But speaking the truth in love, we must grow up in every way into him who is the head, into Christ, from whom the whole body, joined and knit together by every ligament with which it is equipped, as each part is working properly, promotes the body's growth in building itself up in love. (Eph 4:11–16)

This paragraph (4:1–16) begins the exhortation (paraenesis) of the letter ("I beg you . . ." 4:1). Amid the typical ethical language ("lead a life worthy," "with all humility and gentleness," see continuation in 4:17–32), the mention of maintaining "the unity of the Spirit" (4:3) focuses this early section of paraenesis on the theme of oneness of the corporate body ("one body, one Spirit" [4:4], "the unity of the faith" [4:13a]). This unity is grounded in common creed (4:4–6) and in gifts of ministry and leadership (4:7–11). In vv. 12–13 the author strings together six clauses

---

39. Both meanings of the verb are possible here: "filled completely" (see KJV, NKJV) or "fully assured" (NRSV, etc.).

indicating purpose or end.⁴⁰ The first set of three (v. 12) views matters from the perspective of the gifted apostles and teachers. Their ministries are "for bringing the saints to completion, for the work of service, for the building up of the body of Christ."⁴¹ The second set of three (v. 13) restates these ends from the perspective of the saints themselves: "until all of us come to the unity of the faith and of the knowledge of the Son of God, to maturity, to the measure of the full stature of Christ."

For our study on wholeness-perfection, the fifth in the series is of most direct relevance (Greek *eis andra teleion*), but all six contribute to a singular vision of what the church is to reach as a goal. The various gifted ministers aim, first, at "the completion [*ton katartismon*] of the saints." The noun used only here in the NT (*hapax legomenon*) has proven troublesome for translators. Most have resorted to a verbal idea revolving around training or equipping (NRSV: to equip the saints). This, however, ignores the chief sense of the verb, *katartizein*, and its related nouns.⁴²

Katartizō was originally a medical term that described the healing and mending of broken bones. It was then used later in architectural discussions for the completion or repair of a building project, such as the Jerusalem temple or the walls of a city after a siege; in clothing design to describe a finished, completed garment; in pottery to refer to the shaping and completion of a potted vessel; and in pharmaceutical language, to refer to the perfect, completed mixture of ingredients for a healing remedy. Thus, when translating *katartizō*, the chief meaning is best seen as becoming complete.⁴³ Thus, the phrase here is best understood as the completion, restoration, mending, or finishing of the saints. This is not far from the *tamim* concept we have urged elsewhere. That is, the goal of these ministerial gifts is to bring the saints into the shape for which they were originally created.⁴⁴ The author, then, uses two additional images for

---

40. So Barth, *Ephesians*, 440: "six teleological clauses (formulations indicating an intention or goal)."

41. This translation differs from the NRSV by placing a comma between the first two prepositional phrases rather than combining them (NRSV: "to equip the saints for the work of ministry"). For details see Lincoln, *Ephesians*, 251–52.

42. See esp. Page, "Whose Ministry?," 32–35; Hamann, "Translation of Ephesians," 43–45; and Lincoln, *Ephesians*, 254.

43. Spicq, *TLNT*, s.v. καταρτίζω.

44. "He wants them to fulfill their humanity, to be the men and women He envisaged when He created the human race in the first place." Strauss, "Like Christ," 264.

the ministers' task of bringing the saints to completion—they "serve" and "build up" the church.

In v. 13 this same vision of a completed and restored body is expressed from the perspective of the saints themselves in new metaphors. The "unity" mentioned earlier (4:3) will now be reached, specifically a corporate unity in faith and in knowledge of the Son of God. Next comes our *teleios*-phrase, lit. the mature (or complete) man [*andra teleion*]. The focus here is not primarily the *individual's* maturity or completeness, but *corporate* maturity.[45] Among the many suggestions for the identity of this "man [*anēr*]," the corporate body of Christ fits most comfortably.[46] The completion which the saints are to reach as a group is nothing other than the image of Christ himself, the truly complete and developed man, whose body they are. This image was already introduced in the third metaphor in v. 12 ("building up the body of Christ") and is confirmed by the sixth metaphor, "the measure of the full stature of Christ." Thus, this is not a transformation only to be reached at the parousia, but as we suggested for Col 1:28 above, this speaks of the church's behavior and appearance in this world. The ensuing verses 14–15 confirm this reading, speaking of the saints' behavior going forward as mature versus childish, and as "grow[ing] up in every way into him who is the head, into Christ."

Some Remaining "Perfect" Odds and Ends

Paul's letters use *teleios* in a few additional places. Although they are not directly relevant to our study of human wholeness/perfection (since they do not refer to humans as *teleios*), we will consider them briefly for their possible interest as to what the apostle understood by this Greek adjective.

---

45. On this corporate and non-gendered reference of the "mature man," see Matthews, "Christian Maturity," 1–17. Feminist readings, on the other hand, see here a male gender-bias: Vogt, "'Becoming Male,'" 72–83.

46. For discussion of options, see Barth, *Ephesians*, 489–96; and for the above position, Lincoln, *Ephesians*, 256. This Christ-reference explains the male language (*anēr* = male adult), even though clearly all members of the community, regardless of gender, are intended.

Romans 12:2

> Do not be conformed to this world, but be transformed by the renewing of your minds, so that you may discern what is the will of God—what is good and acceptable and perfect.

The letter opened with a depiction of Gentile depravity (1:18–31) in which they failed to "acknowledge [*dokimazein*]" the true God and were given over to "a debased [*adokimon*] mind" (1:28). So now, as the letter draws toward its close, their "minds" are renewed to "understand and agree with what God wants . . . with a view to putting it into practice."[47]

That which they are to discern is the "will of God," and this will of God is *teleios*. Commentators are divided as to whether *teleios*, along with the coordinate words "good" and "acceptable," should be understood as an adjective (e.g., the complete/perfect will of God) or a substantive (the will of God, in other words, the good, the acceptable, the complete). The latter is preferable, although the difference between the two will not be that great.[48] Hence, the will of God can be understood as that which exhibits a fullness and completeness. This may well echo the OT which avoids describing God himself as *tamim/teleios*, but does use these adjectives to speak of his law or his ways (see p. 21 n. 25).[49]

1 Corinthians 13:10

> For we know only in part, and we prophesy only in part; but when the complete [*to teleion*] comes, the partial will come to an end. (1 Cor 13:9–10)

In his paean to the supremacy of love, Paul first contrasts the lasting character of love ("love never ends" or "never fails" [NIV]) with the temporary value of *charismata* like prophecy and tongues ("they will come to

---

47. Moo, *Epistle to the Romans*, 757, on the meaning of *dokimazein* in 12:2.

48. See Dunn, *Romans 9–16*, 715.

49. Though not from Paul, a similar combination of concepts appears in Heb 13:20–21.

> Now may the God of peace . . . make you *complete* in everything *good* so that you may do his *will*, working among us that which is *pleasing* in his sight, through Jesus Christ, to whom be the glory forever and ever.

Note the combination of "good," "acceptable," and "will of God" in reference to believers' behavior. Rather than using *teleioō* for "make complete," this author substitutes the quite similar *katartizō* (to mend, fit, perfect). On the meaning of this term and its semantic overlap with *teleios/teleioō*, see the notes on its occurrence in Eph 4:12 above.

an end" or "pass away" [NIV] and "cease") (13:8). He then notes the character of knowledge and prophecy as partial or fragmentary (13:9). Then, continuing both these temporal and quantitative comparisons of vv. 8–9, he speaks of a future point ("when ... comes") at which these temporary and partial *charismata* will be no more, and *to teleion* will remain.

With *to teleion* Paul refers to a future state of completion and wholeness in contrast to the current state of partial and temporary knowledge. Thus, we shall then see with full clarity ("face to face") versus the current indirect ("as in a mirror") or indistinct vision of reality (v. 12). Or, to use another metaphor, we will then trade our current state that is comparable to that of a child with the state of fully developed or mature humanity ("when I became an adult, I put an end to childish ways," v. 11b).

Most interpreters agree that Paul expects this at the eschaton, the *parousia*.[50] As we have seen elsewhere, *teleios* refers to that which is complete, developed, has reached its goal. If applied to the behavior of believers in the present, Paul can say they are now, already *teleioi* (1 Cor 2:6). They demonstrate the maturity and wholeness that the Spirit enables. If speaking of knowledge and revelation, he can reserve this state of *to teleion* for the future (1 Cor 13:10). Thus, while the central meaning of *teleios* remains unchanged, its precise referent depends on the context. It is, therefore, no contradiction for Paul to imply within the same letter that the state of being *teleios* is already present (1 Cor 2:6) and is yet to come (1 Cor 13:10), since the referent of *teleios* differs in these two instances: life-behavior in one, knowledge and revelation in the other.

Colossians 3:14

> Above all, clothe yourselves with love, which binds everything together in perfect harmony. (NRSV)

> And over all these put on love, that is, the bond of perfection. (NAS)

The paraenesis beginning in 3:1 centers around the behavior appropriate to the "new humanity" (3:10) in contrast to the evil deeds characterizing the "old" (3:9). This new humanity in Christ is explained with the image of taking off one set of clothes and putting on a new set (3:9–10). On the positive side, believers are to "clothe [them]selves with compassion, kindness," and other virtues. Although a verb is missing in v. 14a (lit. "and above all these things love"), the majority of interpreters and translations

---

50. See the commentaries by Conzelmann, Fee, and Thiselton.

are surely correct to see a continuation of the exhortation to "put on" from verse 12. This final virtue, love, is more than a simple addition to the others, but is itself "the bond of perfection [*teleiotētos*]" (NAS), or better, "of wholeness" or "completeness."[51] This means either that love bundles these virtues (or persons) into a whole or unity, or that it leads to completeness.[52] This may echo the love-completeness called for by Jesus (Matt 5:48; Mark 12:29–31) or the love-bond that leads to the wholeness of the mystical body of Christ (Col 2:19).[53]

Summary

Like the OT, Jesus, and the Greco-Roman world around him, Paul continues to use *teleios* and cognates to refer to someone or something that is complete or whole, which fulfills its intent. We found no evidence that he understands it in a novel way as sinlessness. Like the word "saints [*hagioi*, lit. holy ones]," Paul uses *teleioi* as a present-day descriptor of those in Christ, those who love God and walk by his Spirit. "Among the *teleioi* we speak wisdom" (1 Cor 2:6). As argued above, *teleioi* refers here not to an advanced subset of believers, but is another way of designating all believers. The same is true of *teleioi* in Phil 3:15 ("those of us . . . who are *teleioi*").

Like the designations "righteous" or "holy," *teleios* refers to a status conferred at entry into Christ by grace through faith. Yet, it is a status that must be lived out, not merely taken for granted. The apostle must continue to "warn," "teach," and "pray" to assure their continuance in this state of completeness (Col 1:28; 4:12). That status is both given and conditional: "provided that you continue securely established and steadfast in the faith, without shifting from the hope promised by the gospel that you heard, which has been proclaimed to every creature under heaven" (Col 1:23). Continuance as *teleioi* is not automatic, but requires moral exertion, prayer, and community, "until all of us come to the unity of the faith and of the knowledge of the Son of God, to maturity [lit. to a

---

51. Delling, *telos, etc.*, 78–79.

52. "Is the metaphor that of a strap or band that holds the bundle of virtues together and completes it? Or does it mean that agape is that which produces perfection or completeness because it makes the other virtues cohere? Or does it mean that agape produces perfection by making not the virtues but the persons in question into a unity?" Moule, "New Life in Colossians 3:1–17," 491.

53. For these options, see Dunn, *Epistles to the Colossians*, 232.

teleion man], to the measure of the full stature of Christ" (Eph 4:13). It is a moral maturity that can grow and increase "from one degree of glory to another" (2 Cor 3:18).

But what of transformation at the parousia? Does Paul speak of this as the point at which believers are transformed from creatures who sin into those who do not?[54] He certainly envisions some sort of transformation.

> Listen, I will tell you a mystery! We will not all die, but we will all be changed, in a moment, in the twinkling of an eye, at the last trumpet. For the trumpet will sound, and the dead will be raised imperishable, and we will be changed. For this perishable body must put on imperishability, and this mortal body must put on immortality. When this perishable body puts on imperishability, and this mortal body puts on immortality, then the saying that is written will be fulfilled: "Death has been swallowed up in victory." (1 Cor 15:51-54)

> He will transform the body of our humiliation that it may be conformed to the body of his glory, by the power that also enables him to make all things subject to himself. (Phil 3:21)

The text in 1 Corinthians makes clear that Paul thinks here primarily of the transformation of bodies at the resurrection. The perishable and mortal body becomes an imperishable one, a "spiritual body" (v. 44). Believers become "conformed to the body of his glory" (Phil 3:21). Whereas Adam (and Israel) fell short of reflecting the divine glory and image, the recovery of this original divine intent will be brought to its completion at the Parousia when believers are thus "glorified" (Rom 8:29-30; also 2 Cor 3:18). In none of these texts does Paul appear to be envisioning sinlessness as the result of this transformation.[55]

---

54. A common conception runs as follows. At conversion we are set free from the penalty of sin. In this life we are progressively, but only partially, set free from the power of sin. At the end we are set free from the very presence of all sin. The chief evidence for this last idea in the NT is 1 John 3:2: "Beloved, we are God's children now; what we will be has not yet been revealed. What we do know is this: [underline]when he is revealed, we will be like him[underline], for we will see him as he is." On this text, see the discussion in ch. 10 below.

55. He does speak of believers appearing "blameless" (Col 1:28; Phil 2:15; Eph 4:13), but, as we argued above, these texts refer not to an eschatological transformation á la sinlessness, but to believers appearing "without blemish in the midst of a crooked and perverse generation" (Phil 2:15), i.e., before the watching world both during this age and at the final presentation.

Chapter 9

Cracking Some Tough Theological Nuts Raised by Paul's Use of *Teleios*

God is happiest, when his children are at play.[1]

Our discussion of Pauline texts has revealed that the apostle saw human completeness, a *teleios*-life, as achievable. In fact, he expected this of his converts. For this Jewish apostle, such a life was intertwined with God's guidance for such life, his Torah. Even for Gentiles, although their relationship to Torah was different than for Jews, a *teleios*-life still amounted to "the fulfilling of the law" (Rom 13:10b; see also Rom 8:4), discerning the whole will of God (Rom 12:2). Paul's ethical instructions nearly always had a strong relationship to Torah's guidance, whether in reference to the written Torah or to the therein-revealed will of God made known to Gentiles by the Spirit.[2] But this raises a thorny issue of biblical (esp. Pauline) theology. Did Paul think Jews, Christ-believers, or humans for that matter, were capable of obeying Torah? And, if so, did he think anyone (besides Christ) had actually kept it? And, if there were people capable of following the law, what then was the need for Christ?—a question we address at the end of this chapter.

---

1. Statement from Old Hardy Greaves in the film, *The Legend of Bagger Vance*.
2. See Schrage, *Ethics of the New Testament*, 201–7; and Rosner, *Paul, Scripture and Ethics*.

Cracking Some Tough Theological Nuts

Sweeping Away a Misunderstanding: By Whose Power?

Before diving into the details, we need to clarify one crucial matter when we ask about human capability. Are we speaking of what human beings can accomplish *on their own unaided strength, will, and ability*? This is normally the assumption when we answer "no" as to human capability in obeying the law. That is, left to ourselves, with no strength, guidance, or influence from outside, i.e., from God, are human beings capable of consistent and adequate obedience? Nearly the entire Christian theological tradition would answer a resounding "no"![3]

I suspect that Paul and Jewish tradition generally would answer similarly *if the question were to be put as above*. But, I would suggest, this is not a question they thought they were answering. From the very beginning the human in Scripture was seen as a weak lump of clay caused to live—to move, think, act, and choose—only by the breath of God blown into its nostrils. Should this divine breath (*ruah-pneuma-spirit*) be withdrawn, the person returns to dust. Thus, the idea of persons acting *on their own unaided strength, will, and ability* would not typically suggest itself. Every human act and thought was only possible because of the divine enlivening.[4]

And if the question is then put this way—are human beings as divinely inbreathed creatures of dust capable of obeying God?—the answer would be "yes." This seems to be the expectation in the Adam and Eve

---

3. The great exception would appear to be Pelagius who held that "man can, by his own efforts, perfectly fulfil God's commands without sinning." Erickson, *Christian Theology*, 633. For a more sympathetic reading of Pelagius on perfection, see Bonner, *Myth of Pelagianism*, 69–73, 142–46.

4. This misunderstanding (Jews thought they could obey by their own unaided strength) is a crucial problem in many studies of Paul and Judaism/Law. It has become almost second nature to argue that Paul has a more pessimistic anthropology than most strands of Judaism (Laato, Sprinkle, etc.). Whereas Jews thought they could keep Torah on their own power, Paul thought only by the Spirit would this be possible. Thus, as to human vs. divine agency, Paul will be thought to tend toward monergism or unconditionality (i.e., God is the primary agent in human action), whereas most strands of Jewish tradition will be thought to give the unaided human agent more of a role (synergism, conditionality). My contention, which I cannot argue in detail here, is that most of these allegedly more optimistic Jews were equally convinced that human wisdom and action presumed spirit enablement. Sprinkle, who seems more sensitive to this issue, allows that the hymnic material in the DSS generally presumes divine agency or enablement, but then argues from silence that in the didactic material "there is little (if any) emphasis on such obedience being divinely empowered." Sprinkle, *Paul and Judaism Revisited*, 199.

story (albeit disappointed), as well as in the stories of Abraham, David, and the righteous in Israel. Not, of course, that they would obey God without a single misstep—they are, after all, frail creatures of dust—but they can follow God's ways. They can pray with the Psalms, "I was blameless [*tamim*] before him, and I kept myself from guilt" (Ps 18:23). Again, for a Jewish reader none of this would be thought to happen *by their own unaided power*, but only because God had granted to them life by his breath-spirit.[5]

Can Human Beings Keep the Law?

So, with that possible misunderstanding out of the way, let's return to our question and Paul's response: Did Paul think Jews, or humans for that matter, were capable of obeying Torah? And, if so, did he think anyone (besides Christ) had actually kept it? For those who assumed the standard for obedience was perfection (e.g., Luther), the answer was an obvious "no." And these folks could marshal a considerable body of texts that certainly seemed to point this way.

- "Even the circumcised do not themselves obey the law." (Gal 6:13)
- "For 'no human being will be justified in his sight' by deeds prescribed by the law, for through the law comes the knowledge of sin.... All have sinned and fall short of the glory of God." (Rom 3:20, 23)
- "For this reason the mind that is set on the flesh is hostile to God; it does not submit to God's law—indeed it cannot." (Rom 8:7)

If, however, the standard was not such impossible, flawless obedience, but consistent faithfulness, a heart and life given to following the ways of the Lord, what do such "negative" texts mean, and did Paul think some human beings had actually obeyed God adequately? We will first look at some texts (representative, not exhaustive) which show that Paul did,

---

5. According to Levison, the OT (14–103) and some Second Temple literature (118–53) use "spirit" to refer to the creational spirit, the spirit-breath, constitutive of every human being, and essential for life, wisdom, and skill. Levison, *Filled with the Spirit*, 14–86. Levison, however, disagrees that Paul carried on this tradition (236–316). See, however, his subsequent work, Levison, *Inspired*, esp. 186–201, which appears to open the door just a bit wider for a NT "pneumatology of creation" (á la Moltmann and Pannenberg).

Cracking Some Tough Theological Nuts

indeed, think some human beings had kept the law. Then we will examine those texts often brought to argue the opposite.

A number of Pauline texts refer to "fulfilling the law" via loving others or following the Spirit.

- "Bear one another's burdens, and in this way you will fulfill the law of Christ." (Gal 6:2)
- "For God has done what the law, weakened by the flesh, could not do: by sending his own Son in the likeness of sinful flesh, and to deal with sin, he condemned sin in the flesh, so that the just requirement of the law might be fulfilled in us, who walk not according to the flesh but according to the Spirit." (Rom 8:3–4)
- "Owe no one anything, except to love one another; for the one who loves another has fulfilled the law. The commandments, 'You shall not commit adultery; You shall not murder; You shall not steal; You shall not covet'; and any other commandment, are summed up in this word, "Love your neighbor as yourself." Love does no wrong to a neighbor; therefore, love is the fulfilling of the law." (Rom 13:8–10)

At the very least, these texts reveal that the apostle was not as averse to using the language of "fulfilling the law" as we might suppose. Commentators continue to dispute whether the first two have Torah's actual, concrete demands in view ("the law of Christ," "the just requirement of the law"),[6] but the third seems inescapable. It is explicitly Torah's commands to avoid adultery, murder, theft, etc. that are in view in this "fulfilling of the law." The love-command, which itself is taken from Torah (Lev 19:18), is not a replacement of Torah's various commands (i.e., instead of observing all these, now one need only follow the love-command), but is the summation of them. The sense is clear from Jesus and from the later rabbis . . . one can boil all the commands down to a few, or even to one.[7] Paul was confident that believers, now filled with the love of God himself (Rom 5:5), would be characterized by such love as the fruit of God's Spirit (Gal 5:22). Such love among one another he expected, and this amounted to the fulfilling of the law. This is very reminiscent of Jesus

---

6. On Gal 6:2 ("law of Christ"), see Stanton, "What Is the Law of Christ?," 47–59; and Wilson, "Law of Christ," 123–44. On Rom 8:4 ("the just requirement of the law"), see Thompson, "How Is the Law Fulfilled in Us?" 31–40.

7. See Mark 12:32–33; Luke 10:26–28; *b Sabb.* 31a; *Sipra* on Lev 19:18; also Gal 5:14; further, Dunn, *Romans 9–16*, 778–79.

who, in Matthew's Sermon on the Mount, interprets the commands of Torah ("you have heard") in light of the centrality of divine mercy and love (5:43–48). The same point recurs when he tells a wealthy young Jewish man that his admirable following of Torah's commands does not yet amount to the fulfilling of Torah unless it issues from the kind of other-centered mercy entailed by discipleship to Jesus (Matt 19:16–22).[8]

Paul's Blamelessness (Phil 3:6)

Perhaps the clearest expression of Paul's own sense of having kept or fulfilled the law is Phil 3:6: "as to righteousness under the law, blameless." Two issues require resolution in order to properly understand this text: 1) What does "blameless" mean? 2) Why is Paul making such a seemingly self-serving statement?

To the first question (the meaning of "blameless"), *amemptos* was widely used in Hellenistic circles to refer to a person "of exceptional merit" or "of extraordinary civic consciousness," i.e., above public reproach.[9] Jewish texts used it similarly, but reflected the standard for such blame or reproach found in the will of God. Texts using this term for persons are focused on the person's reputation, whether before society or God. Such persons deserve high regard having demonstrated a life characterized by widely valued virtues. It certainly does not imply they are perfect or flawless individuals. Thus, ancient worthies like Abraham or Job are "blameless" regarding God's or Torah's expectations.[10] Paul is here tapping into his Jewish *tamim* tradition, which we have studied previously. His use of *amemptos* should be not at all surprising, since this Greek word was one of the chief translations of *tamim* in the LXX. This clearly refers not to a sinless perfection in their cases, but to a way of life given to following Yahweh. It is this same consistent faithfulness, this blameless wholeness in following the Lord, which Paul also expects of himself (1 Thess 2:10), his converts (Phil 2:15),[11] and which will be confirmed for all believers at the parousia (1 Thess 3:13). As Thielman summarizes for Paul's use of

---

8. See ch. 6 for the more detailed treatment of these passages.

9. BDAG, s.v. *amemptos, amemptōs*. The adjective stems from the verb (*memphomai*) meaning "to blame, scold, upbraid"; see Grundmann, "μεμφομαι, etc.," 571.

10. Gen 17:1; Job 1:1, 8; 2:3; 9:20; 12:4.

11. This same expectation is expressed in 1 Tim 6:13–14: "In the presence of God . . . I charge you to keep the commandment without spot or blame until the manifestation of our Lord Jesus Christ."

"blameless" in Phil 3:6, "he probably means that he observed the commandments as conscientiously as possible and that when he transgressed them he used the means prescribed in the law itself to atone for his sin."[12] Thus, as Paul looks back on his pre-Christian life as a Pharisee, he most certainly did think he had been able to, and, in fact, had, kept the law.[13] This reading of Phil 3:6 is confirmed by Luke's report of Paul's attitude. "Brothers, up to this day I have lived my life with a clear conscience before God" (Acts 23:1; cf. also 24:16).

But, second, *why* is Paul pointing to his blamelessness under Torah? Is this some sort of boasting in self-achievement that he will ultimately reject as "loss" and "rubbish" (Phil 3:7–8)? Is he saying, "I used to think of myself this way (as a law-keeper), but no longer"? Or does he still, as a follower of Christ, think he actually fulfilled the law at that time? And, if so, why is he saying this here?

At Phil 3:2 Paul turns rather abruptly to a warning ("beware of the dogs"). Commentators differ as to the precise target of such warnings for the letter as a whole (Jewish intruders, libertines, etc.), but 3:2–11 seems to have a Jewish issue in view ("mutilate the flesh," "circumcision," "member of the people of Israel," etc.). If others seek to promote a confidence in Jewish identity ("confident in the flesh"), Paul can out-do them ("I have more [confidence in the flesh]").[14] The final element in his superior Jewish pedigree highlights his blameless walk in line with Torah. He makes the same claim to better-than-average faithfulness elsewhere (Gal 1:14).

---

12. Thielman, *Paul and the Law*, 155. Thus, just as *amemptos* and *teleios* overlapped in meaning and were used by the LXX interchangeably to translate *tamim* (see OT chapter), so Paul's claim to be *amemptos* overlaps with Jesus's call to be *teleios*. Paul, like any faithful Jew, is describing his faithfulness in terms known from the stories of Abraham, Noah, David, etc.

13. Das largely agrees with this reading of Phil 3:6: Das, *Paul, the Law, and the Covenant*, 215–22. However, since he is trying to combat a supposed New Perspective commitment to Paul as perfect law-keeper ("The 'new perspective' interpretation of Paul and the law has been wrong in cite Phil 3 as proof that Paul did not have a problem with perfect obedience of the law," 220), he then stresses that this does not mean Paul thought he was sinless or perfect. For most NPP proponents this will seem an unnecessary, or even irrelevant, comment, since they agree that Paul did not think he had perfectly kept Torah in this sense.

14. "Flesh (*sarx*)" here does not suggest unaided (fallen, evil) *human nature* (contra Moehring, "Some Remarks on *Sarx*," 432–36; Hawthorne, *Philippians*, 127–28), but has in view Jewish covenantal confidence in circumcision of the foreskin-flesh (cf. Gal 6:13). This is clear from the covenantal grounds of such confidence he will append in v. 5: circumcision, people of Israel, tribe of Benjamin.

In light of the meaning of "blameless" (see above), Paul is not claiming perfection, but consistent faithfulness. Some, however, think he still did not mean that he *actually* fulfilled Torah's demands. Perhaps he meant, "I *used* to think I fulfilled Torah, but now (as a Christ-follower) I see I was wrong," either because he was self-deceived about his own former goodness, or because he now views the law's demands differently (i.e., more stringently than he once thought).[15] But this misses the point as to why Paul is making these boasts. He will indeed go on to say that these grounds of confidence have now lost their relative value; he views them now as "loss" instead of "gain," as "rubbish" in comparison to the knowledge of Christ. But the reason for this loss of comparative value is not that Paul's former view of them was faulty, but because something better has now come. "These I have come to regard as loss *because of Christ*" (Phil 3:7). This is clear when we look at all these grounds together, rather than focusing only on the last one of "blamelessness." Paul and other Jews were not wrong when they formerly saw circumcision, membership in Israel, zeal for Torah, and righteous faithfulness as covenantal identity markers. *These all still do have value.* "Circumcision indeed is of value if you obey the law" (Rom 2:25). But it is no longer the value they once had as markers of the righteous people of God. With Christ's coming that has all changed. Now it is faith in Christ, and not adherence to Israel's covenant identity ("works of law"), which marks out the people of God (see on Gal 3:10 above).

Thus, Paul actually believed as a zealous Pharisee, and still believes as a zealous Christ-follower, that he obeyed Torah adequately, blamelessly, righteously. However, since the revelation of Christ, that faithfulness has become irrelevant *as far as determining who belongs to God's chosen people*; this is now through faith in Christ alone.[16]

---

15. Moule represents the traditional opinion, namely that Paul "is *looking from Judaism's view point*, and speaks so. *Granted those premises*, he has, in an eminent degree, what his adversary claims to have." Moule, *Epistle to the Philippians*, 59; italics added. Paul is not saying he actually "has" such a confidence, but hypothetically (from a false Jewish point of view) he "might have" such. Numerous translations push the reader in this direction, as well: "although I myself *might have confidence* even in the flesh" (NAS; also KJV, NKJV); "though I *could have confidence* in my own effort *if anyone could*" (NLT).

16. For a similar treatment of this passage, see Dunn, "Philippians 3.2–14," 469–90. "The impact of Jesus the Christ had been so overwhelming for him that it completely relativized every other set of revealed and traditional values by which he had hitherto lived. The completeness of reversal of values could hardly be expressed more sharply. Even so, however, it need not mean that Paul now denied all value to these things he

The "Doers of the Law" (Rom 2:13)

We come now to another Pauline text that seems to assume almost in passing that human beings, including Gentiles, can keep God's law. As with other such texts, this one, too, has been a major point of controversy in figuring out Paul's own views.

> For he will repay according to each one's deeds: to those who by patiently doing good seek for glory and honor and immortality, he will give eternal life; while for those who are self-seeking and who obey not the truth but wickedness, there will be wrath and fury. There will be anguish and distress for everyone who does evil, the Jew first and also the Greek, but glory and honor and peace for everyone who does good, the Jew first and also the Greek. For God shows no partiality. All who have sinned apart from the law will also perish apart from the law, and all who have sinned under the law will be judged by the law. For it is not the hearers of the law who are righteous in God's sight, but the doers of the law who will be justified. When Gentiles, who do not possess the law, do instinctively what the law requires, these, though not having the law, are a law to themselves. They show that what the law requires is written on their hearts, to which their own conscience also bears witness; and their conflicting thoughts will accuse or perhaps excuse them on the day when, according to my gospel, God, through Jesus Christ, will judge the secret thoughts of all. (Rom 2:6–16)

In this passage Paul seems to envision people who "do good" and are rewarded with eternal life, glory, honor, and peace (vv. 7, 10), as well as "doers of the law" who "will be justified" (v. 12) and Gentiles who "do instinctively what the law requires" (v. 14). No other passage appears to state as strongly Paul's understanding of Torah as capable of human fulfillment.

Of course, matters are not quite that simple.[17] Interpreters remain split between those who accept these statements as Paul's own Christian conviction (i.e., some have been able to keep Torah) and those who deny

---

had previously counted as so important. . . . *The sharpness of the contrast is not so much to denigrate what he had previously counted as gain, as to enhance to the highest degree the value he now attributes to Christ, to the knowledge of Christ, and to the prospect of gaining Christ"* (475).

17. See the history of interpretation in Riedl, *Das Heil der Heiden*, 7–172.

that these express Paul's own doctrine.[18] The major objection of those holding the latter, or hypothetical,[19] point of view is Paul's apparent belief in universal human sinfulness (e.g., Rom 3:9–20, 23), which would seem incompatible with a simultaneous belief in actual human law-keeping. I will take the wind out of this particular sail in a moment by arguing that Paul does not, in fact, assert human sinfulness *without exception* in Rom 3:9–20 and 23, at least not quite in the way traditionally formulated.

Those holding the former position (some have actually obeyed the law), fall largely into two groups. One contends that these law-keepers, esp. in v. 14, are Gentile *Christians* empowered by the Spirit.[20] Thus, Rom 2:12–16 is saying only slightly less clearly what Paul will later elucidate.

> so that the just requirement of the law might be fulfilled in us, who walk not according to the flesh but according to the Spirit (Rom 8:4)
>
> the one who loves another has fulfilled the law (Rom 13:8)

Some of these interpreters point to v. 16—"on the day when, according to my gospel, God, through Jesus Christ, will judge the secret thoughts of all"—to support this Christian supposition. However, little in the preceding verses (1–15) would suggest such a *Christian* scenario informed by

---

18. Dunn summarized part of a 1994 Durham-Tübingen Research Symposium, which dealt with this text by saying, "discussion became stuck on the unresolved issue of whether the law-doing Gentile of 2.14, 26–27 was a real or hypothetical figure, and whether he was or could (in Paul's view) only be a Christian gentile." Dunn, *Paul and the Mosaic Law*, 321. See the overview of positions in Gathercole, "Law Unto Themselves," 27–30.

19. I.e., Paul is speaking hypothetically here (*imagine* one could keep the law), rather than envisioning a real-life situation. For analysis and critique of this approach, see Yinger, *Paul, Judaism, and Judgment*, 175–78.

20. For this ancient approach, see Augustine, followed in modern times by Karl Barth, C. E. B. Cranfield, N. T. Wright, and, more recently, Gathercole, "Law Unto Themselves," 27–49.

the cross and resurrection,[21] and these Gentiles do what the law requires "instinctively"[22] (2:14), not by the Spirit.

The remaining position—some Gentiles *qua* Gentiles have kept the law—will be the one taken here.[23] Elsewhere I have detailed how Rom 2:6–11 is part of an argument (2:1–16) designed to show that Gentiles *qua* Gentiles (not Spirit-filled Gentile believers) are not disadvantaged in judgment vis-à-vis Jews.[24] Both Jews and Gentiles will be judged impartially according to their works (2:6–11). Even Jewish possession of Torah ("hearers of the law," 2:13) does not constitute a salvific advantage. It is doing the law that matters, and even Gentiles can "do instinctively the things of the law" (2:14, NAS), since they have "the work of the law written in their hearts" (2:15, NAS).[25]

Since my 1999 book, it has become clearer to me that this Pauline belief in human ability paired with a belief in general human failure is precisely what we should expect from a first-century Jewish thinker, especially one like Paul who sees himself aligned with the Israel-critical prophetic tradition. Biblical scholars are generally agreed that the OT and many Second Temple Jewish writers held to what many refer to as an optimistic anthropology. "On the basis of free will man has not only the capacity always to *choose* good instead of evil. He has also the power

---

21. The strongest argument is that "the work of the law written in their hearts" (2:15, NAS) points to the new covenant promise in Jer 31:33 ("I will put my law within them, and I will write it on their hearts"). However, besides the fact that this phrase may equally reflect the widespread Hellenistic(-Jewish) notion of a universal "unwritten law," its fatal weakness is that it vitiates Paul's argument in ch. 2. He is trying to show that on the basis of commonly accepted *Jewish* principles (e.g., impartial recompense according to deeds), Jews have no salvific advantage over Gentiles *qua* Gentiles. To suddenly slip in Spirit-filled Gentiles vs. Jews at this point dooms his argument as unfair.

22. The dative *physei* (instinctively, by nature) modifies the phrase that follows (instinctively doing the things of the law) rather than that which precedes (Gentiles who do not have the law by nature/birth). On this interpretation, adopted by native Greek-speaker John Chrysostom, see Collins, "Echoes of Aristotle"; contra Gathercole, "Law Unto Themselves," 35–37. See further Dunn, *Romans 1–8*, 1:98; and Kuhr, "Römer 2:14f," 255–58.

23. See also Snodgrass, "Justification by Grace," 72–93; Davies, *Faith and Obedience*, 60–67; Dunn, *Romans 1–8*, 1:93–107; and Longenecker, *Eschatology and the Covenant*, 185–89.

24. Yinger, *Paul, Judaism, and Judgment*, 146–82.

25. Here Paul shares with other Second Temple Jews and the wider Hellenistic world a belief in a widespread moral sensitivity, a law within. Dunn, *Romans 1–8*, 1:98–102.

always to *do* good."²⁶ In fact, as we noted in the chapter on perfection in Jewish tradition, they could identify specific individuals who had chosen the right path and were considered righteous, whole-hearted, and obedient (Abraham, Noah, etc.). Simultaneously, they were pessimistic regarding *how many* were actually following this path. Israel has been a stubborn and rebellious people (Deut 9:6, 13; 31:27; 2 Kgs 17:14; Neh 9:29; Ps 78:8; etc.). The righteous among the chosen nation could frequently echo Elijah's complaint, "the Israelites have forsaken your covenant, thrown down your altars, and killed your prophets with the sword. I alone am left" (1 Kgs 19:10). Even some among non-Jews, most of whom were generally viewed as given over hopelessly to idolatry and immorality, were considered obedient to the light they had.²⁷ Thus, it should come as no surprise that Paul holds Gentiles as well as Jews, viewed here as groups, to be under the power of sin (Rom 1:18–31; 3:9–20, 23), yet still believes that some within these groups, both Jews and (perhaps more rarely) Gentiles, have been able to live their lives according to God's ways, whether Torah or the law of nature.

Since Paul will make essentially the same point in Rom 2:25–27, we can dispense with a lengthy exegesis and simply quote this text, which testifies to Paul's belief that some, indeed, can and have kept God's law.

> Circumcision indeed is of value if you obey the law; but if you break the law, your circumcision has become uncircumcision. So, if those who are uncircumcised keep the requirements of the law, will not their uncircumcision be regarded as circumcision? Then those who are physically uncircumcised but keep the law will condemn you that have the written code and circumcision but break the law.

---

26. Laato, *Paul and Judaism*, 67–77, citation p. 73. Laato is correct that Judaism possessed an "optimistic" anthropology, but his overly dichotomous portrayal misses the clear pessimistic notes in Jewish sources, as well as the equally complex interplay of optimistic and pessimistic notes in Paul.

27. 4 Ezra 3:36; TNaph 8:3; Philo, *Spec. Leg.* II.42–48; *Quod Omnis Probus Liber* 62–74.

Doesn't Romans 3 Assert that No One Can Keep Torah (Perfectly)?

Of course, an easy retort to my suggestion that human beings, as Spirit-infused creatures of dust, are capable of adequate obedience to God's ways might simply be to cite Rom 3:23:

> all have sinned and fall short of the glory of God.

Does not this verse teach that all fail, that no human being succeeds in obeying God? That is, every human being, without a single exception (except, of course, Christ), is a sinner (cf. Rom 3:9–20; 5:12–14) who has failed to obey God's ways perfectly, or even adequately.[28] This is put forward as the reason (*gar*) why God's righteousness can come only by faith and not through Torah (Rom 3:21–22).

However, if we try to follow Paul's argument in Romans, this is actually not the point the apostle is needing to make.[29] From the beginning of the letter, one of his goals has been to sort out whether the Jewish people have a soteriological (covenantal) advantage over Gentiles. As he puts it directly in ch. 3, "Then what advantage has the Jew?" (3:1); "Are we [Jews] any better off [than the Gentiles]?" (3:9). Thus, 1:18–32 lays out the typical Jewish perspective on Gentiles as wicked idolaters and prone to sexual immorality. They are "without excuse" and "deserve to die" (1:20, 32). Then, in ch. 2 he turns to his own Jewish people. Without denying the lasting advantages of Jewish identity (possession of Torah, circumcision, etc.), he does deny that these are any protection for Jews who "do evil" (2:9) or "break the law" (2:23). This, then, is the argumentative background for his statements in ch. 3 as to sinfulness. The assertion in 3:9b ("all, both Jews and Greeks, are under the power of sin") answers the question, "Are we [Jews] any better off [than Gentiles]?" (3:9a) Since "now ... the righteousness of God has been disclosed" (3:21), even we

---

28. This last sentence expresses what, in Christian theology, is usually covered under doctrines such as original sin, universal sinfulness, and human depravity. See, for example, Berkhof, *Systematic Theology*, "Sin in the Life of the Human Race" (244–54). The human being "is unable to do any spiritual good" (247).

29. As many have pointed out, if Paul's point has been to prove that all human beings without exception are sinners, he has done a singularly poor job. Not only would his charges of Jews stealing, committing adultery, and robbing temples (2:20–22) fail to strike the consciences of most Jews, his argument about Gentiles "who do instinctively what the law requires" (2:14) argues the exact opposite. See, for example, Carras, "Romans 2:1–29," 183–207, esp. 196–202.

Jews need this righteousness of faith, "for there is no distinction [between Jew and Gentile], since we [both groups] have sinned" and "are now justified by his grace as a gift, through the redemption that is in Christ Jesus" (3:23-24). As John Ziesler puts matters, "Paul is not concerned with every single human individual, but with peoples, and . . . the aim is to show that as a people the Jews are under the power of sin, just as the Gentiles as peoples are."[30] Thus, "both Jews and Gentiles are sinful, and under the power of sin, and need the rescue that Jesus Christ provides. Into the question of whether in some way every single human being must be regarded as helplessly sinful, Paul simply does not go."[31] The "all" who have sinned at this point in Paul's argument are not all human beings without exception, but all sorts of humanity (Jew or Gentile) without distinction.[32]

Some might object that the OT citations preceding "all have sinned" certainly seem to speak of every human without exception as a sinner. For example,

> There is no one who is righteous, not even one; there is no one who has understanding, there is no one who seeks God. All have turned aside, together they have become worthless; there is no one who shows kindness, there is not even one. (Rom 3:10-12)

This repeated "not even one" certainly looks like a universal declaration admitting no exceptions. But looks can be deceiving.

This passage is a carefully constructed collection of six (or seven)[33] OT texts, all but one from various Psalms. The quotations follow the LXX wording with some modifications and constitute "the most extensive grouping of OT quotations in the entire Pauline corpus."[34] It is possible

---

30. Ziesler, *Paul's Letter to the Romans*, 100. Ziesler's entire summary of this section is well worth reading (99-100).

31. Ziesler, *Paul's Letter to the Romans*, 100.

32. For this interpretation, see also Johnston, "Which 'All' Sinned?" 153-64. For the opposite reading, that *all without exception* are meant and not merely the two groups, see Bell, *No One Seeks for God*, 210-22.

33. Dunn and many others suggest Eccl 7:20 ("Surely there is no one on earth so righteous as to do good without ever sinning.") as the source for the initial quote (3:10, "There is no one who is righteous, not even one"), since Paul's key word "righteous (*dikaios*)" occurs in it, but not in Ps 14:1-3. For the view followed here, that Rom 3:10-12 is a modified quotation of Ps 14:1-3 (LXX 13:2-4), see Davies, *Faith and Obedience*, 82, and 89 n. 83.

34. Longenecker, *Epistle to the Romans*, 261.

they were a preexisting Jewish collection of texts[35] asserting that no one is righteous before God, and are here employed by Paul to underscore his point that "Jews and Gentiles alike are all under sin" (3:9b, NIV).

If one reads these quoted passages in their original contexts, the point becomes readily apparent. Each is a denunciation of the wicked, usually as a cry of the righteous who are being oppressed by these evildoers.[36] They are clearly not seeking to assert that every human being, or every single Israelite, fits these descriptions that "none is righteous" and "none seeks after God." A couple of examples will demonstrate this point.

The first quotation (Rom 3:10–12) follows Ps 14:1–3 (LXX 13:2–4) with some modifications, particularly the insertion of Paul's keyword "righteous (*dikaios*)" at the beginning.

Rom 3:10–12	Ps 14:1–3 (LXX 13:2–4) Brenton
	The fool has said in his heart, There is no God. They have corrupted themselves, and become abominable in their devices;
There is no one who is righteous [*dikaios*], not even one;	there is none that does goodness [*chrēstotēta*], there is not even so much as one.
	The Lord looked down from heaven upon the sons of men,
there is no one who has understanding [*suniōn*], there is no one who seeks [*ekzētōn*] God.	to see if there were any that understood [*suniōn*], or sought after [*ekzētōn*] god.
All have turned aside [*ekseklinan*], together they have become worthless [*ēchreōthēsan*]; there is no one who shows kindness [*chrēstotēta*], there is not even one.	They are all gone out of the way [*ekseklinan*], they are together become good for nothing [*ēchreōthēsan*], there is none that does good [*chrēstotēta*], no not one.

The Psalm's opening verses (1–3) give the impression of a universal indictment with their repeated "not even one." Particularly v. 2 (omitted in Paul's quotation) seems to suggest that all humanity is in view: "The Lord looked down from heaven upon the sons of men." However, this universalizing assumption cannot be correct, for the latter half of the Psalm contrasts these evildoers with "my people," also called "the righteous

---

35. Although not accepted by all commentators, see the substantial arguments in favor: Longenecker, *Epistle to the Romans*, 261–62, 273–75. Also, Albl, *And Scripture Cannot Be Broken*, 172–74.

36. See esp. Davies, *Faith and Obedience*, 82–88.

generation" and "the poor" (vv. 4–7). Thus, these evildoers, who are identified in the opening of the Psalm as "fools" who ignore God, are not the whole mass of humanity.[37] These universal-sounding indictments actually mean "there is no one *among these evildoers* who is righteous." Whether these "fools" are Gentiles or other Israelites is not clear,[38] but the psalmist and the pious worshipper repeating the Psalm in the temple are not meant to see themselves in this group of evildoers. It is not an assertion of universal human sinfulness.

The last quotation also comes from a Psalm.

Rom 3:18 NIV	Ps 36:1b (LXX 35:2b) Brenton
There is no fear of God before his eyes.	The transgressor, that he may sin, says within himself, that there is no fear of God before his eyes.

This Psalm contrasts the transgressor and sinner (vv. 1, 11–12) who does not fear God, with the "upright in heart" who plead for God's protection against these evildoers (vv. 10–11). The charge of "no fear of God" applies not to these upright, but to their oppressors, whether within or without the nation. Again, in its original context it is not intended as a universal indictment of human sinfulness.

This same pattern of universal-sounding language ("no one is," "all are") addressed to a group of evildoers, not to all humanity, is repeated in the other texts quoted in Rom 3:10–18. What then was Paul's point in citing them? Of course, Paul could have been "proof-texting" as it is sometimes called. That is, maybe he simply picked texts that sounded like they were asserting universal human sinfulness, even though he was probably aware they were actually doing no such thing.[39] His theological end justified this misreading of Scripture. Many of us are justifiably nervous if this kind of "proof" constitutes the strength of our biblical-theological convictions.

Thus, Pauline scholars are increasingly taking the apostle seriously as a Jewish interpreter of Scripture. If so, and if these quoted texts originally denounced evildoers whether Jew or Gentile, perhaps this was

---

37. Psalm commentators are generally in agreement. "'[E]veryone' must refer to those outside 'my people.'" Goldingay, *Psalms*, 1:214.

38. In favor of a possible Jewish referent, these evildoers "eat up my people as they eat bread" (v. 4) just as Israel's leaders "eat the flesh of my people" (Mic 3:3).

39. Bell agrees largely with our interpretation of the Psalms; thus, his argument for *all without exception* here leads him to the conclusion that "Paul has radically altered the original meaning" of the Psalm quotes; Bell, *No One Seeks for God*, 221.

Paul's desired point in quoting them. Although the Jewish people possess a distinct covenantal advantage (3:1–2), this will not constitute an excuse or privilege (3:9) for them before God if they are found to be unrighteous and deceitful with no fear of God (3:10–18). These denunciations will apply equally to them. Thus, as Paul will conclude (3:19–20), this collection of indictments "speaks to those who are under the law," i.e., to the Jewish people. The "whole world," both Jew and Gentile, are "held accountable to God," and so is fulfilled one further OT text, "no human being will be justified in his sight" (Ps 143:2) on account of their Jewish identity.

Jewish accountability for sin rather than universal human sinfulness is Paul's aim. And this fits perfectly with what he has been seeking to demonstrate thus far as we noted above. God will show no partiality (2:11).

Romans 7: Every Human's Losing Battle with Sin?

Of course, no discussion of Paul and Torah can skirt Rom 7 with its pessimistic words about incapacity for doing good.

> I was once alive apart from the law, but when the commandment came, sin revived and I died, and the very commandment that promised life proved to be death to me. (vv. 9–10)

> For I do not do what I want, but I do the very thing I hate.... For I know that nothing good dwells within me, that is, in my flesh. I can will what is right, but I cannot do it. (vv. 15, 18)

If Paul is talking here about his own experience, then the discussion is over. He would be acknowledging his powerlessness to keep God's law, even to do good at all. The urge to evil triumphs in him (and, hence, in all human beings) at every turn.[40]

At least as early as John Chrysostom, however, this autobiographical reading has been challenged, and the argument made that the "I" in Rom 7 refers not to Paul's own personal experience, but is a rhetorical figure used by the apostle to make his point.[41] He has already used this technique earlier in Romans: "But if through my falsehood God's truthfulness

---

40. See, for example, Nygren, *Commentary on Romans*, 277–303.

41. See the groundbreaking and still important, Kümmel, *Römer 7*, 1–160; and more recently, Stowers, "Romans 7.7–25," 180–202. On the overall debate, see Lambrecht, *Wretched "I"*.

abounds to his glory, why am I still being condemned as a sinner?" (3:7).[42] Although this debate as to the identity of the "I" is far from over, the tide has clearly shifted away from the once dominant autobiographical reading.[43] Among the numerous alternative suggestions for the identity of the "I," the figure of Israel has the strongest claim in my view.[44] In which case the apostle is not speaking about a supposed inability of human nature, but of Israel's historical failure vis-à-vis Torah. Israel was "once alive apart from the law" (i.e., prior to Sinai), "but when the commandment came" (at Sinai), "sin revived and Israel died" (most notably at the Golden Calf incident, but repeatedly in Israel's history). Israel has consistently failed to do what she wants (7:15–17); she can "will what is right, but [she] cannot do it" (7:18). She "delight[s] in the law of God" but is "captive to the law of sin that dwells in [her] members" (7:22–23). As the prophets point out, her history is one of repeated stiff-necked double-mindedness, ending finally in the covenant curse of exile.

Paul tells this story of Israel at this point in Romans in order to answer a question that his point about being "no longer under the law" has raised (e.g., 7:6). Is the law at fault in all this (7:7)? Is the law bad, a negative element in Israel's history? And his answer, based on Israel's own story, is a resounding "no." The law remains holy and good (7:12). The culprit in this sad story is Sin, which "seiz[ed] an opportunity in the commandment, deceived [Israel] and through it killed [her]" (7:11).

Read this way, the point of Rom 7 is not that human beings are incapable of obeying God, but that Israel as a nation has, in her history, failed to obey God. Paul's point is about salvation-history, not human anthropology.

Then Why Did Christ Have to Die for Sinners?

If we did not need to keep Torah perfectly, and some have, in fact, kept it adequately (e.g., Paul in Phil 3:6), why is the cross necessary? Or to put matters differently, if some were justified under the law (e.g., Abraham,

---

42. "I" = hypothetical Jewish interlocutor; see Moo, *Epistle to the Romans*, 194.

43. Among other reasons for rejecting the autobiographical reading, it is highly unlikely that a first-century Jew, whose entire life from circumcision to death was defined by Torah, would say, "I was once alive apart from the law" (Rom 7:9).

44. Wright, *Climax of the Covenant*, 196–200; Wright, *Paul and the Faithfulness*, 10.3.iv.c; Moo, *Epistle to the Romans*, 426–31.

Noah), and as a matter of principle "the doers of the law are justified" (Rom 2:13), why did Christ have to die for them?

First, "There can be no doubt as to where the centre of gravity of Paul's theology is to be found. It lies in the death and resurrection of Jesus.... His gospel ... focused on the cross."[45] This saving event was needed not just for particularly wicked Gentiles or for unfaithful Jews, but equally for Paul himself, an avowedly blameless follower of the covenant God. To Peter he says,

> We ourselves are Jews by birth and not Gentile sinners; yet we know that a person is justified not by the works of the law but through faith in Jesus Christ. And we have come to believe in Christ Jesus, so that we might be justified by faith in Christ, and not by doing the works of the law, because no one will be justified by the works of the law. (Gal 2:15–16; see also Phil 3:7–11)

To the question "Is there anyone for whom Christ did not need to die?" Paul's answer would be an unequivocal "absolutely not."

Yet Paul nowhere lays out fully or systematically his answer to the question, "*Why* is this so?" We can only attempt to pull together various hints scattered here and there and see if any coherent reasoning is discernible. What follows should be seen as no more than an attempt to fill in the blanks. [46]

For those, both Jew and Gentile, who fall clearly into the category of the wicked, the answer is straightforward: Christ's atoning death is necessary for the forgiveness of their sins and for their redemption from slavery to wickedness. That "Christ died *for our sins*" (1 Cor 15:3) is the answer Christian theology has always provided.[47]

But the more pressing questions our study raises vis-à-vis atonement are: What about those OT saints, like Abraham, who were considered righteous and blameless, and who, according to Paul, were already justified by faith before the coming of Christ (Rom 4)? Or, what about

---

45. Dunn, *Theology of Paul the Apostle*, 208, 209. The entire chapter ("§9: Christ Crucified," 207–33) lays out clearly the centrality and rich meaning of the cross in Paul's theology.

46. Working out the details of a theology of atonement go far beyond the scope of this book. For a challenging reconsideration of this key doctrine, see Wright, *Day the Revolution Began*.

47. See the helpful survey of history and opinions on this issue in Berkhof, *Systematic Theology*, 368–72.

Paul, who considered himself "blameless" (Phil 3:6)? Were he and Abraham not "sinners" (Rom 3:23) needing the atoning sacrifice of Christ?

Here I think our modern individualist framework has blinded us to the more central communal meaning of the cross. We want to see the cross primarily in terms of "Christ died for *my* sins," to win forgiveness and atonement *for me*. And there is most certainly an appropriate personal application of the cross. But this personal application is not what explains the necessity of the cross. For that we must recapture the communal way of thinking common to most ancient peoples, including Israel.

To the extent that ancient peoples asked "Who am I?," their answer did not revolve first around personal achievement (career, charitable action, income, possessions, etc.), but derived first of all from the group to which they belonged. Note how Paul begins his own self-description: "circumcised on the eighth day, a member of the people of Israel, of the tribe of Benjamin, a Hebrew born of Hebrews" (Phil 3:5). These were not "individual achievements," but Paul's statement of group identity.

One's own fate in the ancient world was intimately tied to the fate of one's group, one's people. Thus, Judah as a rebellious nation was sent into exile to Babylon. Even individuals in the nation who were not rebels against Yahweh were sent into exile because they were part of the nation. Their identity was tied to the group. The same could be said of the aged Simeon in the Jerusalem temple in Luke 2. Although described as "righteous and devout" he, too, suffered the fate of the nation under Roman domination.

This same reality of group solidarity and identity explains why every one of us, without exception, needs the deliverance and forgiveness of the cross. Every one of us, even the most exemplary, even the "blameless" like Paul and the "perfect" like Abraham, are part of a rebellious nation (for Jews) and a lost humanity (for Gentiles). We are all "sinners." When the Bible declares Christ died *for our sins*, this last phrase refers chiefly and fundamentally to our group's rebellion (in the case of Israel) and idolatry (in the case of Gentiles). The divine intention for humanity and for Israel and the nations had been thwarted by sin, by Israel's hard-heartedness and the nations' idolatry. The forgiveness of sins was necessary to move this divine intention forward.

Chapter 10

Wholeness-Perfection in Other Apostolic Voices

Perfection is not sinlessness, but the loyalty of the soul by faith to Christ when all is said and done.... Perfection is wholeness.[1]

The remaining NT witnesses to human wholeness contribute substantially to our picture. Here we encounter what may be the single truly sinless human being, yet also learn that Christ himself had to become whole (*teleios*) in some sense (Hebrews). And 1 John will seem to argue both for and against human sinlessness. Although adding some new dimensions, these texts, including James, will confirm our thesis that NT perfection-wholeness largely continues the *tamim* theology we discovered in the Jewish tradition.

Completion-Perfection in Hebrews

Nearly one-third of all the NT occurrences of *teleios* and cognates are found in the letter to the Hebrews, and many consider the term a central, if not the central, concept essential for understanding the letter.[2] However, its employment of this terminology is distinctive in the NT. Our task

---

1. Forsyth, *Christian Perfection*, 36.
2. 14x: 2:10; 5:9, 14; 6:1; 7:11, 19, 28; 9:9, 11; 10:1, 14; 11:40; 12:2, 23. Among the many fine studies of the concept in this letter, that by Peterson is the best in English, with an excellent brief treatment provided by Koester. Peterson, *Hebrews and Perfection*; Koester, *Hebrews*, 122–25.

will be to trace this distinctive use and to inquire if there is any overlap with the meaning we have discerned in other biblical materials thus far.

The basic lexical meaning of *teleios* and cognates in Hebrews remains the same as we have seen elsewhere, namely bringing someone or something to its end or purpose, its *telos*. This is applied first of all to Christ himself.

- It was fitting that God, for whom and through whom all things exist, in bringing many children to glory, should make the pioneer of their salvation perfect [*teleiōsai*] through sufferings. (2:10)
- Although he was a Son, he learned obedience through what he suffered; and having been made perfect [*teleiōtheis*], he became the source of eternal salvation for all who obey him. (5:8–9)
- For the law appoints as high priests those who are subject to weakness, but the word of the oath, which came later than the law, appoints a Son who has been made perfect [*teteleiōmenon*] forever. (7:28)

Not surprisingly, our common English translations of these verses ("made perfect") seemed to suggest there was something "imperfect" about Christ that then had to be "perfected." Many earlier interpretive debates revolved around explaining how the perfect, sinless Son of God could be thought to have been imperfect (committing sin?), since our author obviously considers him "without sin" (4:5). As we have seen, *teleios* and cognates, including the verb *teleioun*, have more to do with bringing something to completion, to its intended end or goal, than with some abstract notion of flawless perfection. What is it then about Christ that the author to the Hebrews thinks had to be "brought to completion"?[3]

Turning first to Heb 2:10, the preceding paragraph (2:5–9) addresses Christ's apparent lowliness as a suffering human being. That is, why did he not look superior to angels? The preacher finds the answer in Ps 8: "What are human beings that you are mindful of them, or mortals, that you care for them? You have made them for a little while lower than the angels; you have crowned them with glory and honor, subjecting all things under their feet" (Heb 2:6–8). Although originally spoken about Israel or humanity, our author interprets the words as referring to "Jesus, who for a little while was made lower than the angels, now crowned with

---

3. Along with nearly all other NT scholars, I consider Hebrews to have been authored by someone other than Paul.

glory and honor because of the suffering of death, so that by the grace of God he might taste death for everyone" (Heb 2:9). This lowering was "fitting" so that he might be "made perfect through sufferings," or better, "completed" in some way through them (2:10). As Peterson elaborates, this completion through suffering refers to the process of his earthly suffering leading up to and including death and exaltation, all of which equipped him, made him completely adequate, for his priestly office. To be thus readied and qualified required that he: 1) identify with his people via incarnation ("made lower than angels"); 2) "taste death for everyone," so as to defeat the devil and free people from fear; and 3) pioneer the way for the "many sons" to glory and exaltation.[4]

The second text referring to Christ's perfecting (5:8-9) moves in a similar direction. Hebrews 5 begins the main central section of the homily dealing with the theme of Christ's high priestly work (5:1—10:18). The literary context relates the perfecting in 5:9 to his office of high priest (4:14-15; 5:1, 5-6, 10). The two paragraphs of 5:1-10 compare the qualities and qualifications of high priests generally with those of Christ as high priest, and do this in the form of a chiasm.

vv. 1-4, High Priesthood—*General* Character and Qualifications: "every high priest" (v. 1)

A. makes atonement for sin (v. 1)
   B. sympathizes with the people (vv. 2-3)
      C. called by God (v. 4)

vv. 5-10, High Priesthood—*Christ's* Character and Qualifications: "thus also Christ" (v. 5)

      C. appointed by God (vv. 5-6)
   B. able to empathize with humanity (vv. 7-8)
A. became source of eternal salvation (vv. 9-10)

This has nothing to do with any perfecting of Christ's being or nature, and everything to do with his completed qualification to be high priest of the new covenant. Thus, again, translations would be more helpful to say something like "and having been fully readied [as high priest], he became

4. Peterson, *Hebrews and Perfection*, 66-73.

the source of eternal salvation for all who obey him." Also as in 2:10, this vocational readiness is intimately related to Christ's humiliation, suffering ("tested as we are," 4:15; "subject to weakness," 5:2; "with loud cries and tears," 5:7), and heavenly exaltation ("who has passed through the heavens," 4:14).

The third and final Christ-related perfection text (7:28) makes crystal clear that our author uses *teleioun* in reference to Christ to mean *completely readied as high priest*. Chapter 7 revolves around the priesthood of Christ "according to the order of Melchizedek" (v. 17). The author explores the superiority of this new (non-levitical) priesthood, since its priest "remains . . . forever" (v. 3; cf. also vv. 16–17, 24), was superior to Abraham and Levi (vv. 4–10), and is part of a "better covenant" (v. 22). He concludes this series of contrasts between the two orders of priesthood with our verse.

> For the law appoints as high priests those who are subject to weakness, but the word of the oath, which came later than the law, appoints a Son who has been made perfect forever. (Heb 7:28)

In contrast to the Aaronic high priests who were subject to personal weakness and were appointed by the law, Christ was appointed by divine oath and "has been made perfect forever." This weakness of the earthly priests refers in context to their mortality ("prevented by death," 7:23) as well as their character (their "own sins," 7:27). In contrast, Christ "holds his priesthood permanently, because he continues forever" (7:24), and, since he is without sin (cf. 4:15), "has no need to offer sacrifices . . . for his own sins" (7:27).[5] Whereas the earthly priests, owing to their own mortality and weakness, could never reach the ultimate goal of covenantal priesthood, Christ has reached that *telos*. He "has been made perfect forever," which refers "to the whole process by which Jesus was personally prepared and vocationally qualified for his continuing ministry in the

---

5. References to Jesus's sinlessness in Hebrews (4:15; 7:26–28; cf. also 2 Cor 5:21 ["knew no sin"]) raise theological issues. Does this imply Jesus was not truly human? That his humanity was somehow different from ours or even from pre-Fall Adam's? And for our study of human *teleios*, does this sinlessness of Christ present a model of humanity different from the wholeness and faithfulness, but not sinlessness, we have been sketching? Or, could Christ's being "without sin" in 4:15 refer to something other than lifelong sinlessness in all respects? Could it mean he never deviated from his calling, never rebelled? For brief reflections, see Peterson, *Hebrews and Perfection*, Appendix A, "Sinlessness of Christ and His Perfecting," 188–90.

presence of God."⁶ This application of *teleios* language to Christ is unique to Hebrews as is its focus on Christ's completed qualification for heavenly high priestly ministry.

The remaining perfection texts in Hebrews speak of Israel's (or humanity's) completion.⁷ In an extended exhortation (5:11—6:20) the author urges the hearers to press on to completion (6:1), and starts this with a reproof to awaken them to their need (5:11–14). He accuses them of being "dull in understanding," of needing "milk" or the "basic elements of the oracles of God" rather than "solid food." Unlike their current immature state needing elementary instruction, he speaks of those who are *teleioi* (complete, mature, whole, perfect), who can distinguish good from evil, i.e., who are ethically and educationally complete.⁸

> But solid food is for the mature [*teleiōn*], for those whose faculties have been trained by practice to distinguish good from evil. (5:14)

Although the hearers themselves are not considered to have reached this completeness (6:1), it is a desirable and realizable goal for them in the author's mind. The term in this context does not describe sinless people, but those who have reached the ethical and noetic goals for human beings expected by the gospel, and thus is not that much different from what we have discovered about human wholeness elsewhere.

Several of the perfection texts in Hebrews deal with the law's inability to bring about such completeness contrasted with Christ's effectiveness to do the same.

> . . . the law made nothing perfect [*eteleiōsen*] (7:19a)

> Since the law has only a shadow of the good things to come and not the true form of these realities, it can never, by the same sacrifices that are continually offered year after year, make perfect [*teleiōsai*] those who approach. (10:1)

---

6. Lane, *Hebrews 1–8*, 196.

7. One text speaks neither of Christ's nor humanity's completion, but of "the greater and [more] perfect [*teleioteras*] tent (not made with hands, that is, not of this creation)" (9:11). This refers to the heavenly tabernacle, which is more complete than the earthly, since it partakes of the heavenly new-creation reality rather than being of this (old) creation.

8. See Koester, *Hebrews*, 302; Peterson, *Hebrews and Perfection*, 176–83.

Contrast this with Christ, who "by a single offering ... has perfected [*teteleiōken*] for all time those who are sanctified" (10:14).

Torah's inability to bring *teleios* is given extended explanation in chapters 9 and 10. They open with a description of the wilderness tabernacle under the "first covenant" (9:1–5), and then move on to describe the priestly ministry in that tabernacle (10:6–10). Subsequently, the author will contrast this with Christ's heavenly high priestly ministry (9:11–14).

OT priesthood, tabernacle and sacrifices	Christ in the heavenly sanctuary
enter continually (9:6)	enters once for all (9:12)
offer blood of goats and bulls (9:13)	offers his own blood (9:12)
purify the flesh (9:13)	purifies the conscious from dead works (9:14)

Whereas the old system could only purify the external flesh (9:10) and "cannot perfect the conscience" (9:13), Christ's sacrifice "purif[ies] our conscience from dead works to worship the living God." This "conscience" refers not so much to an internal moral arbiter as we might think today ("Is this or that path right?"), but to a consciousness regarding past behavior, usually an awareness of wrongdoing, "an evil conscience" (10:22).[9] More than simply an internal ethical voice, this conscience "is directed toward God and embraces the whole person in his relation to God."[10] It is the awareness that one's relationship with God is in order, that one has a "good conscience" (13:18), or does not (10:22). The old system "sanctifies those who have been defiled so that their flesh is purified" (9:13). It provided an effective and repeated restoration of the Israelites in their covenantal relationship with Yahweh. It restored them as a nation annually to their place as a holy people before God. However, what it could not do was change their hearts. As Lane notes, "Although the ritual of the Day of Atonement might effect temporary relief, the renewal was short lived. The annual repetition of the solemn ceremonies indicated that sin had again come into remembrance (10:3–4)."[11] Christ's work, on the other hand, results in a "true heart in full assurance of faith, with our hearts sprinkled clean from an evil conscience" (10:22). This is connected, in our author's mind, with Jeremiah's new covenant promise.

---

9. Hebrews speaks of the conscience in 9:9, 14; 10:2, 22; and 13:18. Only in the last-mentioned is a "clear conscience" in view. On the whole, see Pierce, *Conscience in the New Testament*.

10. Lane, *Hebrews 9–13*, 225.

11. Lane, *Hebrews 9–13*, 225.

Wholeness-Perfection in Other Apostolic Voices

> For by a single offering he has perfected for all time those who are sanctified. And the Holy Spirit also testifies to us, for after saying, [quoting Jer 31] "This is the covenant that I will make with them after those days, says the Lord: I will put my laws in their hearts, and I will write them on their minds," he also adds, "I will remember their sins and their lawless deeds no more." Where there is forgiveness of these, there is no longer any offering for sin. (Heb 10:14–18)

Through Christ's once-for-all offering of himself, their hearts are purified as promised in Jeremiah's new covenant. Koester summarizes well the sense of this saying. "Although completion finally means everlasting life in God's presence, Hebrews can say that those who are sanctified by Christ have already been made complete in the sense of being brought into right relationship with God."[12]

This inability of Torah is further described in the next chapter.

> Yet all these, though they were commended for their faith, did not receive what was promised, since God had provided something better so that they would not, apart from us, be made perfect [*teleiōthōsin*]. (Heb 11:39–40)

This statement derives from the fact that the law, as we have just discussed, brought nothing to completion (7:19; 9:9; 10:1). Thus, those like Moses, Joshua, etc., who lived under the law's administration, could not achieve the fullness or completion of this relationship with Yahweh until Christ had come. They had, of course, "received approval as righteous" (11:4), "pleased God" (11:5), and were genuine heirs of the promises (11:7). However, "all of these died in faith *without having received the promises*, but from a distance they saw and greeted them" (11:13). While Torah could bring many of the promised divine blessings, it could not bring the full enjoyment, the *teleios*, of God's promised blessings.

This bringing to completion, this perfecting, belongs to Christ.

> Looking to Jesus the pioneer and perfecter [*teleiōtēn*] of our faith, who for the sake of the joy that was set before him endured the cross, disregarding its shame, and has taken his seat at the right hand of the throne of God. (12:2)

In contrast to the OT saints whose faith looked from afar at this completion (ch. 11), the new covenant saints experience the completion of their

---

12. Koester, *Hebrews*, 123.

faith by Jesus, who himself led the way to this completion and through his suffering brings theirs to completion.[13] This text does not speak directly of human perfection or wholeness, but of the completion of faith by Jesus. The focus here is probably not so much on each individual's own believing being completed (although that would also be correct), but to the faith generally, which has just been detailed throughout chapter 11. This faith was not brought to completion in the era of Torah, but has now been completed by Christ.[14]

And now that Christ has opened the way to this completeness, even those who lived under the old arrangement can partake. They, too, are included in "the assembly of the firstborn who are enrolled in heaven" and "the spirits[15] of the righteous made perfect [*teteleiōmenōn*]" (12:23). As Peterson notes, this "speaks of the fulfillment of 11:40, so that believers of pre-Christian days and Christians together enjoy the consummation of their hopes."[16]

What we have seen about *teleios* in Hebrews thus far will be confirmed in the final verses to consider (7:11, 19). In chapter 7 the author retraces the story of Abraham's encounter with Melchizedek (7:1–10; cf. Gen 14), and then turns to another Melchizedek text ("You are a priest forever, according to the order of Melchizedek," Ps 110:4) whose two phrases he will unpack to show the superiority of Christ's priesthood. First he explores Christ's priesthood "according to the order of Melchizedek" (7:11–14), and then his being such a priest "forever" (7:15–19).[17]

The first paragraph opens with an observation based upon Ps 110:4:

> Now if perfection [*teleiōsis*] had been attainable through the levitical priesthood—for the people received the law under this priesthood—what further need would there have been to speak of another priest arising according to the order of Melchizedek, rather than one according to the order of Aaron? (7:11)

---

13. Since this particular noun form, *teleiōtēs*, seems to be unknown in the LXX or in contemporary Greek literature, it is possible that our author coined it to contrast with "pioneer [*archēgos*]"; so Lane, *Hebrews 9–13*, 141.

14. So Peterson, *Hebrews and Perfection*, 171.

15. The reference to the "spirits of the righteous" does not seek to differentiate spirit/soul from body, but is "an idiom for the godly dead" in Jewish apocalyptic literature: Lane, *Hebrews 9–13*, 470–71.

16. Peterson, *Hebrews and Perfection*, 164.

17. On the structure of his section, see esp. Koester, *Hebrews*, 356–58.

That is, the divine affirmation of a different, non-Levitical, priesthood in Ps 110, one acknowledged in the Abraham story to be greater (7:1–10), implies that there was something deficient in the Aaronic priesthood. It was unable to bring completion or perfection.[18] Even though this completion is not defined here, we have seen plenty of hints as to the author's meaning. "[E]arlier passages have spoken about the hope of being crowned with glory and honor (2:5–10), entering God's promised rest (4:9–10), and inheriting the blessing that God promised to Abraham and his heirs (6:7, 12)."[19] And this culminates in "approach[ing] God" (7:19). Thus, Koester speaks for many when he concludes that this completion refers to "the establishment of right relationship with God through the cleansing of the conscience and the consummation of this relationship in everlasting glory, rest, and celebration in God's heavenly city."[20] As we have noted everywhere with the *telei-* word-group, the central sense is that something or someone reaches their goal or purpose (*telos*), the aim of their being or nature is fulfilled. In this instance, it is the divine intention for God's people that is in view.[21] And this contrasts with the old covenant people of God who could not receive what was promised and be made complete apart from the new covenant ones (11:39–40).

Wholeness-Perfection in James

The short but weighty letter of James adds its voice to the human *tamim* theology we have been discovering elsewhere in biblical tradition. Commentators are largely agreed that James's use of perfection terminology is rooted in the Jewish *tamim* tradition.[22] This expectation of human completeness is clear right in the opening section.

> My brothers and sisters, whenever you face trials of any kind, consider it nothing but joy, because you know that the testing of your faith produces endurance; and let endurance have its full

---

18. Apart from Luke 1:45 ("And blessed is she who believed that there would be a fulfillment of what was spoken to her by the Lord."), this is the only NT use of the noun *teleiōsis*.

19. Koester, *Hebrews*, 358.

20. Koester, *Hebrews*, 353. Similarly Peterson, *Hebrews and Perfection*, 129: "the fulfillment of the promises of the New Covenant in the priestly ministry of Christ."

21. Heb 10:14: "he has perfected for all time those who are sanctified."

22. Hartin, "Call to Be Perfect," 483–84; Du Plessis, *Teleios*, 233–40; Allison, *Critical and Exegetical Commentary*, 154–58.

effect, so that you may be mature [*teleioi*] and complete, lacking in nothing. (Jas 1:2–4)

The full effect of holding fast to faith in God, of enduring in the face of testing, is the wholeness and completeness anticipated for human beings in the Jewish tradition. This connection of endurance under trials and perfection-completion through wisdom had already been made in Jewish tradition.[23] As does Philo, James pairs *teleios* with a synonym, *holoklēros* [complete], further testifying to this *tamim* concept.[24]

Our understanding of this human wholeness here in James, and in Jewish tradition generally, assumes he is thinking of this occurring in the here-and-now. It is in this life that we face this testing of faith, and it is in this life that such enduring of testing produces human wholeness. However, Hartin and others think James's "that you may be mature [*teleioi*]" refers to "perfection of the eschatological age."[25] They have good grounds.

1. Testing and endurance are often connected with eschatological context in Christian and Jewish texts.

2. Similar statements in 1 Pet 1:7 and Rom 5:3–4 have eschatological contexts.

3. Jas 1:12 ties endurance to "the crown of life" (life in the age to come?).

However, while an eschatological component should not be excluded, neither should the more common Jewish understanding of human *teleios* be omitted.[26] The this-worldly, non-eschatological, understanding of *teleios* is clear in 3:2 (see below), as Hartin himself seems to acknowledge.[27]

A second testimony to this understanding of human wholeness occurs in Jas 3:2.

---

23. Gowan, "Wisdom and Endurance," 145–53.

24. Foerster, "Ολόκληρος," 3:766.

25. Hartin, "Call to Be Perfect," 481–83. Klein argues similarly, Klein, *Ein vollkommenes Werk*, 81, 163–84; as does Allison, *Critical and Exegetical Commentary*, 159–60.

26. Allison cites 4 Macc 9:8, "where suffering works both virtue in the present and eschatological reward in the future: 'through this severe suffering and endurance, we will have the prize of virtue and will be with God.'" Allison, *Critical and Exegetical Commentary*, 160.

27. "The person who performs 'the perfect work' shows a total dedication to carrying out God's will. Faced with trials and testing, such a person is not deflated from total allegiance to God." Hartin, "Call to Be Perfect," 484. Dibelius rejects the eschatological interpretation in favor of the ethical, arguing that the language and the concatenation of virtues (x works y leads to z) favor the ethical interpretation. Dibelius, *James*, 72–74.

Wholeness-Perfection in Other Apostolic Voices

> For all of us make many mistakes. Anyone who makes no mistakes in speaking is perfect, able to keep the whole body in check with a bridle.

This comes in a paragraph about the use of the tongue (3:1–12), which can teach (3:1), boast (3:5), bless, and curse (3:10).[28] Whether limited to teaching or other speech, the problem lies in the fact that "all of us make many mistakes [or stumble: *ptaiomen*]." This verb typically referred to literal stumbling, but came to be widely used metaphorically for erring or sinning.[29] It was a commonplace in both Jewish and Hellenistic culture that we all stumble, err, transgress, especially in the arena of speech.[30]

James continues the focus on speech by noting that a *teleios* person is one who "makes no mistakes in speaking [lit. does not stumble or sin in speech]." It is not entirely clear whether the author thinks such mistake-less speech, and thus perfection, is possible or not. Since he has just said we all make such mistakes (3:2a), and will later admit "no one can tame the tongue" (3:8), many think such perfection impossible. On the other hand, the opening reference to *teleios* (1:4) raised expectations of its achievement. The solution depends in large part on just what we understand by a "mistake in speaking." While our English translation might suggest speech that never includes any error or is never harsh and censorious, this is probably pressing the language beyond its intent. Both Hellenistic and Jewish tradition held it possible, though difficult, to exercise self-control, including control of one's speech.[31] Our author turns to this in vv. 3–4 with the images of bits controlling horses and rudders guiding ships. His aim in all of this seems to be to avoid the duplicitous behavior seen in vv. 9–12—a mouth that brings forth both blessing and cursing. This is the "double-minded" person (1:7), who is the opposite

---

28. Commentators differ as to whether the section maintains a focus on teachers (v. 1), or moves into a more general admonition on human speech. Allison may well be correct to refuse to choose one or the other. "One can imagine the section serving well in a variety of settings. Wherever there are teachers, some think too highly of themselves, and wherever there are human beings, some speak ill of others." Allison, *Critical and Exegetical Commentary*, 518.

29. Schmidt, "πταίω," 6:883–84.

30. For widespread evidence, see Allison, *Critical and Exegetical Commentary*, 523–24. Commentators are divided over whether the author here refers to the Hellenistic commonplace that we all make mistakes, or the Jewish concept of general human sin. See Dibelius, *James*, 183–84 and n. 116, who favors the former.

31. Johnson, *Letter of James*, 263–64, though Johnson thinks James differs from the Jewish tradition as to its achievability.

of the perfect one (1:4). Perhaps, then, James is speaking not so much of mistake-less speech, but of consistent speech. Such consistency, such completion, is, indeed difficult ("we all stumble"), but it is not impossible, especially with the help of divine wisdom (1:5).

Finally, although 2:10 does not use perfection language, its call to "keep the whole law" makes this verse relevant for our study.

> For whoever keeps the whole law but fails in one point has become accountable for all of it.

A common approach to this verse sees in it a demand that acceptable obedience to the law must achieve 100 percent conformity. A single act of disobedience spells damnation.[32] This approach, however, ignores that James may be using a typically Jewish way of speaking about Torah obedience. Thus, for instance, "in m.Qidd. 1.10, the one who fails to perform one... commandment in the law will not have life in the world to come."[33] In such Jewish tradition the point was not the idea of flawless, 100 percent obedience, but was a rejection of partiality in Torah obedience. One may not pick and choose in obedience to God. As James notes in the following verse 11,[34] one cannot pick between adultery and murder; to violate either one is to violate Torah. Our hearts may not claim to follow God's desires while simultaneously declaring, "this one command I will ignore." Such a person is not wholehearted, complete.[35]

Perfection in 1 John

Although the first epistle of John does not contain a great deal of perfection language (5x, see below), it presents the reader with perhaps the greatest paradox in the NT regarding human perfection. It seems, in fact, to assert that believers can and must be sinless. "We know that those who

---

32. Gal 3:10 ("Cursed is everyone who does not observe and obey *all* the things written in the book of the law.") and 5:3 ("he is obliged to obey *the entire law*") support this view according to these interpreters.

33. Cited in Allison, *Critical and Exegetical Commentary*, 412, with several additional Jewish statements of the same.

34. "For the one who said, 'You shall not commit adultery,' also said, 'You shall not murder.' Now if you do not commit adultery but if you murder, you have become a transgressor of the law."

35. This was, likewise, Paul's point when speaking similarly to Gentiles who desired circumcision in Gal 5:3 ... they are "obliged to obey the entire law," not simply part of it or only the parts more amenable to Gentile sensibilities.

Wholeness-Perfection in Other Apostolic Voices

are born of God do not sin" (5:18a). Yet, simultaneously it condemns anyone who would claim to be sinless. "If we say that we have not sinned, we make him a liar" (1:10a). Our task here is to sort out this jarring paradox and to discover the meaning of this "perfect love" (4:18) which never sins.

The letter is concerned with behavior right from the beginning. Because God himself is light with no darkness (1:5), so those who claim fellowship with him must "walk in the light as he himself is in the light" (1:7). "Walking" is a well-known Jewish metaphor for human behavior and is used with light and darkness here to refer to good or evil behavior. This is well illustrated by Eph 5:8–9.

> For once you were darkness, but now in the Lord you are light. Live [lit. walk] as children of light—for the fruit of the light is found in all that is good and right and true.

Apparently, one of the problems this author must deal with is a group who seem to be claiming something akin to sinless perfection.[36]

> <u>If we say that we have no sin</u>, we deceive ourselves, and the truth is not in us. If we confess our sins, he who is faithful and just will forgive us our sins and cleanse us from all unrighteousness. <u>If we say that we have not sinned</u>, we make him a liar, and his word is not in us. (1 John 1:8–10)

The second underlined assertion ("we have not sinned" [*ouk hēmartēkamen*]) is usually understood as a denial that one has committed post-baptismal sin, i.e., as a believer.[37] While the first assertion ("we have no sin" [*hamartian ouk echomen*]) sounds identical, its different wording opens the possibility that something else may have been in mind. Perhaps such individuals thought the very root of sin, i.e., their sinful inclination, had been eradicated. Or, that as believers they would no longer carry any liability (in judgment) for sins committed.[38] Whichever the case, the author brands such perfectionistic views as lies and self-deception. Here and at several other points in the letter it becomes obvious he does not think believers will remain fully sinless.[39]

---

36. For the many proposals as to the specific identity of such an opposing group in the Johannine literature, see von Wahlde, *Commentary*, 339–45.

37. "[P]robably entailed a denial of having sinned since becoming a believer," Brown, *Epistles of John*, 234.

38. The first view is held by von Wahlde, *Commentary*, 49, "the inclination to sin"; and the second by Brown, *Epistles of John*, 205–6, "free from the guilt of sin."

39. 1:9 ("if we confess our sins"); 2:1–2 ("if anyone does sin"); 5:16 ("if you see your

But what, then, are we to do with the two passages that seem to assert precisely such sinlessness for believers?

> Everyone who commits sin is guilty of lawlessness; sin is lawlessness. You know that he was revealed to take away sins, and in him there is no sin. <u>No one who abides in him sins</u>; no one who sins has either seen him or known him. Little children, let no one deceive you. Everyone who does what is right is righteous, just as he is righteous. Everyone who commits sin is a child of the devil; for the devil has been sinning from the beginning. The Son of God was revealed for this purpose, to destroy the works of the devil. <u>Those who have been born of God do not sin</u>, because God's seed abides in them; <u>they cannot sin, because they have been born of God</u>. The children of God and the children of the devil are revealed in this way: all who do not do what is right are not from God, nor are those who do not love their brothers and sisters. (1 John 3:4–10)

> We know that <u>those who are born of God do not sin</u>, but the one who was born of God protects them, and the evil one does not touch them. (1 John 5:18)

There are numerous ways a reader could try to understand this sinlessness and, thereby, reconcile it with the author's simultaneous denial of sinlessness.[40]

1. Some think *different groups* are in view with the differing statements. The assertions of sinlessness apply to an elite group in the church, while acknowledgment of sin applies to the rest. Or, varying slightly from this, perhaps there were two different mentalities being addressed—one which supposed they were sinless and another which claimed sinning didn't matter. The two types of statements were not meant to be harmonized, but addressed different issues.

2. Others think statements like they "do not sin" express an *ideal*. They could be translated "ought not to sin," thus allowing that, in fact, they might and do sin.

3. Some surmise that the *literary context* of the two types of statements separates them. The acknowledgments of sin in believers are

brother or sister committing what is not a mortal sin").

40. For various interpretive solutions and their supporters, see Brown, *Epistles of John*, 413–15; and Marshall, *Epistles of John*, 178–82. Rarely, a few scholars will suggest two different authors are at work making contradictory statements.

Wholeness-Perfection in Other Apostolic Voices

pastoral in nature. They seek to apply the gospel of forgiveness to believers who fail. "If we confess our sins, he who is faithful and just will forgive us our sins" (1 John 1:9). The stark assertions of sinlessness, on the other hand, arise from an apocalyptic context. This is the "last hour" when antichrists arise (2:18), "lawlessness" reigns under the "lawless one" (1 John 3:4; 2 Thess 2:3–10; both using *anomia*), and the world hates the saints (1 John 3:13). Jewish apocalyptic literature envisioned this final period as a time when the persecuted followers of the God of Israel would be without sin.[41] The sinlessness spoken of in 1 John is an apocalyptically colored picture of end-time conditions, not a neutral or objective statement of fact.[42]

4. Perhaps the most common solution is to see two *different types of sin* at work in the paradoxical statements. Believers do commit unintentional, venial, or occasional minor sins, but they do not commit deliberate, mortal, or habitual sin. Or, perhaps, the particular sin they do not and cannot commit is apostasy, the "sin leading to death" (5:16), turning from the love of Christ and the brethren.[43]

The first two options can be eliminated in my opinion. First, there is (against #1) little indication of two different fronts in the church or that these statements are addressed only to a part of the church. Instead it is "those [i.e., *all those*] who are born of God [who] do not sin." Second, since the fact of sinning or not sinning is presented as a way to differentiate true from false believers ("The children of God and the children of the devil are revealed in this way," 3:10a), this must refer to observable behavior, not to one's intentions or some unrealized, i.e., non-observable ideal (against #2).

Some revision and combination of options #3 and #4 will probably be closer to the truth. The apocalyptic reading is increasingly popular and has much to be said in its favor. De la Potterie is correct that 1 John's doctrine of impeccability arises out of Jewish apocalyptic expectations.

---

41. Ezek 36:29; 1 En 5:8–9; Jub 5:12; TLevi 18:9; 1QS 4:21–23. For this interpretation, see esp. de la Potterie, "Impeccability," 175–96.

42. Thus, as de la Potterie concludes, Christians do, in fact, sin "under their empirical aspect" (i.e., in actual behavior), but do not sin when considered as participants of the end. De la Potterie, "Impeccability," 186.

43. This is the sin of "unbelief" according to Bogart, *Orthodox and Heretical Perfectionism*.

"At the end of time, the chosen people will be a holy people, a people without sin; this sanctity, this impeccability, will be due to the active presence of the Spirit, wisdom, and law within the hearts of the chosen ones. From their relationship with God they will receive the strength to sin no longer and the gift of life."[44] The only change I would make is to clarify more precisely the shape of this anticipated sinlessness.[45] As we have seen from the OT, the DSS, and other Second Temple literature, claims to be "without sin," to be perfect or *tamim*, refer to wholeness and whole-hearted loyalty, but not to sinlessness. This, and not actual sinlessness, is also what the apocalyptic texts are envisioning. When 1 John asserts believers do not sin, he means they do not depart from the path of faithfulness and whole-hearted obedience to God.

When, on the other hand, the letter acknowledges that believers commit sins, it is speaking of individual acts of disobedience to God and to his commandments. They are what Scripture and Jewish tradition typically identify as transgression. Such infractions of the divine will are to be confessed and forgiven (1 John 1:9). They are violations of God's commandments (2:1–6). As we saw in the chapters treating Jewish tradition, it was common to acknowledge that even the righteous, the complete [*tamim*], could and did disobey the divine will at times, "out-of-character" as it were. This did not, however, invalidate their status as those who were pure, single of heart, obedient, and whole-hearted. The same paradox we have discovered in 1 John was common to Jewish tradition. Thus, both the OT Psalms and the hymns from Qumran are full of confessions that the worshiper has indeed committed transgressions, while simultaneously claiming that the worshiper continues to walk in faithfulness and integrity.[46]

44. De la Potterie, "Impeccability," 178; his convincing support from Second Temple literature can be found on 178–81.

45. Furthermore, de la Potterie's attempt to resolve the paradox against this background is unpersuasive. Claiming an apocalyptic context for only the sinlessness assertions hardly helps. Surely in 1 John's narrative world, the acknowledgments of sinfulness are also being applied to those who are living in the last hour. Though supporting de la Potterie, Brown admits this is a "serious difficulty": Brown, *Epistles of John*, 415.

46. My interpretation is not that distant from the common appeal to different types of "sin" as an explanation of the paradox (#4 above). It advances the argument, however, by positing a different background or rationale. Instead of relying on appeals to Greek present tense ("continues to sin," "does not sin continually"), now rendered dubious by Greek verbal aspect theory, my reading appeals to an existing Jewish pattern of speech about sin, perfection, and righteousness.

Wholeness-Perfection in Other Apostolic Voices

This reading, which draws from our study of wholeness, is confirmed by the five occurrences of *teleios* language in 1 John.

- But whoever obeys his word, truly in this person the love of God has reached perfection [*teteleiōtai*]. (2:5)
- No one has ever seen God; if we love one another, God lives in us, and his love is perfected [*teteleiōmenē estin*] in us. (4:12)
- Love has been perfected [*teteleiōtai*] among us in this: that we may have boldness on the day of judgment, because as he is, so are we in this world. (4:17)
- There is no fear in love, but perfect [*teleia*] love casts out fear; for fear has to do with punishment, and whoever fears has not reached perfection [*teteleiōtai*] in love. (4:18)

Every instance above is connected with love, both love for and from God and love for one another. As Jesus noted in agreement with Jewish tradition, to love God and others has always been the heartbeat of biblical devotion, of the OT path of Torah and *tamim* (Matt 22:36–40). This divine love comes to its fullness in those who obey what God says (1 John 2:5) and love one another (4:12). Such biblically whole people live a life of "perfect love" and no longer need live in fear of divine wrath (4:18).

One final text in 1 John, although not using *teleios* language, has often been invoked in debates over human perfection.

> Beloved, we are God's children now; what we will be has not yet been revealed. What we do know is this: when he is revealed, *we will be like him*, for we will see him as he is. (3:2)

A common, popular understanding reads, "We will never know a total absence of sin until we are with the Lord in glory: 'When Christ appears, we shall be like him.'"[47] That is, the sinless perfection that eludes us in this life will be ours when transformed at Christ's second coming. This understanding of "like him" as moral transformation is certainly possible. The letter focuses throughout on sin and ethics in the lives of believers as we noted earlier. And the same note is sounded in the verses immediately preceding ("Everyone who does right has been born of him," 2:29) and following ("And all who have this hope in him purify themselves, just as he is pure," 3:3).

---

47. GotQuestions.org. https://www.gotquestions.org/continue-to-sin.html.

This interpretation, however, raises problems of its own. Whatever "like him" means, it is something believers do not yet see, experience, or understand: "what we will be has not yet been revealed" (2:2a). But as we discovered, the letter has made clear that "not sinning" is something already predicated of believers: "No one who abides in him sins" (3:6a). The perfection of divine love is already a reality.[48]

Thus, many point to the sharing of divine glory as the meaning of this "like him."[49] John's gospel speaks of a future vision of Christ's glory (John 17:1, 5, 24; see also 1:14) and Paul envisions believers sharing this glory at the parousia (Rom 8:17–21; Col 3:4), particularly in the glorification of their bodies at the resurrection (Phil 3:21; 1 Cor 15:42–44). This may be John's way of expressing the thought found in 2 Cor 3:18: "And all of us, with unveiled faces, seeing the glory of the Lord as though reflected in a mirror, are being transformed into the same image from one degree of glory to another; for this comes from the Lord, the Spirit." In the end we may simply have to acknowledge that "John does not state explicitly in what new ways we shall be like Jesus at the parousia."[50]

---

48. Perhaps "like him" simply means the occasional transgressions that still mark believers and must be confessed will be removed, but are already dealt with and forgiven, but this hardly justifies the sense of wonder at this transformation (3:1–3).

49. See Schnackenburg, *Johannine Epistles*, 157–60; and Marshall, *Epistles of John*, 172.

50. Marshall, *Epistles of John*, 172.

Part Three

The Church's Pursuit of Perfection

Chapter 11

The Reception of Perfection in Christian History and Theology

> The distinctive character of each religion and confession
> is best recognized in its ideal of perfect piety.[1]

The central thesis of this chapter is that the post-NT church by and large lost the earthy, this-worldly, Jewish inspired vision of human wholeness we discovered in the previous chapters. This does not mean that it lost interest in such perfection. Far from it! The quest for godlikeness, for the perfecting of the human being, for the vision of God and the *summum bonum*, became central points of preaching and discussion, but the goal of this quest, the nature of human perfection, would look quite different.[2]

It would, in fact, move the perfect human from earth to heaven, and locate such perfection more in the realm of mind than body. Humans reaching perfection would be more angelic, even sexless, and separated from the passions or impulses that so move us earthly creatures. Perfection would be found in the vision of God, the contemplation of the Ideal, and was a strongly interior matter, though, to be sure, it would have visible consequences (e.g., taming passions). This became the dominant understanding of perfection and lies behind most patristic and medieval discussions as well as the mystical tradition of Christian spirituality.[3]

---

1. Flew, *Idea of Perfection*, 377 n. 374 (author's translation), citing Adolf von Harnack, *Albrecht Ritschl*.

2. On this quest in church history, see esp. Flew, *Idea of Perfection*.

3. Kirk states this development as follows. "Christianity came into a world

In order to manage this mass of material, we will look at:

- Patristic voices on perfection (including Augustine)
- The monastic/ascetic quest for perfection
- The medieval quest (including Aquinas)
- Reformation voices on perfection
- Modern thoughts on perfection

The Decisive Turn: Patristic Voices on Perfection

The several centuries following the apostolic period witnessed the decisive turn toward a view of Christian perfection or wholeness quite different from what we have seen in most of the OT and Jewish perspectives. This should not be entirely surprising, since the leading theologians of the second-century church and beyond were almost all non-Jews and often well-schooled in Greek philosophy. Although they would give serious attention to Scripture, frequently their understanding of those texts and concepts, including those dealing with human wholeness, would be informed more by their Greek philosophical framework and an allegorical interpretive method than by an attempt to recapture a Jewish way of looking at matters.[4] Thus, for example, the body or flesh was no longer simply the human lump of clay as in the OT, in itself morally neutral, but now a negative aspect of human existence connected with the inferior world of materiality. Similarly, "soul" was no longer simply a term describing the human being as a living, spirit-infused clay being, but was an immaterial "part" of a human that can be separated from the body at death.

Yet, in this very turn to a more philosophical understanding they were preceded, and to some extent guided, by a Jewish thinker we have

---

tantalized with the belief that some men at least had seen God, and had found in the vision the sum of human happiness. . . . Their quest was primarily a selfish one; their motive to secure for themselves, either here or hereafter, an all-absorbing religious experience. . . . [T]he Church undertook the amazing task of transforming this self-centred cult of the divine into an ideal of disinterested worship and service." Kirk, *Vision of God*, 54.

4. Burgeoning anti-Judaism in the early church may also have played a role in their general lack of interest in Jewish ways of understanding matters.

already noted, Philo, who himself had drunk deeply of Plato's well.[5] We now know that some of Philo's voluminous writings were known already in second-century Alexandria to such influential Christian thinkers as Origen and Clement. It may well have been Origen who brought his extensive library of Philo's works to Caesarea where they were preserved for the church.[6]

As we saw earlier, Philo had already proposed a more Platonic view of perfection. Characteristic of this Platonic quest was "the way by which the human soul will be able to return to its origins, to the bosom of the divine. All of Plato's ideas are characterized by his concern with the eternal and divine."[7] Thus, for Clement of Alexandria also, "Moses . . . describes the perfect man as being neither God nor man, but . . . something on the border between uncreated and the perishable nature" (*Somn.* 2,234).[8] And reference in Genesis to Noah as "a just man, perfect in his generation . . . does not mean merely to use the common expressions for a rational mortal animal" but refers to one who has "driven away all the untameable and furious passions and brutal wickednesses of the soul" (*Abr.* 31–32). For Philo, human perfection refers to virtues of mind freed of the passions of the flesh.[9] Thus, Philo hears the call to Abraham to "walk before me and be blameless" (Gen 17:1) as akin to the calls to priests and prophets to raise themselves "above all the objects of the mere outward senses" and to fix their views "on that world which is perceptible only by the intellect," the world of "incorruptible incorporeal ideas" (*Gig.* 61–62).

This more Platonizing worldview will surface repeatedly in key church fathers throughout the second through fourth centuries and will deeply influence the way they think about the goal of human development and the way to reach that goal.[10] The world of ideas, mind, spirit is to be desired over the visible world of flesh and materiality. The latter, in fact, carries particular dangers to the development toward human perfection, particularly the downward pull of human passions. Perfection was seen as the ascent to pure being (Mind), the return to the original state of being, and the elimination of passion and hindrances of living in the

---

5. On Philo see ch. 4.

6. On this fascinating intersection of Philo and early Christian thinkers, see Runia, "Philo of Alexandria," 143–60.

7. Karavites, *Evil*, 25.

8. Yonge translation.

9. *Deus* 116–18; *QG* 1,97.

10. So Flew, *Idea of Perfection*, ch. 6, "The Christian Platonists" (138–57).

flesh (asceticism). It would, however, be unfair to portray these patristic fathers as Platonists first, and Christians second, as though theirs was but a surface "Christianizing" of Platonic pre-commitments. Their commitment to Christ, Scripture, prayer, church tradition, and bodily holiness are heartfelt, and their devotional intensity is still moving to read. This Christian foundation can be seen in Clement of Alexandria, for whom the Greeks' prizing of knowledge of forms was inadequate, being replaced by the knowledge of God through Christ and mediated through Scripture.[11]

Nevertheless, their philosophical framework made a difference. Since this Platonizing of Christian spirituality in the patristic period has been fully studied by others,[12] we will be content to provide here a sampling of selected fathers to give the reader a feel for this development.

Continuing Echo of Biblical Wholeness: Clement of Rome

Those closest to the apostolic era still speak of human wholeness or perfection in ways that are more reminiscent of Jewish tradition and the NT. As the apostolic age was closing out, Clement of Rome's words about perfection still sound much like what we heard in the NT documents.[13]

> Let him who has love in Christ perform the commandments of Christ.... In love were all the elect of God made perfect [*eteleiōthēsan*]. Without love is nothing well pleasing to God.... [T]hose who were perfected [*teleiōthentes*] in love by the grace of God have a place among the pious who shall be made manifest at the visitation of the Kingdom of Christ.... Blessed are we, beloved, if we perform the commandments of God in the concord of love, that through love our sins may be forgiven.[14]

The perfection or wholeness of the saints is connected above all with love and the keeping of Christ's commands. They can be currently described as whole or perfect in spite of "unwilling sin,"[15] and this integrity of an obedient life in love must be maintained until "the visitation of the Kingdom of Christ," i.e., the future coming of Christ.

---

11. Karavites, *Evil*, 145–50.
12. See, for instance, the classic study by Louth, *Origins*.
13. Clement was active ca. 100 CE in Rome.
14. *1 Clem.* XLIX–L.
15. *1 Clem.* II:3.

The Reception of Perfection

Intimations of Change: Irenaeus (130–202 CE)

As we noted in Jewish literature, human beings could regularly be referred to as *tamim*, whole or perfect. For Irenaeus the first perfect human being was Christ, not Adam, Noah, or anyone else in the OT.[16] As did Clement, Irenaeus strove to adhere to what he found in Scripture. When arguing against Valentinian dualism he expressed himself thus:

> For this reason does the apostle declare, "We speak wisdom among them that are perfect," terming those persons "perfect" who have received the Spirit of God ... whom also the apostle terms "spiritual," they being spiritual because they partake of the Spirit, and not because their flesh has been stripped off and taken away, and because they have become purely spiritual.[17]

Although Irenaeus remained close to the biblical tradition in many ways, what is striking in his comments about human perfection is the subtle change in the concept itself. Rather than the covenantal-relational *tamim* theology, describing a realistic path of life in obedience to the God of Israel, Irenaeus saw perfection more ontologically. That is, the very make-up of the human person must change. The body and its passions must come into subservience to the soul (mind) led by the divine spirit.[18]

Irenaeus's anthropology is key in all this. The human body, although not evil *per se*, is lower than the realm of spirit, and must be "commingled" and united with spirit and soul (mind).[19] This necessitates a God-guided growth to human perfection in gradual stages.[20] The goal of this process "is the exaltation of the creature formed by God from mud until it comes to share in the uncreated glory of God: it is the coming to be of humankind in the image and likeness of God."[21] This perfection only truly occurs in the eschaton, when corruptible bodies are made incorruptible.

---

16. *Haer.* 4.38; 5.1.1.

17. *Haer.* 5.6.1.

18. Behr, *Asceticism*, 25–127. According to Behr, Irenaeus does not, however, adopt the Hellenistic anti-passion stance seen in the Alexandrians (below).

19. "The perfect man consists in the commingling and the union of the soul receiving the spirit of the Father, and the admixture of that fleshly nature which was moulded after the image of God" (*Haer.* 5.6.1; trans. from Roberts et al., *Ante-Nicene Fathers*, vol. 1).

20. See Minns, *Irenaeus*, 69.

21. Minns, *Irenaeus*, 70.

God and Human Wholeness

The Alexandrian Turn to Plato

> [H]eathen syncretism ... was united with the doctrine of the Church. The task, which had been begun by Philo ... was now undertaken in the Church. Clement led the way in attempting a solution of the problem, but the huge task proved too much for him. Origen took it up under more difficult circumstances and ... brought it to a conclusion.[22]

If Irenaeus gives testimony to subtle changes in the church's understanding of human wholeness and the path to it, the Alexandrians, Clement, and Origen, mark a sea change.

Clement of Alexandria (150–215 CE)

Though we know little of Clement's early life,[23] by the time we meet him in Alexandria he was a well-known Christian scholar and teacher, and his writings give evidence of an intimate and wide-ranging knowledge of Greek philosophy. Like many other Christian leaders in Alexandria of the second and third centuries, and not unlike Philo in the world of Jewish thought, Clement found in Platonic ideas, or more precisely Neoplatonic, a helpful key to understanding the gospel of Christ.[24] The unseen world of ideas and knowledge carries a higher value than the visible material realm. The spirit is the willing partner, while the flesh is weak. Thus, human perfection will occur most fully in the realm of spirit and mind rather than flesh.

> For if there is one function belonging to the peculiar nature of each creature, alike of the ox, and horse, and dog, what shall we say is the peculiar function of man? He is ... compounded of a rational and irrational part, of soul and body. Well, the

---

22. Harnack, *History of Dogma*, 2:11.

23. There is some evidence for his birth in Athens. According to Epiphanius, *Panarion* 32.6, some called Clement an Alexandrian, others an Athenian.

24. See esp. Lilla, *Clement of Alexandria*. Throughout this section on the church fathers, I will use "Platonic" as a catch-all for the philosophical views of the fathers. "It is not pure Plato. What we have found in Philo and Plotinus has other philosophical debts than those to Plato. Middle Platonism, of which Philo, as we have seen, can be regarded as an example, and neo-Platonism are indebted to Aristotle and the Stoics for some of their emphases. But it is not by chance that they are called 'Platonist': Plato is their acknowledged master." Louth, *Origins*, 51.

> body tills the ground, and hastes to it; but the soul is raised to God: trained in the true philosophy, it speeds to its kindred above, turning away from the lusts of the body.... As slaves the Scripture views those "under sin" and "sold to sin," the lovers of pleasure and of the body; and beasts rather than men.... The severance, therefore, of the soul from the body, made a life-long study, produces in the philosopher gnostic alacrity, so that he is easily able to bear natural death, which is the dissolution of the chains which bind the soul to the body.[25]

Thus, Clement regularly refers to those advancing toward perfection as "gnostics" and the aim of their quest as the true apprehension of unseen reality.

> Being ruler therefore of himself and of all that belongs to him the gnostic makes a genuine approach to truth, having a firm hold of divine science. For the name science would fitly be given to the knowledge and firm hold of intellectual objects. Its function in regard to divine things is to investigate what is the First Cause and what that through which all things were made and without which nothing has been made, what are the things that hold the universe together.[26]

Unlike Montanists and the gnostic movement, however, Clement's commitment to Scripture did not allow him to demonize the material world. For Clement, God's created world was still good, though it was not the best.[27] The result was a split-level spirituality or search for perfection.[28] Clement sees the mass of Christians in two groups, the neophytes and the gnostics. The former are instructed in *Paedagogus* in a life of virtue and moderation based upon the gospel. "In a word, whatever things are natural to men we must not eradicate from them, but rather impose on

---

25. *Stromateis* 4.3; *ANF* translation.

26. *Stromateis* 7.3.17; citation from Oulton and Chadwick, *Alexandrian Christianity*, 103.

27. "Those, then, who run down created existence and vilify the body are wrong." *Stromateis* 4.26.

28. For the following, see esp. Behr, *Asceticism*, ch. 5–6 (152–207). This division of humanity into the perfect, the gnostics or initiated, on the one side, and the average, uninstructed, unenlightened on the other side, was widespread among the philosophers and mysteries of the day.

them limits and suitable times."²⁹ This training [*askēsis*] aims especially at "curbing the irrational impulses."³⁰

The gnostics are instructed in *Stromateis*. Their training continues this *askēsis* but goes beyond what was expected of the neophyte. When discussing marriage, for example, Clement notes, "All things which are created for man's use, such as marriage and procreation, are good, when used with moderation; yet it is 'better than good' to become free from passion (*apathēs*). So the gnostic does not reject such things as bad, but aims 'to do things that are better than good,' which, not being essential, are also more difficult."³¹ His Platonizing piety comes through clearly in his instructions on prayer to the more advanced gnostics.

> So also we raise the head and lift the hands to heaven, and stand on tiptoe at the closing utterance of the prayer, following the eagerness of the spirit directed towards the intellectual essence; and endeavouring to detach the body from the earth, by lifting it upwards along with the uttered words, constraining the soul, winged with the desire of better things, to ascend into the holy place, magnanimously despising the fetters of the flesh. For we know well that the Gnostic willingly departs from the whole world, just as the Jews did from Egypt, showing clearly, above all, that he will be as near as possible to God.³²

One notes here Clement's Christian piety (prayer) combined with his underlying Platonism ("directed toward the intellectual essence," "despising the fetters of the flesh"). Thus, we see in Clement many of the Platonic seeds that will soon flower throughout the patristic church and in the monastic movement. Asceticism with its suppression of bodily needs and fleshly urges will be seen as the path for those who seek perfection. Like Christ's instruction to the young man in Matt 19:21, they go beyond the good path of saving obedience to find perfection in radical Christlikeness. Perfection itself will be understood more in a Platonizing direction and less as the more earthy, covenantal Jewish view of *tamim*. Similar to Greeks who saw the intellectual apprehension of reality and participation in that reality to be the *telos* of human beings, so Christians would increasingly speak of the vision of God, the beatific vision, and

---

29. *Paed.* 2.5.46.1.
30. *Paed.* 1.9.75.2.
31. *Strom.* 4.23.147–149.8.
32. *Strom.* 7.7.40.1–2; cited in Behr, *Asceticism*, 194.

theosis, as the apex of human perfection.³³ As to perfection in the sense of sinlessness, Clement remains ambivalent.³⁴

Origen (184–253 CE)

Following in Clement's footsteps catechizing Alexandrian Christians came Origen, arguably "the greatest genius the early church ever produced."³⁵ Like his predecessor, Origen was steeped in Greek philosophy and had largely adopted a Neoplatonic framework, which will have formative influence on his understanding of human perfection. At the same time, we will misunderstand him and his teaching on perfection if we assume he was a Neoplatonist first, and a Christian or biblical thinker only secondarily.³⁶ Unlike the Platonists, Origen does not view the material world as evil *per se*. For him it is God's good creation, which also makes a place for Christ's own materiality in the incarnation. The human body is not something that must ultimately be shed in order to unite with pure Mind. As divine creation makes clear, a body is, in fact, necessary for true humanity and perfection. Even resurrected life is embodied, though, of course, in a celestial body rather than the coarse terrestrial ones we know.

The hindrance to human perfection lies not then in our materiality, but in the passions, the urges, that arise from it. It has become "a source of excess, inflamed passions and spiritual trial."³⁷ The bodily desires for food, drink, sex, etc. are not evil in themselves, but drag the soul down when it chooses carnal satisfaction over the desires of the spirit. Thus, the path to perfection is that of training (*askēsis*) in virtue, of renunciation of

33. See esp. Flew, *Idea of Perfection*, 138–51.
34. Karavites, *Evil*, 46. See *Paed.* 1.94.1; 1.4.3.
35. McGuckin, *Westminster Handbook to Origen*, 25.
36. In the fifth and sixth centuries a number of Origen's teachings were condemned as heretical, in part because they seemed more indebted to Greek philosophy than to the Bible and church tradition. This same view of Origen as most fundamentally a Neoplatonist constitutes the weakness of many earlier studies of Origen's doctrine, including Flew and Burgess. Since the 1950s Origen's reputation has been on the mend among patristic scholars, and he is now increasingly viewed as most fundamentally a man of the church and the Bible, without denying the powerful influence of his Neoplatonic commitments. Our presentation of Origen's doctrine of human perfection will follow these more recent studies: Blosser, *Become Like the Angels*; Scott, *Journey Back to God*; and earlier, Völker, *Das Vollkommenheitsideal des Origenes*.
37. Blosser, *Become Like the Angels*, 192.

carnal desires and of seeking the likeness of Christ in prayer, obedience, and the knowledge of God.

Like Clement, Origen acknowledged that some, the more spiritual or mature, would advance more quickly in this life toward perfection than others. The bulk of Christians should occupy themselves with growth in the virtues (love, self-control, etc.) through prayer and harkening to Scripture and church teaching. "As the soul advances spiritually, it slowly strips away layers of sin and evil, leading to progressively higher states of virtue and enlightenment."[38] Those who make good progress in this, both in this life and after resurrection, move on to grasping the nature of the visible world (its ephemeral character), and then to contemplative knowledge.[39]

While there may be a few who come near such perfection in this life, for nearly all this is a post-mortem, post-resurrection experience.[40] This ascent finds its final rest in union with God, in the vision of God, in *theosis*.[41] At this point, human beings attain an angel-like existence.

> We may entertain the hope that by a virtuous life, and by acting in all things agreeably to reason, we may rise to a likeness with all these; that men, when made perfect, become like the angels.[42]

Origen envisions this entire process in two stages, a pre- and a post-resurrection one, as can be seen in his comments on Israel's exodus as a guide to the Christian pilgrimage.

> One is the means of training the soul in virtues through the Law of God when it is placed in flesh; and by ascending through certain steps it makes progress, as we have said, from virtue to virtue, and uses these progressions as stages. And the other journey is the one by which the soul, in gradually ascending to the heavens after the resurrection, does not reach the highest

---

38. Scott, *Journey Back to God*, 101–2.

39. Scott, *Journey Back to God*, 118–19. Scott notes that this three-stage ascent to perfection mirrors the three branches of Greek learning: ethics (virtue and self-mastery); science (nature of the world); contemplation.

40. Origen compares these rare individuals with Enoch. "Someone like this, even if he seems to be still in the world and to dwell in flesh, nonetheless will not 'be found.' Where will he not be found? In no worldly deed, in no fleshly thing, in no vain conversation is he found. For God has taken him across from these pursuits and placed him in the realm of the virtues." *HomNum* 27.12, quoted in Scott, *Journey Back to God*, 114.

41. On this see esp. Völker, *Das Vollkommenheitsideal des Origenes*, 117–44.

42. *Contra Celsum* 4.29.

point unseasonably, but is led through many stages. In them it is enlightened stage by stage; it always receives an increase in splendor, illumined at each stage by the light of Wisdom, until it arrives at the Father of lights Himself.[43]

Like the Greeks, Origen can express the fulfillment of human existence with the term perfection (*teleios*). He means, however, by this something much closer to the Greek vision of the triumph of the rational over the earthly passions, much as was the case with Clement before him. While Origen's human perfection is not quite the disembodied union with the universal Mind of the Greeks, neither is it the earthy communion of humans in love and in fellowship with God we discovered in Jewish tradition. He and Clement witness to a fundamental change in how human perfection is understood in the Christian tradition,[44] a change that will be adopted with gusto by the monastic movement we will examine next, as well as by the church at large.

The Alexandrian Seed Flowers in the Desert: Ascetic Monasticism

According to Athanasius, the young St. Antony (251–356 CE) "went into church just when the Gospel was being read and he heard the Lord saying to the rich man: 'If you wish to be perfect, go and sell all your belongings; give [the proceeds] to the poor. Then come and follow me and you will have treasure in heaven' [Matt 19:21]."[45] This call to perfection through voluntary renunciation initiated Antony's life as a solitary desert monk, an anchorite. The story is also typical of a great many of the early desert monks for whom Christ's call to renunciation framed the door to perfection.

Whether Antony had been directly influenced by Origen's teaching or not, the similarity of thought on the human quest for perfection is clear.[46]

---

43. *HomNum* 27.6, quoted in Scott, *Journey Back to God*, 109–10.

44. Although Origen does seem to view sinlessness as a possibility for a few who advance toward perfection, he is very halting in proposing this, and is equally certain that all humans remain sinners. Völker, *Das Vollkommenheitsideal des Origenes*, 162–68.

45. Athanasius, *Vit. Ant.* 2.2-3, quoted in Wortley, *Book of the Elders*, Introduction.

46. Finn argues that such influence is "probable": Finn, *Asceticism*, 112–17.

> [Antony] used to say that one should give all one's time to the soul rather than to the body. True, because necessity demands it, a little time should be given to the body; but on the whole we should give our first attention to the soul and look to its advantage. It must not be dragged down by the pleasures of the body, but rather the body must be made subject to the soul.[47]

In Jesus's call to "be perfect" (Matt 5:48) we found the focus to be on imitating God's liberal kindness to all. Though it would be unfair to accuse Antony and the desert monks of forgetting Christian charity toward others, it is clear that their focus has turned inward on the perfecting of one's own self.[48]

> [W]e have no need to go abroad for the Kingdom of Heaven nor to cross the sea to obtain virtue. The Lord has told us in advance: *The Kingdom of Heaven is within you.* Virtue, therefore, has need only of our will, since it is within us and springs from us. Virtue exists when the soul keeps in its natural state. It is kept in its natural state when it remains as it came into being. Now it came into being fair and perfectly straight. . . . For the soul is said to be straight when its mind is in its natural state as it was created.[49]

A constant element of this path to perfection is the denial of bodily demands.

> Hate everything in the world and repose of the body, for these made you an enemy of God. As a person who has an enemy fights with him, so we ought also to fight against the body to allow it no repose.[50]

This could often lead to rather bizarre extremes.

> They used to say of Abba Pior that he used to eat walking around. When somebody inquired why he ate like that, he said . . . "[It is] so that my soul may experience no physical pleasure even when I am eating."[51]

---

47. Athanasius, *Life of Saint Antony*, §45 (58).

48. The development of monastic communities, versus the lone monk in the desert, would bring love for one another and to outsiders back into focus, but even here the central pursuit remained individual ascent to God.

49. Athanasius, *Life of Saint Antony*, §20 (37).

50. Isaiah, *Abba Isaiah of Scetis*, 26.

51. Taken from Ward, *Sayings of the Desert Fathers*, Pior 2.

By such extremes of fasting and other forms of self-denial the monk "dries up the channels of delights," i.e., of bodily delights that draw off the soul from its true focus.[52] But the monks fought not only against their own urges, the soul is equally embattled by the demonic realm. Demonic powers can work through the body and mind—stimulating cravings or lascivious thoughts—or can attack the monk directly and harmfully. Thus, the stories of the monks are full of tales of warfare with these spiritual enemies.

Whether expressed in philosophical terms or not, the monks view the various passions and urges arising from life in a human body as a danger to the soul's ascent to pure reason, to the knowledge of God. Even seemingly harmless human interactions could pose a threat. Thus, we hear of monks who would burn letters from their families rather than allow the reading of them to arouse passions such as loneliness or longing for absent loved ones. The goal of this quest is pure contemplation of God, conformity of one's mind and soul to the One Mind and Soul of all being. And to this end one must remove all urges and passions of body and mind, one must seek *apatheia*, a passionless state much prized by the Stoics.

The difference between this monastic ascetic view of perfection and what I am calling the *tamim*-view, is made clear by the most common term for Egyptian ascetics, "renunciants [*apotaktikos*]." This name is tied to Jesus's command to "renounce [*apotassein*] possessions" (Luke 14:33) with obvious connection to the "be perfect ... sell all" of Matt 19:21. As we have sought to show, however, Jesus's call to be *tamim/teleios* in Matt 19 envisions embracing the wholeness of embodied human beings in loving covenant with God and one another, not the renunciation of the desires of the body in favor of the life of the mind.

Excursus:
Windisch and Early Perfection Teaching

Before winding up this section on the church fathers and perfection, it is only fair to engage briefly with an important voice who argued an opposing thesis. In 1908 Hans Windisch published *Baptism and Sin in Earliest Christianity until Origen*.[53] There he

---

52. Ward, *Sayings of the Desert Fathers*, Hyperechios 3.
53. Windisch, *Taufe und Sünde*. His thoughts were preceded by Wernle, *Der Christ*, and have been recently revived by Umbach, *In Christus getauft*.

argued that many of the church fathers believed baptism enabled true sinlessness. Simultaneously, he argued, they could not but recognize the presence of sin in the lives of believers. Ultimately Windisch chalked this contradiction up to logical inconsistency.

Windisch, however, consistently misinterpreted the language of perfection, blamelessness, uprightness, etc. to refer to sinlessness rather than to the sort of less-than-perfect completeness I have argued for. As he notes, the Psalms "promise to the pious a sinless life."[54] Windisch seemed unaware of the meaning of *tamim*, *teleios*, etc. Had he recognized that *tamim* and related terms envision human uprightness rather than sinless perfection, his contradiction would have found a straightforward solution.

Augustine (354–430 CE)

Augustine's importance for the development of theology in the Western (or Latin) church, and of the Western church's reflections on perfection, can hardly be overstated. "The West becomes Augustinian, either directly, when it seeks to develop the insights of the 'Doctor of Grace,' or indirectly, when, trying to free itself from a dominant Augustinianism; it . . . concerns itself with the problems that engaged Augustine."[55] Augustine's view of the goal of the human quest for perfection can be seen vividly in a passage from his *Confessions*, in a discussion with his mother, Monica, very near the end of her life.

> So we said: if to any man the tumult of the flesh grew silent, silent the images of earth and sea and air; and if the heavens grew silent, and the very soul grew silent to herself and by not thinking of self mounted beyond self: if all dreams and imagined visions grew silent, and every tongue and every sign and whatsoever is transient—for indeed if any man could hear them, he should hear them saying with one voice: We did not make ourselves, but He made us who abides forever: but if, having uttered this and so set us to listening to Him who made them, they all grew silent, and in their silence He alone spoke to us, not by them but by Himself: so that we should hear His word, not by any tongue of flesh nor the voice of any angel nor the

---

54. Windisch, *Taufe und Sünde*, 15.
55. Louth, *Origins*, 129.

The Reception of Perfection

sound of thunder nor in the darkness of a parable, but that we should hear Himself whom in all these things we love, should hear Himself and not them: just as we too had but now reached forth and in a flash of the mind attained to touch the eternal Wisdom which abides over all: and if this should continue, and all other visions so different be quite taken away, and this one should so ravish and absorb and wrap the beholder in inward joys that his life should eternally be such as that one moment of understanding for which we had been sighing—would this not be: "Enter thou into the joy of Thy Lord"? But when shall it be? Shall it be when "we shall all rise again" and "shall not all be changed"?[56]

Human perfection lies beyond this transient world of language, sight, and sensation. It comes not in this world but only at the resurrection when we see God, our beloved, face to face. As with many of those we have been reviewing in the early church, Augustine, too, like his mentor Ambrose was indebted to Neoplatonism.[57]

Augustine stated his own views on human perfection in an anti-Pelagian essay, "The Perfection of Human Righteousness."[58] He is responding here to a tract, *Definitions*, allegedly written by Caelestius, a disciple of Pelagius, which apparently argued for the possibility (necessity?) of Christians leading sinless lives. With his belief in the utter corruption of human nature at the fall, Augustine vigorously denies any possibility of human perfection qua sinlessness in this life.[59]

However, he is aware that his Latin Bible describes some individuals as "perfect [*perfectus*]" and calls believers to "be perfect [*estote perfecti*]." In order to interpret these texts he abandons his basic understanding of perfection as sinlessness in favor of an alternate meaning. Noah's "perfection" means "that he was perfect as far as citizens of the city of God can be

---

56. *Confessions* IX. x. 23–5 (Sheed translation).

57. See Brown, *Augustine of Hippo*. When speaking of Abraham's perfection, Ambrose describes him as "in training night and day, ever on the lookout, never indulging in sleep but on perpetual watch, intent on God, so as to understand the things that are and to comprehend the causes of each," and as one who has a "virtuous mind ... so that it might rule the body, not being captivated by carnal pleasures, but that submissive flesh might cater to the mind in appropriate servitude." *On Abraham*, 2.10.76–77; citation taken from Louth and Conti, *Genesis 1–11*, 51–53.

58. The translation used here is: Augustine, "Perfection of Human Righteousness," 279–316.

59. "It is one thing to be without sin; Scripture said this exclusively of the Only-Begotten in this life"; Augustine, "Perfection of Human Righteousness," 301.

perfect during the pilgrimage of this present life, not, of course, as perfect as they are to be in that immortal life in which they will be as perfect as the angels of God."[60] That is, "people can be called righteous who *draw so close to the perfection* of righteousness that *they are right next to it*, and we do not deny that many persons have been able to do this, even in this life in which we live from faith."[61] Thus, biblical texts that speak of humans as actually being righteous, blameless, etc. in this life are speaking of this alternate ("close to perfection") understanding, while those that call for true, complete perfection and righteousness are using the other, setting it as an unattainable ideal that should be always pursued with the aid of divine grace. The confusion in terminology is patent and will continue to crop up in further discussions of perfection, especially in Wesley.

Medieval Perfection

Leading medieval theologians such as Aquinas and Bonaventure continued the philosophical bent of the patristic era.[62] Like Aristotle, they located human perfection especially in the realm of the intellect, in contemplation.[63] They combined this, however, with the biblical notion of the centrality of divine benevolence. As God's nature is love, so growing in love, i.e., godlikeness, is the aim of human perfection.[64] Aquinas sets a somewhat different tone here from Aristotle and earlier fathers like Origen, in that *loving* the object is true perfection, not simply *contemplating* it. This perfection will impact both the living of mundane life as well as the life of contemplation.

This may also be an appropriate place to note another important stream in the Christian search for human perfection, namely mysticism.[65] We will adopt McGinn's definition of mysticism as "a special consciousness of the presence of God that by definition exceeds description and

---

60. "City of God," 15.26; *Fathers of the Church* 14:477; cited in Louth and Conti, *Genesis 1–11*, 129.

61. Augustine, "Perfection of Human Righteousness," 301, emphasis added.

62. On this era, see Burgess, "Medieval Models," ch. 6, 149–79.

63. "[M]an's highest function is thinking, and this act is at its highest when man thinks about things divine"; Burgess, "Medieval Models," 164.

64. Burgess, "Medieval Models," 165.

65. For a standard treatment see Louth, *Origins*. A readable introduction is Lamm, *Wiley-Blackwell Companion*.

results in a transformation of the subject who receives it."⁶⁶ Or, even more pithily, "*Mysticism is the art of union with God.*"⁶⁷ Its goal revolves generally around a direct experience of the divine, in many cases extending even to some form of union with God. Not infrequently, the language of a ladder to God comes into play, as the mystic ascends from early or lower stages (e.g., purgation of captivation by the bodily senses) to higher ones. Ultimately, the mystic saint hopes to "see" God (*beatific vision*), to be transformed into Christ's likeness. In some forms of Christian mysticism this can even entail the extinguishing of the human self as God becomes all-in-all, although that certainly need not be essential to all mystical quests.

Perfection in Orthodox Spirituality

Although our historical review has focused more on the Western church than the Eastern, it is worth noting that the perfecting of humanity plays a key role in Orthodox spirituality. As Staniloae notes, "[T]he goal of Orthodox spirituality is the perfection of the believer by his union with Christ. He is being imprinted to an ever-greater degree by the human image of Christ, full of God."⁶⁸ There are two steps in this ascent to deification (*theosis*). First comes asceticism or "moving ahead toward perfection through purification from the passions and the acquiring of the virtues." The second is the more passive and contemplative mystical union, "a life progressively moving ahead in the union with God."⁶⁹ Origen and Clement set the tone for Orthodoxy on many of these points.

A New Chapter: Reformation Voices on Legal Perfection

The Reformation marked a new chapter in the understanding of perfection. Up to this point, most Christian traditions both in East and West took the call to "be perfect" as something incredibly difficult but attainable, at least for some, via discipline, contemplation, self-denial, etc. For the reformers, human sinfulness meant any such quest to eradicate sin in this life was a pipe-dream from the start. Thus, the Augsburg Confession

---

66. McGinn, *Presence of God*, 3:26.
67. McColman, *Big Book of Christian Mysticism*, 26.
68. For this see esp. Staniloae, *Orthodox Spirituality*, 21.
69. Staniloae, *Orthodox Spirituality*, 21–24.

condemns Anabaptists and others as "those who contend that some may attain to such perfection in this life that they cannot sin."[70] Closely allied to this was their firm, but to a large extent novel, conviction that the OT law set its bar at nothing less than sinless perfection. On this point all the reformers spoke with one voice. We cited earlier Luther's Small Catechism on this crucial point.[71] Calvin echoes this.

> God has not promised the reward of life for particular works but he only declares that the man who does them shall live [Lev. 18:5], leveling that well-known curse against all those who do not persevere *in all things* [Deut. 27:26; Gal. 3:10]. The *fiction of partial righteousness* is abundantly refuted by these statements, where no other righteousness than the *complete observance of the law* is allowed in heaven. ... The Lord often testifies that he recognizes no righteousness of works except in the *perfect observance of his law*.[72]

Since perfection is viewed as humanly unattainable and part of the old covenant of works, it is no surprise that the sort of striving for perfection we have seen in the desert monks or in the Roman Catholic "counsels" generally played little role in Lutheran or Reformed churches. When they do reflect positively on perfection, they employ one of two tactics. First, they will understand it not as sinlessness but as a "completely correct" understanding of gospel doctrine and a holy life governed by love.

> Here [Matt 5:48] and everywhere in Scripture "to be perfect" means, in the first place, that doctrine be completely correct and perfect, and then, that life move and be regulated according to it. Here, for example, the doctrine is that we should love not only those who do us good, but our enemies, too. Now, whoever teaches this and lives according to this teaching, *teaches and lives perfectly*. ... What He wants is *an entire, whole, and undivided love*, where one loves and helps his enemy as well as his friend. So I am called a truly perfect man, one who has and holds the doctrine in its entirety. Now, if my life does not measure up to this in every detail—as indeed it cannot, since flesh

---

70. Article XII: Of Repentance. Calvin likewise inveighs "against the illusion of perfection"; *Inst.* 3.3.14; also 4.1.13, 16.

71. Chapter 1 above.

72. *Inst.* 3.14.13, italics added. Interestingly, Calvin does seem aware that the OT's language of perfection refers to "those who cultivate rectitude purely and heartily" rather than those "who are perfect in every respect ... and who lack nothing." Calvin, *Comm. on Genesis*, s.v. Gen 6:9; cited in Burgess, *Reaching Beyond*, 203.

The Reception of Perfection

> and blood incessantly hold it back—that does not detract from the perfection. Only we must keep striving for it, and moving and progressing toward it every day.... Then I have true Christian perfection.[73]

Or, second, they will speak of the imputation of perfection by faith in Christ.

> Through this justification, which occurs through faith, the justified person becomes completely and totally perfect.... Perfection is nothing other than faith in the Lord Jesus and is not in us or ours but in Christ or of Christ for whose sake we are considered perfect before God and thus his perfection is ours by ascription.[74]

The Lutheran Pietist tradition felt the imputation tactic had become too dominant, leading to moral laxity. If believers considered themselves already perfect in Christ, they could relax too much in their striving for holiness. Thus, while the Pietists retained both tactics noted above, they laid heightened stress upon striving for holiness of life. The justified person

> is never completely perfect but he can grow and increase in good works as long as he lives.... Thus the Scripture does not wish to teach that a person can be completely perfect in his life, that he can be without sin or the attraction to sin, but that a person can come to a human strength in Christianity so as to kill the old habits in himself and to conquer his flesh and blood, and that one person is always more perfect than the other.[75]

The Reformed tradition felt the same deficiency in the standard Lutheran treatment, but responded with its doctrine of the third use of the law as a guide and call to Christian holiness. In all of these reformational approaches to perfection, an unavoidable paradox remains. "We are perfect, and we are not perfect." [76]

---

73. Luther, "Sermon on the Mount," 129, italics added.

74. Francke, "On Christian Perfection," 114. Francke, himself a Lutheran, is stating here what he considers the standard Lutheran position.

75. Francke, "On Christian Perfection," 115.

76. Olson, "Pietism," 16. Although Olson speaks here specifically of Pietism, his words apply equally to the reformational position as a whole.

Christian Perfection Finds a Home: John Wesley and Perfect Love

The Reformation's unresolved tension on the matter of perfection, particularly its occasional tendency toward moral laxity, meant the issue would not rest. James Arminius claimed to be doing nothing but echoing Augustine on this point. "[Augustine] thinks it possible for a man to be without sin by means of the grace of Christ and free-will," yet "he does not think that any man has attained to such perfection in this life" except Christ.[77] P. van Limborch, a later follower of Arminius, clarified, "It is not sinless or an absolutely perfect obedience, but such as consists in a sincere love of piety, absolutely excluding every habit of sin."[78] This interest in a positive place for perfection reached its climax in John Wesley.[79] His *Plain Account of Christian Perfection* was first published in 1766 as an attempt to clarify what he had consistently taught on this subject since 1725 and to engage with the misunderstandings and slander it had engendered. As Wesley scholars now generally agree, he did not hold that believers would attain a "sinless perfection" in this life.[80] Instead, his unyielding insistence on perfection referred to

> purity of intention, dedicating all the life to God. It is giving God all our heart; it is one desire and design ruling all our tempers. It is the devoting, not a part, but all our soul, body, substance to God. In another view,[81] it is all the mind which was in Christ, enabling us to walk as Christ walked. It is the circumcision of the heart from all filthiness, all inward as well as outward pollution. It is renewal of the heart in the whole image of God, the full likeness of him that created it. In yet another, it is loving God with all our heart, and our neighbour as ourselves.

---

77. Arminius, *Writings*, 1:256; see also 1:369–71.

78. van Limborch, *Institutiones Theologiae Christianae*, 661a; cited in Platt, "Perfection (Christian)," 732.

79. An outstanding and readable treatment of Wesley and perfection is Noble, *Holy Trinity, Holy People*.

80. This is also true of the entire Wesleyan tradition. "The Wesleyan-Arminian view of sin emphasizes the Johannine view of sin as lawlessness (*anomia*), and excludes from the concept of sin shortcomings due to the infirmities of mind and body (1 John 3:4).... [I]gnorance which results in *hamartia* is excusable, but this is not true of willful negligence (Heb. 2:3). For this reason one may be blameless even though far from faultless—'New Testament perfection is not faultlessness but blamelessness.'" Turner, *Vision Which Transforms*, 102; his citation is from Coats, "Holiness," 745.

81. He means here different ways of expressing perfection.

> Now, take it in which of these views you please (for there is no material difference), and this is the whole and sole perfection, as a train of writings prove to a demonstration, which I have believed and taught for these forty years, from the year 1725 to the year 1765.[82]

Although he preferred the term perfect love, he was equally comfortable with the simple term perfection and used it indiscriminately in his speaking and writing. For his opponents, this unqualified use of perfection led to charges of an outrageous perfectionism teaching. Wesley was not helped by some of his followers who were less careful than he and added fuel to the fire by claims to sinlessness. Since Wesley himself did not actually mean what the English term perfection normally implies (flawlessness, sinlessness), one wonders why he didn't simply defuse his opponents' attacks by ceasing the use of the word perfection.[83]

Fringe Groups: Perfection as Freedom to Sin

Although always a fringe occurrence in the Christian tradition, we should mention the existence of groups who viewed themselves as already so perfected, so touched and transformed by the Spirit, that sin and evil have no effect on them. One of these groups from the Middle Ages is described as follows:

> Because the [Brethren of the] Free Spirit believed God to be in themselves, not in the Church, and considered themselves in a state of perfection without sin, they felt free to do all things commonly prohibited to ordinary man. Sex and property headed the list. They practiced free love and adultery and were accused of indulging in group sex in their communal residences. They encouraged nudity to demonstrate absence of sin and shame. As "holy beggars," the Brethren claimed the right to use and

---

82. Wesley, *Plain Account*, 17. Quotation taken from Noble, *Holy Trinity, Holy People*, 86.

83. This point is argued by Peters, *Christian Perfection*, esp. 53–54, 63. As to why Wesley insisted on using the term, his own answer would certainly have been that it is a biblical word. When arguing for the biblical roots of his perfection teaching he once commented, "this perfection cannot be a delusion, unless the Bible be a delusion, too." John Wesley to Lawrence Coughland, August 27, 1768, in *Letters*, 5:102. Quoted in Bratton, *Witnesses of Perfect Love*, 16 n. 16. In addition, Wesley was deeply influenced by the stress on "perfection" in the Christian mystical tradition. See Tuttle, *Mysticism*, 147–57.

take whatever they pleased, whether a market woman's chickens or a meal in a tavern without paying. This included the right, because of God's immanence, to kill anyone who forcibly attempted to interfere.[84]

Recent Developments and Summary[85]

As the notes in the previous chapters have revealed, reflection on biblical and theological perfection has not ceased. However, if interest reached somewhat of a climax with Wesley's movement (and the reaction to it),[86] it seems to have cooled a bit in the intervening years. Controversies over perfection, whether academic or ecclesiastical, are not common. On the other hand, intensive research into OT and Jewish thought on human wholeness has been leading very recently to an increasing emphasis on human flourishing and happiness. We will note this in a bit more detail in the concluding chapter.

Hopefully the reader has discerned via this brisk walk through church history that the topic of perfection has played a notable role throughout the church's reflections on how to live before God. Yet, in nearly all those reflections the connection to the OT *tamim*-tradition went missing, replaced by understandings of perfection drawn from other quarters such as Greek philosophy, English language usage, etc. Perhaps it is time we sought to return to the sources of biblical perfection-wholeness teaching.

---

84. Tuchman, *Distant Mirror*, 316.

85. The topic of human perfection has been of interest not only to biblical scholars and theologians, but also to ethicists generally, as well as philosophers, psychologists, scientists, architects; in fact, in nearly all human endeavors. Helpful entrée to the study of perfection in other fields can be found in: Hurka, *Perfectionism*; Hyde, *Perfection*. For reflection on perfection in Western philosophy and its relation to biblical perfection, see esp. Foss, *Idea of Perfection*.

86. For the reaction, see esp. Warfield, *Perfectionism*.

Chapter 12

Righteous Imperfection: Conclusions and Reflections

Perfection is like "God on a good day."[1]

In this final chapter we will summarize some of the more notable conclusions of this study regarding human wholeness or perfection in biblical and theological tradition, and will reflect on some of the theological and practical ramifications of what we have discovered.

1. The Hebrew and Greek terms glossed with some form of the English word "perfect" denote something or someone who is whole, intact, complete, sound, wholehearted, mature, blameless, etc. In no instance do they denote what our English "perfect" most typically implies, i.e., flawless, without error, without sin. Most English translations have wisely eliminated the word "perfect" in OT texts, and in many NT passages. However, probably due to the strength of tradition, translators continue to resist this move for several crucial texts such as Matt 5:48 ("be perfect"). So as not to mislead English readers, translations should avoid forms of "perfect."

2. The Torah called for Israel's faithfulness to God, for wholeheartedness in relation to him and his ways, and for god-like lovingkindness toward others. This expectation was expressed through a variety of overlapping terms such as *tamim* (whole, complete, upright), *shalem* (full, complete, whole), *tsaddiq* (righteous), *yashar* (upright), etc. The OT did not demand or expect flawless obedience to its commandments in order

---

1. Hyde, *Perfection*, 19.

for an individual to be considered righteous, upright, or *tamim*. Scripture marked out many who exemplified this fullness of true human life, such as Noah ("a righteous man, blameless (*tamim*) in his generation" [Gen 6:9]), Job ("blameless [*tam*] and upright" [Job 1:1]), and many others.

3. This means, furthermore, that God's Torah (instruction, guidance, law) was doable, just as Deut 30:11 insists: "this commandment that I am commanding you today is not too hard for you." God did not set up an arrangement with Israel that was beyond her ability. Israel, and individual Israelites, could keep the law. They could adhere faithfully to what God set forth for them. They could be righteous, upright, wholehearted, and could experience the wholeness of life walking with God, which he desired for them. "So now, O Israel, what does the LORD your God require of you? Only to fear the LORD your God, to walk in all his ways, to love him, to serve the LORD your God with all your heart and with all your soul, and to keep the commandments of the LORD your God and his decrees that I am commanding you today, for your own well-being" (Deut 10:12–13).

Let's be clear, this does not mean they could do this by their own unaided human ability and willpower. Always and everywhere the OT assumes that Israel's obedience flows (or should flow) out of their relationship with God himself. Like Adam and Eve, all human beings are creatures of dust animated by the divine breath (*ruach*, spirit). Their every thought and movement is possible only because of God's prior action. No one obeys "on their own." The upright know their own weakness apart from God.[2] If the question of agency is posed—Who is the active agent in human obedience, God or the human being?—the answer must be *both*.[3]

This conclusion—adequate obedience to Torah is achievable—carries major theological implications, especially for the reformational wing of the church. The longstanding answer to the question, Why could the law not save?, must be rethought. Luther's answer—because no one can keep the law perfectly—proves unhelpful. First, because Torah never envisioned or demanded such flawless obedience. And second, because an

---

2. There are, of course, the "fools" in the OT, who think they can live without God (Ps 14:1) and who "trust in their own wits" rather than in God's wisdom (Prov 28:26) and exalt themselves and their own abilities (Prov 30:32). As Kellenberger argues, the upright see God at work in every aspect of their lives, while "the fool does not find God's presence in his life." Kellenberger, "Fool of the Psalms," 100.

3. Much work of late has been done on this question of divine and human agency. For those interested in further study, see Barclay and Gathercole, *Divine and Human Agency*; and Maston, *Divine and Human Agency*.

adequate obedience was, indeed, achievable, even under the old covenant arrangement.

This conclusion about the doability of the Law also impacts the perennial Christian theological question regarding judgment according to deeds. If, as Paul says, we are justified by faith apart from works (Rom 3:28) how can we also be judged according to our deeds (Rom 2:6; 2 Cor 5:10; etc.)? As long as this judgment was thought to compare us to an alleged bar of perfect obedience, the situation seemed hopeless. Who's perfect after all? But if the standard is something less than flawless perfection, what is that standard? Our study suggests that God will measure us at the judgment in regard to our wholehearted faithfulness, whether our lives have been characterized by *tamim*, *shalem*, and integrity. This is little different than faith (*pistis*) in the New Testament. Thus, in the end, justification by faith and judgment according to deeds turn out to be two sides of the very same coin.[4]

4. In the centuries between the last OT prophet and the opening of the NT gospel story this *tamim* language and concept retained its original meaning and its importance for Jewish self-definition. The translation of the OT from Hebrew into Greek (LXX) produced no substantial changes, but provided a new tongue for the same thoughts. Now Greek terms like *teleios*, *amemptos*, etc. continued the expression of this tradition. And the Qumran scrolls give eloquent testimony to the continued centrality of such blameless faithfulness for Jewish self-understanding within Israel's covenantal framework. We discerned no movement during this period toward the sort of perfection teaching we will encounter later.

5. Jesus's striking use of this wholeness/perfection tradition (Matt 5:48; 19:21) continued the Jewish *tamim* tradition. When he called disciples to "be perfect," he referred not to an unachievable level of flawless obedience, but to the achievable wholeness envisioned throughout the OT and Jewish tradition. Jesus's use of the *tamim* tradition in the Sermon on the Mount revolved around loving God and neighbor from the whole heart just as it did in the OT. His teaching "exceeded" the righteous behavior taught by the Pharisees not by being more rigorous than theirs, but by placing mercy at the heart of every commandment.

6. For Luther and most of the Reformation tradition, Gal 3:10 constituted a proof of their perfect law-keeping thesis. Why is everyone "under a curse"? Because no one can "observe and obey all the things written

---

4. On this see Yinger, *Paul, Judaism, and Judgment*.

in the book of the law," i.e., because no one can keep the law perfectly. chapter 7 argued that this misinterprets Gal 3:10. This text does not support the perfect law-keeping thesis, but is a key part of Paul's argument in Galatians that Jewish covenantal identity ("those of Torah-works") no longer marks out who belongs to the people of God. That role in the new eschatological era is born by allegiance to messiah Jesus ("faith in Christ").

7. The apostle Paul continues the Jewish *tamim* tradition when he refers to the followers of Christ as *teleioi* (1 Cor 2:6; Phil 3:15). Like Jesus, Paul expected such wholeness or blamelessness of his converts in this life before the watching world (Phil 2:15). It was not something that awaited believers only in a transformed afterlife. Paul thought Torah was doable. In fact, both before and after meeting Christ, he considered himself to have kept Torah blamelessly (Phil 3:6). This optimistic view is not contradicted by Rom 3:23 ("all have sinned"), since that text intends to teach that both Jews and Gentiles are under Sin's power, not necessarily that every single individual is at root wicked. The cross of Christ was necessary to liberate all of us, whether we belong to Jewish or to Gentile humanity, from our communal sinfulness in the form of rebellion and idolatry.

8. The letter to the Hebrews provides a distinct note to *teleios* in the NT by speaking of Christ's needed "perfecting" as his being qualified for heavenly high priesthood through suffering. This letter also explains why the old covenant was unable generally to bring the *teleios* desired by God since it was not designed to transform the human heart.

9. Following the NT era, the developing Christian movement fairly quickly lost track of this Jewish *tamim* theology. It retained, and even expanded in many ways, the interest in human perfection, but now understood this differently than the biblical tradition. Rather than human wholeness being found within this world and precisely in the context of embodied existence, Neoplatonic influence meant that human perfection took place through the overcoming of this visible world and specifically of the passions and constraints of embodied existence. For example, rather than human sexuality being an integral element of human wholeness, the truly perfect learned to overcome or even suppress sexual urges. This would come to full flower in the early monastic movement. Here perfection necessitated the renunciation of the desires of the body in favor of the life of the mind. Thus the counsels of perfection required celibacy. This has moved a long way from Jesus's Jewish view which embraced the

wholeness of embodied human beings in loving covenant with God and one another.

10. The quest for human perfection has occupied many of the best Christian minds and movements in church history. One thinks particularly of John Wesley and his "Plain Account of Christian Perfection," along with the controversies surrounding his claims. Rarely, and unfortunately, in these church-historical disputes did the parties seek to begin with the Bible's language of *tamim-teleios*, but instead typically assumed an understanding of perfection derived far too much from their own mother-tongue. The Protestant Reformation cemented a new twist in this perfection tradition by positing perfect law-keeping as necessary for the attainment of righteousness under the Jewish framework. This turn has carried with it major consequences for biblical studies and theology, particularly in the Protestant camp.

Suggestion for Further Reflection

A particularly interesting ramification of our understanding of human wholeness in the Bible relates to the renewed quest in Christian theology and spirituality for happiness, human flourishing, and the good life. I say "renewed quest" because the search for the ultimate human good life can be traced at least back to the Greek foundations of Western thought. Aristotle, for instance, asked, "What is the aim, the end or purpose, of the human being?" His answer, *eudaimonia*, referred to the good life, a satisfactory and happy life, or in somewhat more philosophical terms, "the life that is becoming to a human being."[5]

This search for the *summum bonum*, the fulfilled or flourishing human life, has been taken up by a number of Christian and Jewish authors recently. Thus, Hava Tirosh-Samuelson claims for the OT wisdom tradition that "the moral order and in turn human well-being are located in the very structure of the universe. Only the wise man—he who grasps that structure and lives in accordance with it—can flourish, i.e., experience happiness."[6] Similarly, Jonathan Pennington takes up the Sermon on the Mount and shows how it "is Christianity's answer to the greatest

---

5. McCabe, *Good Life*, 8. On philosophy and the good life, see esp. Pawelski, "Introduction to Philosophical Approaches," 284–300.

6. Tirosh-Samuelson, *Happiness in Premodern Judaism*, 55–56. See also McConville, *Being Human in God's World*, who stresses the OT's "call to realize the full potential of the human in God's world" (59).

metaphysical question that humanity has always faced—*How can we experience true human flourishing?* What is happiness, blessedness, *shalom*, and how does one obtain and sustain it?"[7] And Paul Wadell explores Aristotle and Aquinas to argue "we will be happy when we are what God wants us to be—people of goodness, kindness, mercy, and forgiveness; people who come to life in loving and serving others."[8]

The understanding of perfection as human wholeness proposed in this book dovetails well with this renewed emphasis on human flourishing. Some have suggested recently that we would do well to translate the beatitudes in precisely this fashion, "flourishing are the . . ." rather than "blessed are the . . . ."[9] And Ellen Charry has coined the term "asherism" (from Heb *ashre* = happy, blessed, flourishing) to describe the Bible's vision of human flourishing.[10] I have sought to demonstrate that the Bible's consistent call to be *tamim-teleios* is nothing other than a summons to precisely the sort of flourishing God-centered human existence envisioned by the one who created and redeemed us. On the human side, this, and not an impossible perfection, is what God was after when creating humanity in the garden.

---

7. Pennington, *Sermon on the Mount*, 14.

8. Wadell, *Happiness*, 2. See also the essays in Volf and Crisp, *Joy and Human Flourishing*.

9. See Pennington, *Sermon on the Mount*, ch. 2.

10. Charry, "God and the Art of Happiness," 238–52.

Bibliography

Abrahams, Israel. *Studies in Pharisaism and the Gospels*. First and Second Series. New York: KTAV, 1967.

Agourides, S. "Apocalypse of Sedrach." In *The Old Testament Pseudepigrapha*, edited by James H. Charlesworth, 1.605–13. Garden City, NY: Doubleday, 1983.

Albl, Martin C. *And Scripture Cannot Be Broken: The Form and Function of the Early Christian Testimonia Collections*. Leiden: Brill, 1999.

Alexander, Philip S. "Torah and Salvation in Tannaitic Literature." In *Justification and Variegated Nomism*. Vol. 1, *The Complexities of Second Temple Judaism*, edited by Donald A. Carson, Peter T. O'Brien, and Mark A. Seifrid, 261–301. Grand Rapids: Baker Academic, 2001.

Allen, Diogenes, and Eric O. Springsted. *Philosophy for Understanding Theology*. 2nd ed. Louisville: Westminster John Knox, 2007.

Allison, Dale C. *A Critical and Exegetical Commentary on the Epistle of James*. ICC. New York: Bloomsbury, 2013.

———. "The Structure of the Sermon on the Mount." *JBL* 106.3 (1987) 423–45.

Anderson, Gary A. "Intentional and Unintentional Sin in the Dead Sea Scrolls." In *Pomegranates and Golden Bells: Studies in Biblical, Jewish, and Near Eastern Ritual, Law, and Literature in Honor of Jacob Milgrom*, edited by David P. Wright, David Noel Freedman, and Avi Hurvitz, 49–64. Winona Lake, IN: Eisenbrauns, 1995.

Annas, Julia. *The Morality of Happiness*. New York: Oxford University Press, 1993.

Arminius, Jacobus. *Writings*. Translated by James Nichols. 3 vols. Grand Rapids: Baker, 1956.

Arnold, Bill T. *Genesis*. Cambridge: Cambridge University Press, 2009.

Arnold, Bradley. *Christ as the Telos of Life: Moral Philosophy, Athletic Imagery, and the Aim of Philippians*. WUNT 2.371. Tübingen: Mohr Siebeck, 2014.

Athanasius. *The Life of Saint Antony*. Translated by Robert T. Meyer. Westminster, MD: Newman, 1950.

Atkinson, Kenneth. "Enduring the Lord's Discipline: Soteriology in the *Psalms of Solomon*." In *This World and the World to Come: Soteriology in Early Judaism*, edited by Daniel M. Gurtner, 151–55. LSTS 74. London: T. & T. Clark, 2011.

Augustine. "The Perfection of Human Righteousness." In *The Works of Saint Augustine, Pt.1, Vol. 23: Answer to the Pelagians*, edited by John E. Rotelle, translated by Roland J. Teske, 279–316. Hyde Park, NY: New City, 1997.

Barclay, John M. G. "Constructing a Dialogue: *4 Ezra* and Paul on the Mercy of God." In *Anthropologie und Ethik im Frühjudentum und im Neuen Testament: Wechselseitige*

Bibliography

Wahrnehmungen, edited by Matthias Konradt and Esther Schläpfer, 3–22. WUNT 322. Tübingen: Mohr Siebeck, 2014.

———. *Paul and the Gift*. Grand Rapids: Eerdmans, 2015.

Barclay, John M. G., and Simon J. Gathercole, eds. *Divine and Human Agency in Paul and His Cultural Environment*. Early Christianity in Context. London: T. & T. Clark, 2006.

Barker, Paul A. "The Theology of Deuteronomy 27." *TynBul* 49.2 (1998) 277–303.

Barth, Markus. *Ephesians: Introduction, Translation and Commentary on Chapters 4–6*. AB 34A. New York: Doubleday, 1974.

Barth, Markus, and Helmut Blanke. *Colossians: A New Translation with Introduction and Commentary*. Translated by Astrid B. Beck. AB 34B. New York: Doubleday, 1994.

Bauckham, Richard. "Apocalypses." In *Justification and Variegated Nomism*, edited by D. A. Carson, Peter Thomas O'Brien, and Mark A. Seifrid, 135–87. Grand Rapids: Baker Academic, 2001.

Behr, John. *Asceticism and Anthropology in Irenaeus and Clement*. New York: Oxford University Press, 2000.

Bell, Richard H. *No One Seeks for God: An Exegetical and Theological Study of Romans 1:18—3:20*. WUNT 106. Tübingen: Mohr Siebeck, 2013.

Benner, David G. *Human Being and Becoming: Living the Adventure of Life and Love*. Grand Rapids: Brazos, 2016.

Berkhof, Louis. *Systematic Theology*. 4th rev. and enl. ed. Grand Rapids: Eerdmans, 1941.

Betz, Hans Dieter. *Galatians: A Commentary on Paul's Letter to the Churches in Galatia*. Hermeneia. Philadelphia: Fortress, 1979.

———. *The Sermon on the Mount: A Commentary on the Sermon on the Mount, Including the Sermon on the Plain (Matthew 5:3—7:27 and Luke 6:20–49)*. Hermeneia. Minneapolis: Fortress, 1995.

Black, Matthew. *The Scrolls and Christian Origins: Studies in the Jewish Background of the New Testament*. repr. ed. Chico, CA: Scholars, 1983.

Blosser, Benjamin P. *Become Like the Angels: Origen's Doctrine of the Soul*. Washington, DC: Catholic University of America Press, 2012.

Bogart, John. *Orthodox and Heretical Perfectionism in the Johannine Community as Evident in the First Epistle of John*. Missoula, MT: Scholars, 1977.

Bonner, Ali. *The Myth of Pelagianism*. Oxford: Oxford University Press, 2018.

Bratton, Amy Caswell. *Witnesses of Perfect Love: Narratives of Christian Perfection in Early Methodism*. Toronto: Clements Academic, 2014.

Braun, Herbert. "Vom Erbarmen Gottes über den Gerechten: zur Theologie der Psalmen Salomos." *ZNW* 43.1–2 (1950–1951) 1–54.

Brown, Peter. *Augustine of Hippo: A Biography*. Berkeley: University of California Press, 2000.

Brown, Raymond E. *The Epistles of John: Translated, with Introduction, Notes, and Commentary*. AB 30. Garden City, NY: Doubleday, 1982.

Brueggemann, Walter. *Genesis*. Interpretation. Louisville: Westminster John Knox, 2010.

———. *Solomon: Israel's Ironic Icon of Human Achievement*. Columbia: University of South Carolina Press, 2005.

Bibliography

Büchler, Adolf. *Types of Jewish-Palestinian Piety: From 70 B.C.E. to 70 C.E.: The Ancient Pious Men*. Repr. ed. Farnborough: Gregg, 1969.

Burgess, Stanley M. "Medieval Models of Perfectionism." In *Reaching Beyond: Chapters in the History of Perfectionism*, edited by Stanley M. Burgess, 149–79. Peabody, MA: Hendrickson, 1986.

Burgess, Stanley M., ed. *Reaching Beyond: Chapters in the History of Perfectionism*. Peabody, MA: Hendrickson, 1986.

Campbell, Douglas A. *The Deliverance of God: An Apocalyptic Rereading of Justification in Paul*. Grand Rapids: Eerdmans, 2009.

Carlston, Charles. "The Vocabulary of Perfection in Philo and Hebrews." In *Unity and Diversity in New Testament Theology: Essays in Honor of George E. Ladd*, edited by Robert A. Guelich, 133–60. Grand Rapids: Eerdmans, 1978.

Carras, George P. "Romans 2:1–29: A Dialogue on Jewish Ideals." *Biblica* 73.2 (1992) 183–207.

Carter, Warren. *Households and Discipleship: A Study of Matthew 19–20*. Sheffield: Sheffield Academic, 1994.

Cavin, Robert L. *New Existence and Righteous Living: Colossians and 1 Peter in Conversation with 4QInstruction and the Hodayot*. Berlin: De Gruyter, 2013.

Charles, R. H. *The Apocalypse of Baruch*. London: A. & C. Black, 1896.

Charlesworth, James H. "Prayer of Manasseh: A New Translation and Introduction." In *The Old Testament Pseudepigrapha*, edited by James H. Charlesworth, 2.625–37. Garden City, NY: Doubleday, 1983.

Charry, Ellen T. "God and the Art of Happiness." *Theology Today* 68.3 (2011) 238–52.

Coats, Robert Hay. "Holiness (NT and Christian)." In *Encyclopædia of Religion and Ethics*, edited by James Hastings, John A. Selbie, and Louis H. Gray, 743–50. New York: C. Scribner's Sons, 1908–1926.

Collins, C. John. "Echoes of Aristotle in Romans 2:14–15: Or, Maybe Abimelech Was Not So Bad After All." *Journal of Markets and Morality* 13.1 (2010) 123–73.

Collins, John Joseph. *The Apocalyptic Imagination: An Introduction to the Jewish Matrix of Christianity*. New York: Crossroad, 1984.

Condra, Ed. *Salvation for the Righteous Revealed: Jesus Amid Covenantal and Messianic Expectations in Second Temple Judaism*. Leiden: Brill, 2002.

Conzelmann, Hans. *1 Corinthians: A Commentary on the First Epistle to the Corinthians*. Translated by James W. Leitch. Hermeneia. Philadelphia: Fortress, 1975.

Cousland, J. R. C. *The Crowds in the Gospel of Matthew*. Leiden: Brill, 2002.

Cranfield, C. E. B. *A Critical and Exegetical Commentary on the Epistle to the Romans*. 6th ed. 2 vols. Edinburgh: T. & T. Clark, 1975.

Cranford, Michael. "The Possibility of Perfect Obedience: Paul and an Implied Premise in Galatians 3:10 and 5:3." *NovT* 36.3 (1994) 242–58.

Curran, Thomas, and Andrew P. Hill. "Perfectionism Is Increasing Over Time: A Meta-Analysis of Birth Cohort Differences from 1989 to 2016." *Psychological Bulletin* (Dec. 28, 2017).

Cuvillier, Élian. "Torah Observance and Radicalization in the First Gospel: Matthew and First-Century Judaism: A Contribution to the Debate." *NTS* 55.2 (2009) 144–59.

Das, A. Andrew. "Galatians 3:10: A 'Newer Perspective' on an Omitted Premise." In *Unity and Diversity in the Gospels and Paul: Essays in Honor of Frank J. Matera*, edited by Christopher W. Skinner and Kelly R. Iverson, 203-23. Atlanta: SBL, 2012.

———. *Paul, the Law, and the Covenant*. Peabody, MA: Hendrickson, 2001.

David, Susan, Ilona Boniwell, and Amanda Conley Ayers, eds. *The Oxford Handbook of Happiness*. Oxford: Oxford University Press, 2013.

Davies, Glenn N. *Faith and Obedience in Romans: A Study in Romans 1-4*. JSNTSup 39. Sheffield: JSOT, 1990.

Davies, W. D. *The Setting of the Sermon on the Mount*. BJS 186. AtlantaA: Scholars, 1989 [orig. 1964].

Davies, W. D., and Dale C. Allison. *A Critical and Exegetical Commentary on the Gospel According to Saint Matthew*. ICC. 3 vols. Edinburgh: T. & T. Clark, 1988.

de la Potterie, Ignace. "The Impeccability of the Christian According to 1 Jn 3,6-9." In *The Christian Lives by the Spirit*, edited by I. de la Potterie and S. Lyonnet, 175-96. Staten Island, NY: Alba, 1971.

Deasley, Alex R. G. "The Idea of Perfection in the Qumran Texts." Diss., University of Manchester, 1972.

———. *The Shape of Qumran Theology*. Carlisle, Cumbria: Paternoster, 2000.

Deissler, Alfons. "Perfection: The Old Testament." In *Encyclopedia of Biblical Theology: The Complete Sacramentum Verbi*, edited by Johannes Baptist Bauer, 658-63. New York: Crossroad, 1970.

Delitzsch, Franz, and Carl Friedrich Keil. *The Pentateuch*. Translated by James Martin. 3 vols. Grand Rapids: Eerdmans, 1949.

Delling, Gerhard. "*telos, etc.*" In *TDNT* 8:49-87.

DeSilva, David Arthur. "Grace, the Law and Justification in *4 Ezra* and the Pauline Letters: A Dialogue." *JSNT* 37.1 (2014) 25-49.

Dibelius, Martin. *James: A Commentary on the Epistle of James*. Translated by Michael A. Williams. Hermeneia. Philadelphia: Fortress, 1976.

Dickson, John Irwin. "The Idea of Perfection in the Old Testament." Diss., Vanderbilt University, 1954.

Dihle, Albrecht. "Das Streben nach Vollkommenheit nach Philon und Gregor von Nyssa." In *Ausgewählte kleine Schriften zu Antike und Christentum*, edited by Georg Schöllgen, 260-66. JAC Ergänzungsband 38. Münster: Aschendorff Verlag, 2013.

Douglas, Mary. *Purity and Danger: An Analysis of Concept of Pollution and Taboo*. New York: Routledge, 2005.

Du Plessis, Paul Johannes. *Teleios: The Idea of Perfection in the New Testament*. Kampen: Kok, 1959.

Dunn, James D. G. *A Commentary on the Epistle to the Galatians*. Black's New Testament Commentaries. Peabody, MA: Hendrickson, 1993.

———. *The Epistles to the Colossians and to Philemon: A Commentary on the Greek Text*. NIGTC. Grand Rapids: Eerdmans, 1996.

———. *The New Perspective on Paul: Revised Edition*. Grand Rapids: Eerdmans, 2008.

———. "Philippians 3.2-14 and the New Perspective on Paul." In *The New Perspective on Paul: Revised Edition*, by James D. G. Dunn, 469-90. Grand Rapids: Eerdmans, 2008.

———. *Romans 1-8, 9-16*. WBC 38a-38b. Dallas: Word, 1988.

———. *The Theology of Paul the Apostle*. Grand Rapids: Eerdmans, 1998.

Dunn, James D. G., ed. *Paul and the Mosaic Law*. Grand Rapids: Eerdmans, 2001.

Bibliography

Edlund, Conny. *Das Auge der Einfalt: Eine Untersuchung zu Matth. 6,22–23 und Luk. 11,34–35*. Acta Seminarii Neotestamentici Upsaliensis XIX. Uppsala: Almqvist & Wiksells, 1952.

Eisenbeis, Walter. *Die Wurzel שלם im Alten Testament*. BZAW 113. Berlin: de Gruyter, 1969.

Enns, Peter. *Evolution of Adam: What the Bible Does and Doesn't Say About Human Origins*. Grand Rapids: Baker, 2012.

Epstein, I., ed. *Sanhedrin*. Translated by Jacob Shachter and H. Freedman. The Babylonian Talmud 19. London: Soncino, 1994.

Erickson, Millard J. *Christian Theology*. Grand Rapids: Baker, 1986.

Falk, Daniel. "Psalms and Prayers." In *Justification and Variegated Nomism*. Vol. 1, *The Complexities of Second Temple Judaism*, edited by Donald A. Carson, Peter T. O'Brien, and Mark A. Seifrid, 7–56. Grand Rapids: Baker Academic, 2001.

Fee, Gordon D. *Paul's Letter to the Philippians*. NICNT. Grand Rapids: Eerdmans, 1995.

Feldmeier, Reinhard. "'As Your Heavenly Father Is Perfect': The God of the Bible and Commandments in the Gospel." *Interpretation* 70.4 (2016) 431–44.

Finn, R. D. *Asceticism in the Graeco-Roman World*. Cambridge: Cambridge University Press, 2009.

Flew, R. Newton. *The Idea of Perfection in Christian Theology: An Historical Study of the Christian Ideal for the Present Life*. Oxford: Clarendon, 1968.

Foerster, Werner. "Ὁλόκληρος." In *TDNT*, edited by G. Kittel, G. W. Bromiley, and G. Friedrich, 3.766. Grand Rapids: Eerdmans, 1964.

Forsyth, Peter Taylor. *Christian Perfection*. New York: Dodd, Mead, 1899.

Foss, Martin. *The Idea of Perfection in the Western World*. Princeton: Princeton University Press, 1946.

Francke, August Hermann. "On Christian Perfection." In *Pietists: Selected Writings*, edited by Peter C. Erb. New York: Paulist, 1983.

García Martínez, Florentino. *The Dead Sea Scrolls Translated: The Qumran Texts in English*. Translated by Wilfred G. E. Watson. 2nd ed. Grand Rapids: Eerdmans, 1996.

Garlington, Don. "Paul's 'Partisan ἐκ' and the Question of Justification in Galatians." *JBL* 127.3 (2008) 567–89.

———. "Role Reversal and Paul's Use of Scripture in Galatians 3.10–13." *JSNT* 65 (1997) 85–121.

Gathercole, Simon J. "A Law Unto Themselves: The Gentiles in Romans 2.14–15 Revisited." *JSNT* 85 (2002) 27–49.

Goldingay, John. *Psalms*. 3 vols. Grand Rapids: Baker Academic, 2006.

Gowan, Donald E. "Wisdom and Endurance in James." *Horizons in Biblical Theology* 15 (1993) 145–53.

Graham, Matt Patrick. "Aspects of the Structure and Rhetoric of 2 Chronicles 25." In *History and Interpretation: Essays in Honour of John H. Hayes*, edited by Jeffrey K. Kuan, William P. Brown, and Matt Patrick Graham, 78–89. JSOTSup 173. Sheffield: Sheffield Academic, 1993.

Grindheim, Sigurd. "Apostate Turned Prophet: Paul's Prophetic Self-Understanding and Prophetic Hermeneutic with Special Reference to Galatians 3.10–12." *NTS* 53.4 (2007) 545–65.

———. "Wisdom for the Perfect: Paul's Advice to the Corinthian Church (1 Corinthians 2:6–16)." *JBL* 121.4 (2002) 689–709.

Bibliography

Grundmann, Walter. "μεμφομαι, etc." In *TDNT* 4.571-74.

Guelich, Robert A. "The Matthean Beatitudes: 'Entrance-Requirements' or Eschatological Blessings?" *JBL* 95.3 (1976) 415-34.

Gurtner, Daniel M. *Second Baruch: A Critical Edition of the Syriac Text : With Greek and Latin Fragments, English Translation, Introduction, and Concordances*. New York: T. & T. Clark, 2009.

Hagner, Donald A. *Matthew 1-13*. WBC 33a. Dallas: Word, 1993.

———. *The New Testament: A Historical and Theological Introduction*. Grand Rapids: Baker Academic, 2012.

Hamann, Henry Paul. "The Translation of Ephesians 4:12—A Necessary Revision." *Concordia Journal* 14.1 (1988) 42-49.

Harnack, Adolf von. *History of Dogma*. 7 vols. New York: Russell & Russell, 1958.

Harnisch, Wolfgang. *Verhängnis und Verheissung der Geschichte: Untersuchungen zum Zeit- und Geschichtsverständnis im 4.Buch Esra und in der syr. Baruchapokalypse*. Göttingen: Vandenhoeck & Ruprecht, 1969.

Harrington, Daniel J. "The Rich Young Man in Matthew 19,16-22: Another Way to God for Jews?" In *The Four Gospels, 1992: Festschrift Frans Neirynck*, edited by Frans van Segbroeck, 1425-32. Leuven: Peeters, 1992.

Hartin, Patrick J. "Call to Be Perfect through Suffering (James 1:2-4). The Concept of Perfection in the Epistle of James and the Sermon on the Mount." *Bib* 77 (1996) 477-92.

———. *A Spirituality of Perfection: Faith in Action in the Letter of James*. Collegeville, MN: Liturgical, 1999.

Hauck, Friedrich. "*Amōmos*." In *TDNT* 4:830.

Hawthorne, Gerald F. *Philippians*. WBC 43. Waco, TX: Word, 1983.

Hays, Christopher M. "Rich and Poor." In *Dictionary of Jesus and the Gospels*, edited by Joel B. Green, 800-10. 2nd ed. Downers Grove, IL: IVP Academic, 2013.

Hays, J. Daniel. "Has the Narrator Come to Praise Solomon or to Bury Him?: Narrative Subtlety in 1 Kings 1-11." *JSOT* 28.2 (2003) 149-74.

Hays, Richard B. *The Faith of Jesus Christ: The Narrative Substructure of Galatians 3:1— 4:11*. 2nd ed. Grand Rapids: Eerdmans, 2002.

———. "The Letter to the Galatians." In *The New Interpreter's Bible* 11, 181-348. Nashville: Abingdon, 2000.

Hübner, Hans. *Law in Paul's Thought*. Edinburgh: T. & T. Clark, 1984.

Hurka, Thomas. *Perfectionism*. Oxford Ethics Series. New York: Oxford University Press, 1993.

Hurvitz, Mitchell M., and Sara E. Karesh. *Encyclopedia of Judaism*. New York: Facts on File, 2006.

Hyde, Michael J. *Perfection: Coming to Terms with Being Human*. Waco, TX: Baylor University Press, 2010.

Illman, Karl-Johan. "ŠLM." In *TDOT*, edited by Gerhard Johannes Botterweck and Helmer Ringgren, 97-105. Grand Rapids: Eerdmans, 2006.

Isaacs, Nathan. "Is Judaism Legalistic?" *The Menorah Journal* 7 (1921) 259-68.

Isaiah. *Abba Isaiah of Scetis: Ascetic Discourses*. Translated by John Chryssavgis and Pachomios Penkett. Kalamazoo, MI: Cistercian Publications, 2002.

Johnson, Luke Timothy. *The Letter of James: A New Translation with Introduction and Commentary*. AB 37a. New York: Doubleday, 1995.

Johnson, Marshall D. "Life of Adam and Eve." In *The Old Testament Pseudepigrapha*, edited by James H. Charlesworth, 2.249-95. Garden City, NY: Doubleday, 1983.

Bibliography

Johnston, J. William. "Which 'All' Sinned? Rom 3:23–24 Reconsidered." *NovT* 53 (2011) 153–64.
Jonge, Martinus de, and Harm W. Hollander, eds. *The Testaments of the Twelve Patriarchs: A Commentary*. Leiden: Brill, 1985.
Kaminski, Carol M. *Was Noah Good?: Finding Favour in the Flood Narrative*. New York: Bloomsbury, 2014.
Karavites, Peter. *Evil, Freedom, and the Road to Perfection in Clement of Alexandria*. Leiden: Brill, 1998.
Kedar-Kopfstein, Benjamin. "*Tamam*, etc." In *TDOT*, edited by Gerhard Johannes Botterweck and Helmer Ringgren, 699–711. Grand Rapids: Eerdmans, 2006.
Kee, Howard Clark. "The Ethical Dimensions of the Testaments of the XII as a Clue to Provenance." *NTS* 24.2 (1978) 259–70.
Kellenberger, James. "The Fool of the Psalms and Religious Epistemology." *International Journal for the Philosophy of Religion* 45.2 (1999) 99–113.
Kirk, Kenneth E. *The Vision of God: The Christian Doctrine of the Summum Bonum*. New York: Harper & Row, 1966.
Kissinger, Warren S. *The Sermon on the Mount: A History of Interpretation and Bibliography*. Metuchen, NJ: Scarecrow, 1975.
Kittel, Gerhard, Gerhard Friedrich, and Geoffrey Bromiley, eds. *TDNT*. 10 vols. Grand Rapids: Eerdmans, 1964–1976.
Klein, Martin. *Ein vollkommenes Werk: Vollkommenheit, Gesetz und Gericht als theologische Themen des Jakobusbriefes*. Stuttgart: W. Kohlhammer, 1995.
Knoppers, Gary N. "Dynastic Oracle and Secession in 1 Kings 11." *Proceedings* 7 (1987) 159–72.
Koester, Craig R. *Hebrews: A New Translation with Introduction and Commentary*. AB 36. New York: Doubleday, 2001.
Kugel, James L. *A Walk through Jubilees: Studies in the Book of Jubilees and the World of Its Creation*. Boston: Brill, 2012.
Kuhr, Friedrich. "Römer 2:14f und die Verheissung bei Jeremia 31:31f." *ZNW* 55.3–4 (1964) 243–61.
Kümmel, Werner Georg. *Römer 7 und das Bild des Menschen im Neuen Testament; Zwei Studien*. Theologische Bücherei 53. Munich: C. Kaiser, 1974.
Kushner, Harold S. *How Good Do We Have to Be? A New Understanding of Guilt and Forgiveness*. Boston: Little, Brown & Co., 1997.
Kwakkel, Gert. *According to My Righteousness: Upright Behaviour as Grounds for Deliverance in Psalms 7, 17, 18, 26, and 44*. Oudtestamentische Studiën 46. Leiden: Brill, 2002.
Laato, Timo. *Paul and Judaism: An Anthropological Approach*. Translated by T. McElwain. Atlanta: Scholars, 1995.
LaCocque, Andre. *Jesus the Central Jew: His Time and His People*. Atlanta: SBL, 2015.
Lambrecht, Jan. *The Wretched "I" and Its Liberation: Paul in Romans 7 and 8*. Louvain Theological and Pastoral Monographs 14. Grand Rapids: Eerdmans, 1992.
Lamm, Julia A., ed. *The Wiley-Blackwell Companion to Christian Mysticism*. Malden, MA: Wiley-Blackwell, 2013.
Lane, William L. *Hebrews 1–8*. WBC 47A. Dallas: Word, 1991.
———. *Hebrews 9–13*. WBC 47B. Dallas: Word, 1991.
Lapide, Pinchas. *The Sermon on the Mount, Utopia or Program for Action?* Translated by Arlene Swidler. Maryknoll, NY: Orbis, 1986.

Bibliography

LaRondelle, Hans K. *Perfection and Perfectionism: A Dogmatic-Ethical Study of Biblical Perfection and Phenomenal Perfectionism*. 2nd ed. Berrien Springs, MI: Andrews University Press, 1975.

Levison, John R. *Filled with the Spirit*. Grand Rapids: Eerdmans, 2009.

———. *Inspired: The Holy Spirit and the Mind of Faith*. Grand Rapids: Eerdmans, 2013.

Light, Gary W. "Salvation, Save, Savior." In *Eerdmans Dictionary of the Bible*, edited by David Noel Freedman, 1153–55. Grand Rapids: Eerdmans, 2000.

Lilla, Salvatore Romano Clemente. *Clement of Alexandria: A Study in Christian Platonism and Gnosticism*. London: Oxford University Press, 1971.

Lincoln, Andrew T. *Ephesians*. WBC 42. Nashville: Thomas Nelson, 1990.

Lohfink, Gerhard. "Wem gilt die Bergpredigt? Eine redaktionskritische Untersuchung von Mt 4,23—5,2 und 7,28f." *Theologische Quartalschrift* 163 (1983) 264–84.

Lohse, Eduard. *Colossians and Philemon: A Commentary on the Epistles to the Colossians and to Philemon*. Hermeneia. Philadelphia: Fortress, 1971.

———. "'Vollkommen Sein' Zur Ethik des Matthäusevangeliums." In *Salz der Erde, Licht der Welt*, edited by L. Oberlinner and P. Fiedler, 131–40. Stuttgart: Verlag Katholisches Bibelwerk, 1991.

Longenecker, Bruce W. *2 Esdras*. Sheffield: Sheffield Academic, 1995.

———. *Eschatology and the Covenant: A Comparison of 4 Ezra and Romans 1–11*. JSNTSup 57. Sheffield: JSOT, 1991.

Longenecker, Richard N. *The Epistle to the Romans*. NIGTC. Grand Rapids: Eerdmans, 2016.

———. *Galatians*. WBC 41. Dallas: Word, 1990.

Louth, Andrew. *The Origins of the Christian Mystical Tradition: From Plato to Denys*. 2nd ed. Oxford: Oxford University Press, 2007.

Louth, Andrew, and Marco Conti. *Genesis 1–11*. ACCS. Downers Grove, IL: InterVarsity, 2001.

Luck, Ulrich. "Die Frage nach dem Guten: zu Mt 19,16–30 und Par." In *Studien zum Text und zur Ethik des Neuen Testaments: Festschrift zum 80.Geburtstag von Heinrich Greeven*, 282–97. Berlin: de Gruyter, 1986.

Lundbom, Jack R. *Deuteronomy: A Commentary*. Grand Rapids: Eerdmans, 2013.

Luther, Martin. "The Sermon on the Mount." In *Luther's Works*, edited by Jaroslav Pelikan.Vol. 21. Saint Louis: Concordia, 1956.

Luther, Martin, and Frederick W. Conrad. *Luther's Small Catechism: Explained and Amplified for Use in Classes, Schools, and Families*. Rev. ed. Philadelphia: Lutheran Publication Society, 1886.

Luz, Ulrich. *Matthew 8–20*. Hermeneia. Minneapolis: Augsburg Fortress, 2000.

Madueme, Hans, and Michael Reeves, eds. *Adam, the Fall, and Original Sin: Theological, Biblical, and Scientific Perspectives*. Grand Rapids: Baker Academic, 2014.

Marshall, I. Howard. *The Epistles of John*. NICNT. Grand Rapids: Eerdmans, 1978.

Martyn, J. Louis. *Galatians: A New Translation with Introduction and Commentary*. AB 33a. New York: Doubleday, 1997.

Maston, Jason. *Divine and Human Agency in Second Temple Judaism and Paul: A Comparative Study*. WUNT 2.297. Tübingen: Mohr Siebeck, 2010.

Matlock, R. Barry. "Helping Paul's Argument Work? The Curse of Galatians 3.10–14." In *The Torah in the New Testament: Papers Delivered at the Manchester-Lausanne Seminar of June 2008*, edited by Michael Tait and Peter Oakes, 154–79. New York: T. & T. Clark, 2009.

Bibliography

Matthews, Bradley J. "Christian Maturity in Ephesians and Colossians: Distinctly Masculine or Gender-Relativized in Christ?" *Lexington Theological Quarterly* 42.1 (2007) 1–17.

Mayes, Andrew D. H. "On Describing the Purpose of Deuteronomy." *JSOT* 58 (1993) 13–33.

McBride, S. Dean. "Polity of the Covenant People: The Book of Deuteronomy." *Interpretation* 41.3 (1987) 229–44.

McCabe, Herbert. *The Good Life: Ethics and the Pursuit of Happiness*. New York: Continuum, 2005.

McColman, Carl. *The Big Book of Christian Mysticism: The Essential Guide to Contemplative Spirituality*. Charlottesville, VA: Hampton Roads, 2010.

McConville, J. Gordon. *Being Human in God's World: An Old Testament Theology of Humanity*. Grand Rapids: Baker Academic, 2016.

McFarland, Ian A. "Original Sin." In *T. & T. Clark Companion to the Doctrine of Sin*, edited by Keith L. Johnson and David Lauber, 303–18. New York: Bloomsbury T. & T. Clark, 2016.

McGinn, Bernard. *The Presence of God: A History of Western Christian Mysticism*. 7 vols. New York: Crossroad, 1991.

McGuckin, John Anthony, ed. *The Westminster Handbook to Origen*. Louisville: Westminster John Knox, 2004.

McKeating, Henry. "Divine Forgiveness in the Psalms." *SJT* 18.1 (1965) 69–83.

Metzger, Bruce M. "The Fourth Book of Ezra." In *The Old Testament Pseudepigrapha*, edited by James H. Charlesworth, 1.516–59. Garden City, NY: Doubleday, 1983.

———. "The 'Lost' Section of II Esdras (= IV Ezra)." *JBL* 76.2 (1957) 153–56.

Millar, J. Gary. "Ethics and Human Nature." In *Now Choose Life: Theology and Ethics in Deuteronomy*, by J. Gary Millar, 161–80. Grand Rapids: Eerdmans, 1999.

Minns, Denis. *Irenaeus: An Introduction*. New York: T. & T. Clark, 2010.

Moehring, H. R. "Some Remarks on *Sarx* in Phil 3:3ff." In *Studia Evangelica IV*, edited by F. L. Cross, 432–36. Berlin: Akademie-Verlag, 1968.

Montefiore, Claude G. *Judaism and St. Paul: Two Essays*. New York: Arno, 1973.

Montefiore, Claude G., and H. M. J. Loewe. *A Rabbinic Anthology*. repr. New York: Schocken, 1974.

Moo, Douglas J. *The Epistle to the Romans*. NICNT. Grand Rapids: Eerdmans, 1996.

———. *The Letters to the Colossians and to Philemon*. PNTC. Grand Rapids: Eerdmans, 2008.

Moo, Jonathan. "The Few Who Obtain Mercy: Soteriology in *4 Ezra*." In *This World and the World to Come: Soteriology in Early Judaism*, edited by Daniel M. Gurtner, 98–113. LSTS 74. New York: T. & T. Clark, 2013.

Moore, George Foot. *Judaism in the First Centuries of the Christian Era, the Age of the Tannaim*. 3 vols. Cambridge: Harvard University Press, 1927.

Moule, C. F. D. "New Life in Colossians 3:1–17." *Review and Expositor* 70.4 (1973) 481–93.

Moule, H. C. G. *The Epistle to the Philippians*. Grand Rapids: Baker, 1981.

Mussner, Franz. *Der Galaterbrief*. Herders Theologischer Kommentar zum Neuen Testament 9. Freiburg: Herder, 1974.

Nel, Philip J. "Sh-L-M." In *New International Dictionary of Old Testament Theology and Exegesis*, edited by Willem VanGemeren, 130–35. Grand Rapids: Zondervan, 1997.

Bibliography

The New Merriam-Webster Dictionary. Springfield, MA: Merriam-Webster, 1989.

Nickelsburg, George W. E. *Ancient Judaism and Christian Origins: Diversity, Continuity, and Transformation.* Minneapolis: Fortress, 2003.

Noble, Thomas A. *Holy Trinity, Holy People: The Theology of Christian Perfecting.* Cambridge: James Clarke & Co., 2013.

Nolland, John. *The Gospel of Matthew: A Commentary on the Greek Text.* NIGTC. Grand Rapids: Eerdmans, 2005.

Nygren, Anders. *Commentary on Romans.* Philadelphia: Muhlenberg, 1949.

O'Brien, Peter Thomas. *Colossians, Philemon.* WBC 44. Waco, TX: Word, 1982.

———. *The Epistle to the Philippians: A Commentary on the Greek Text.* NIGTC. Grand Rapids: Eerdmans, 1991.

Olivier, J. P. J. "Tamam." In *New International Dictionary of Old Testament Theology and Exegesis,* edited by Willem VanGemeren, 306–8. Grand Rapids: Zondervan, 1997.

Olson, Roger E. "Pietism: Myths and Realities." In *The Pietist Impulse in Christianity,* edited by Christian T. Collins Winn et al., 3–16. Cambridge, MA: James Clarke & Co., 2012.

Oulton, John E. L., and Henry Chadwick. *Alexandrian Christianity: Selected Translations of Clement and Origen with Introductions and Notes.* Philadelphia: Westminster, 1954.

Page, Sydney H. T. "Whose Ministry?: A Re-Appraisal of Ephesians 4:12." *NovT* 47.1 (2005) 26–46.

Passmore, John Arthur. *The Perfectibility of Man.* 3rd ed. Indianapolis: Liberty Fund, 2000.

Pawelski, James O. "Introduction to Philosophical Approaches to Happiness." In *The Oxford Handbook of Happiness,* edited by Susan David, Ilona Boniwell, and Amanda Conley Ayers, 284–300. Oxford: Oxford University Press, 2013.

Pennington, Jonathan T. *The Sermon on the Mount and Human Flourishing: A Theological Commentary.* Grand Rapids: Baker Academic, 2017.

Peters, John Leland. *Christian Perfection and American Methodism.* New York: Abingdon, 1956.

Peterson, David. *Hebrews and Perfection: An Examination of the Concept of Perfection in the Epistle to the Hebrews.* New York: Cambridge University Press, 1982.

Pierce, Claude A. *Conscience in the New Testament: A Study of Syneidesis in the New Testament, in the Light of Its Sources and with Particular Reference to St. Paul, with Some Observations Regarding Its Pastoral Relevance Today.* London: SCM, 1958.

Piper, John. *The Future of Justification: A Response to N. T. Wright.* Wheaton, IL: Crossway, 2007.

Platt, Frederic. "Perfection (Christian)." In *Encyclopædia of Religion and Ethics,* edited by James Hastings, John A. Selbie, and Louis H. Gray, 9.728–37. New York: C. Scribner's Sons, 1908–1926.

Powell, Mark Allan. "Reading Matthew in Light of a (Recovered) Hermeneutic of Law and Gospel." In *To All the Nations: Lutheran Hermeneutics and the Gospel of Matthew,* edited by Kenneth Mtata and Craig Koester, 27–44. Leipzig: Evangelische Verlagsanstalt, 2016.

Rahlfs, Alfred. *Septuaginta: id est Vetus Testamentum graece iuxta LXX interpretes.* Stuttgart: Württembergische Bibelanstalt, 1971.

Reiser, Marius. "Love of Enemies in the Context of Antiquity." *NTS* 47.4 (2001) 411–27.

BIBLIOGRAPHY

Riedl, Johann. *Das Heil der Heiden nach R 2,14-16. 26. 27*. Vienna: St. Gabriel Verlag, 1965.

Rigaux, Béda. "Révélation des mystères et Perfection à Qumrân et dans le Nouveau Testament." *NTS* 4.4 (1958) 237-62.

Roberts, Alexander, et al., eds. *The Ante-Nicene Fathers: Translations of the Writings of the Fathers Down to A.D. 325*. 10 vols. Grand Rapids: Eerdmans, 1989.

Rohr, Richard. *Falling Upward: A Spirituality for the Two Halves of Life*. San Francisco: Jossey-Bass, 2011.

Rosner, Brian S. *Paul, Scripture and Ethics: A Study of 1 Corinthians 5-7*. Leiden: E. J. Brill, 1994.

Rössler, Dietrich. *Gesetz und Geschichte: Untersuchungen zur Theologie der jüdischen Apokalyptik und der pharisäischen Orthodoxie*. Neukirchen: Neukirchener Verlag, 1962.

Rowe, Christopher Kavin. *One True Life: The Stoics and Early Christians as Rival Traditions*. New Haven, CT: Yale University Press, 2016.

Runia, David T. "Philo of Alexandria and the Beginnings of Christian Thought: Alexandrian and Jew." *Studia Philonica Annual* 7 (1995) 143-60.

Sabourin, Leopold. "Why Is God Called 'Perfect' in Mt 5:48." *Biblische Zeitschrift* 24.2 (1980) 266-68.

Sanders, E. P. "On the Question of Fulfilling the Law in Paul and Rabbinic Judaism." In *Donum Gentilicium: New Testament Studies in Honour of David Daube*, edited by Ernst Bammel, C. K. Barrett, and W. D. Davies, 103-26. Oxford: Clarendon, 1978.

———. *Paul and Palestinian Judaism: A Comparison of Patterns of Religion*. Philadelphia: Fortress, 1977.

———. "Testament of Abraham." In *The Old Testament Pseudepigrapha*, edited by James H. Charlesworth, 1.871-902. Garden City, NY: Doubleday, 1983.

Sappington, Thomas J. *Revelation and Redemption at Colossae*. London: Continuum, 1991.

Schechter, Solomon. *Aspects of Rabbinic Theology: Major Concepts of the Talmud*. New York: Schocken, 1961; Macmillan, 1909.

Schmidt, K. L. "πταίω." In *TDNT* 6:883-84.

Schnackenburg, Rudolf. *Christian Existence in the New Testament*. Notre Dame: University of Notre Dame Press, 1968.

———. *The Johannine Epistles: Introduction and Commentary*. New York: Crossroad, 1992.

Schoeps, Hans-Joachim. *Aus frühchristlicher Zeit, religionsgeschichtliche Untersuchungen*. Tübingen: Mohr, 1950.

Schrage, Wolfgang. *The Ethics of the New Testament*. Translated by David E. Green. Philadelphia: Fortress, 1990.

Schreiner, Thomas R. "Is Perfect Obedience to the Law Possible: A Re-Examination of Galatians 3:10." *Journal of the Evangelical Theological Society* 27.2 (1984) 151-60.

———. "Paul and Perfect Obedience to the Law: An Evaluation of the View of E. P. Sanders." *Westminster Theological Journal* 47.2 (1985) 245-78.

Schweitzer, Albert. *The Mystery of the Kingdom of God: The Secret of Jesus' Messiahship and Passion*. Translated by Walter Lowrie. New York: Macmillan, 1950.

Schweizer, Eduard. *The Letter to the Colossians: A Commentary*. Minneapolis: Augsburg, 1982.

Bibliography

Scott, James M. "'For as Many as Are of Works of the Law Are Under a Curse' (Galatians 3.10)." In *Paul and the Scriptures of Israel*, edited by Craig A. Evans and James A. Sanders, 187–221. Sheffield: JSOT, 1993.

Scott, Mark S. M. *Journey Back to God: Origen on the Problem of Evil*. Oxford: Oxford University Press, 2012.

Scullion, John J. "Righteousness (OT)." In *ABD*, edited by David Noel Freedman, 5:724–36. New York: Doubleday, 1992.

Shults, Fount Lee. "Shalem and Thamim in Biblical Hebrew: An Analysis of the Semantic Field of Wholeness." PhD diss., University of Texas at Austin, 1974.

Silva, Moisés, and Karen H. Jobes. *Invitation to the Septuagint*. 2nd ed. Grand Rapids: Baker Academic, 2015.

Simpson, John Andrew, and Edmund Weiner, eds. *The Oxford English Dictionary*. 2nd ed. New York: Oxford University Press, 1989.

Smith, Barry D. *What Must I Do to Be Saved?: Paul Parts Company with His Jewish Heritage*. Sheffield: Sheffield Phoenix, 2007.

Snodgrass, Klyne. "Justification by Grace—to the Doers: An Analysis of the Place of Romans 2 in the Theology of Paul." *NTS* 32.1 (1986) 72–93.

Spicq, Ceslas. *Theological Lexicon of the New Testament*. Translated by James D. Ernest. Peabody, MA: Hendrickson, 1994.

Sprinkle, Preston M. *Paul and Judaism Revisited: A Study of Divine and Human Agency in Salvation*. Downers Grove, IL: IVP Academic, 2013.

Staniloae, Dumitru. *Orthodox Spirituality: A Practical Guide for the Faithful and a Definitive Manual for the Scholar*. South Canaan, PA: St. Tikhon's Seminary Press, 2002.

Stanley, Christopher D. *Paul and the Language of Scripture: Citation Technique in the Pauline Epistles and Contemporary Literature*. Cambridge: Cambridge University Press, 1992.

Stanton, Graham N. "What Is the Law of Christ?" *Ex Auditu* 17 (2001) 47–59.

Stemberger, Günter. *Introduction to the Talmud and Midrash*. Minneapolis: Fortress, 1992.

Stendahl, Krister. "The Apostle Paul and the Introspective Conscience of the West." In *Paul among Jews and Gentiles*, by Krister Stendahhl, 78–96. Philadelphia: Fortress, 1976.

Stone, Michael E. *Fourth Ezra: A Commentary on the Book of Fourth Ezra*. Hermeneia. Minneapolis: Fortress, 1990.

Stowers, Stanley K. "Romans 7.7–25 as a Speech-in-Character." In *Paul in His Hellenistic Context*, edited by Troels Engberg-Pedersen, 180–202. Minneapolis: Fortress, 1995.

Strauss, Richard L. "Like Christ: An Exposition of Ephesians 4:13." *Bibliotheca Sacra* 143.571 (1986) 260–65.

Stulman, Louis. "Encroachment in Deuteronomy: An Analysis of the Social World of the D Code." *JBL* 109.4 (1990) 613–32.

———. "Sex and Familial Crimes in the D Code: A Witness to Mores in Transition." *JSOT* 53 (1992) 47–63.

Tatarkiewicz, Władysław. *On Perfection*. Edited by Janusz Kuczynski. Warsaw: Warsaw University Press, 1992.

Theissen, Gerd. *Sociology of Early Palestinian Christianity*. Philadelphia: Fortress, 1978.

Bibliography

Thielman, Frank. *Paul and the Law: A Contextual Approach*. Downers Grove, IL: InterVarsity, 1994.
Thiselton, Anthony C. *The First Epistle to the Corinthians: A Commentary on the Greek Text*. NIGTC. Grand Rapids: Eerdmans, 2000.
Thompson, R. W. "How Is the Law Fulfilled in Us? An Interpretation of Romans 8:4." *Louvain Studies* 11 (1986) 31–40.
Thurston, Bonnie Bowman. "Matthew 5:43–48." *Interpretation* 41.1 (1987) 170–73.
Tirosh-Samuelson, Hava. *Happiness in Premodern Judaism: Virtue, Knowledge, and Well-Being*. Cincinnati: Hebrew Union College Press, 2003.
Toews, John E. *The Story of Original Sin*. Cambridge: Casemate, 2013.
Trafton, Joseph L. "What Would David Do? Messianic Expectation and Surprise in Ps. Sol. 17." In *The Psalms of Solomon: Language, History, Theology*, edited by Eberhard Bons and Patrick Pouchelle, 155–74. Atlanta: SBL, 2015.
Tuchman, Barbara W. *A Distant Mirror: The Calamitous 14th Century*. New York: Knopf, 1978.
Turner, George Allen. *The Vision Which Transforms: Is Christian Perfection Scriptural?* Kansas City, MO: Beacon Hill, 1964.
Tuttle, Robert G. *Mysticism in the Wesleyan Tradition*. Grand Rapids: Asbury, 1989.
Tyndale, William. *Expositions and Notes on Sundry Portions of the Holy Scriptures: Together with the Practice of Prelates*. Edited by H. Walter. Cambridge: University Press, 1849.
Umbach, Helmut. *In Christus getauft, von der Sünde befreit: die Gemeinde als sündenfreier Raum bei Paulus*. Göttingen: Vandenhoeck & Ruprecht, 1999.
van Limborch, Philipp. *Institutiones Theologiae Christianae*. 4th ed. Amsterdam, 1715.
VanderKam, James C. *The Dead Sea Scrolls Today*. 2nd ed. Grand Rapids: Eerdmans, 2010.
———. "The Righteousness of Noah." In *Ideal Figures in Ancient Judaism: Profiles and Paradigms*, edited by John J. Collins and George W. E. Nickelsburg, 13–32. SBL Septuagint and Cognate Studies 12. Chico, CA: Scholars, 1980.
VanderKam, James C., and J. T. Milik. "Jubilees." In *Discoveries in the Judeaean Desert XIII; Qumran Cave 4, VIII, Parabiblical Texts, Part 1*, edited by Harold Attridge et al. Oxford: Clarendon, 1994.
Vogt, Kari. "'Becoming Male': One Aspect of an Early Christian Anthropology." In *Women: Invisible in Theology and Church*, edited by Elisabeth Schüssler Fiorenza and Mary Collins, 72–83. Edinburgh: T. & T. Clark, 1985.
Volf, Miroslav, and Justin E. Crisp, eds. *Joy and Human Flourishing: Essays on Theology, Culture, and the Good Life*. Minneapolis: Fortress, 2015.
Völker, Walther. *Das Vollkommenheitsideal des Origenes: Eine Untersuchung zur Geschichte der Frömmigkeit und zu den Anfängen christlicher Mystik*. Tübingen: Mohr-Siebeck, 1931.
———. *Fortschritt und Vollendung bei Philo von Alexandrien: Eine Studie zur Geschichte der Frömmigkeit*. Leipzig: J. C. Hinrichs, 1938.
Von Wahlde, Urban C. *Commentary on the Three Johannine Letters*. The Gospel and Letters of John 3. Grand Rapids: Eerdmans, 2010.
Wadell, Paul J. *Happiness and the Christian Moral Life: An Introduction to Christian Ethics*. 2nd ed. Lanham, MD: Rowman & Littlefield, 2012.
Walters, John R. *Perfection in New Testament Theology: Ethics and Eschatology in Relational Dynamic*. Lewiston, NY: Mellen Biblical, 1995.

Bibliography

Ward, Benedicta. *The Sayings of the Desert Fathers: The Alphabetical Collection.* Rev. ed. Kalamazoo, MI: Cistercian, 1984.
Warfield, Benjamin Breckinridge. *Perfectionism.* Studies in Perfectionism. 2 vols. New York: Oxford University Press, 1931-1932.
Waters, Guy Prentiss. *The End of Deuteronomy in the Epistles of Paul.* WUNT 2/221. Tübingen: Mohr Siebeck, 2006.
Wernle, Paul. *Der Christ und die Sünde bei Paulus.* Leipzig: J. C. B. Mohr, 1897.
Wesley, John. *A Plain Account of Christian Perfection: As Believed and Taught by the Reverend Mr. John Wesley from the Year 1725 to the Year 1777.* Kansas City, MO: Beacon Hill, 1966.
Westermann, Claus. *Genesis: A Commentary.* Vol. 1. Minneapolis: Augsburg, 1984.
Wigoder, Geoffrey, ed. *The New Standard Jewish Encyclopedia.* 7th ed. New York: Facts on File, 1992.
Wilkins, Michael J. *The Concept of Disciple in Matthew's Gospel: As Reflected in the Use of the Term mathētēs.* Leiden: Brill, 1988.
Williamson, Ronald. *Jews in the Hellenistic World: Philo.* Cambridge: Cambridge University Press, 1989.
Wilson, Todd A. "The Law of Christ and the Law of Moses: Reflections on a Recent Trend in Interpretation." *Currents in Biblical Research* 5.1 (2006) 123-44.
Windisch, Hans. *Taufe und Sünde im ältesten Christentum bis auf Origenes: Ein Beitrag zur altchristlichen Dogmengeschichte.* Tübingen: Mohr, 1908.
Winninge, Mikael. *Sinners and the Righteous: A Comparative Study of the Psalms of Solomon and Paul's Letters.* Stockholm: Almqvist & Wiksell, 1995.
Wintermute, O. S. "Jubilees." In *The Old Testament Pseudepigrapha*, edited by James H. Charlesworth, 1.35-142. Garden City, NY: Doubleday, 1983.
Wortley, John. *Book of the Elders: Sayings of the Desert Fathers: The Systematic Collection.* Collegeville, MN: Liturgical, 2012.
Wright, Christopher J. H. *Deuteronomy.* NIBC. Peabody, MA: Hendrickson, 1996.
Wright, N. T. *The Climax of the Covenant: Christ and the Law in Pauline Theology.* Minneapolis: Fortress, 1993. T. & T. Clark, 1991.
———. *The Day the Revolution Began: Reconsidering the Meaning of Jesus's Crucifixion.* San Francisco: HarperOne, 2016.
———. *Justification: God's Plan and Paul's Vision.* Downers Grove, IL: IVP Academic, 2009.
———. *Paul and the Faithfulness of God.* 2 vols. Minneapolis: Fortress, 2013.
Yinger, Kent L. *The New Perspective on Paul: An Introduction.* Eugene, OR: Cascade, 2011.
———. *Paul, Judaism, and Judgment According to Deeds.* New York: Cambridge, 1999.
———. "Review of *In Christus getauft—von der Sünde befreit.*" *BBR* 12.2 (2002) 309-11.
Yonge, Charles Duke. *The Works of Philo: Complete and Unabridged.* New updated ed. Peabody, MA: Hendrickson, 1993.
Young, Norman H. "Who's Cursed—and Why? (Galatians 3:10-14)." *JBL* 117.1 (1998) 79-92.
Ziesler, John A. *Paul's Letter to the Romans.* Philadelphia: Trinity Press International, 1989.
Zoccali, Christopher. "What's the Problem with the Law? Jews, Gentiles, and Covenant Identity in Galatians 3:10-12." *Neotestamentica* 49.2 (2015) 377-415.

Subject Index

agency (divine-human), 15n12, 28, 123–24, 184
alēthinos, 41
amemptos, 41, 127n12
amōmos, 40n5, 41
atonement, 30n12, 34, 38, 138–40

blameless, 22, 126–27
Brethren of the Free Spirit, 181–82

Christ, 115, 117
   "made perfect" in Hebrews, 142–45
   sinless, 1, 84, 93, 142, 144, 179
   See also atonement.

covenantal nomism, 12n4, 47, 48
curse (of the law), 97–100

ethnocentric, 100
eudaimonia, 68, 187–88
exile (continuing), 100

flesh (or *sarx*), 69, 83, 90, 105–6, 109, 124, 125, 127–28, 137, 146, 162, 163, 165, 166

gnostic, 167–68

haplous/haplotēs, 41
holoklēros, 150
human frailty, 7, 34, 37, 123–24, 184

imitatio dei, 61n87, 81–82

justify/justification, 101, 185. See also righteous(ness).

kalal, 16n16

legalism, 44n21, 47n34, 48, 54, 78–79, 89n45, 97n12

mysticism, 176–77, 181n83

obedience
   as pattern of life, 33–34
   how much required, 25, 28–29, 33–34, 93, 152
   perfect
      not required in Judaism, 11–12, 44, 47, 50, 64
      in Protestant theology, 84, 177–79
   to "all" the commandments, 30–33, 98

perfect
   difficulty with Engl. term, 1–2, 5
   Engl. meaning, 3–5
   Greek terms used for, 40–42, 66–67. See also *teleios*, *amōmos* and *amemptos*.
   Heb. terms used for, 14–17. See also *tamam* and *shalem*.
   in Middle English, 82–83
   people in OT (KJV), 12–13

Subject Index

perfect (*continued*)
  used of God, 21n25, 82
  various Engl. translations used for in OT, 13–14, 20–22
  various translations in Matt 5:48, 86

perfection
  and asceticism, 2, 69, 168, 169, 171–173, 177
  and imputation, 74, 179
  as gradual ascent, 163, 170–71, 172, 173, 177
  as vision of God, 60, 61, 90, 161, 168–69, 170, 177
  distinctive in Hebrews, 141–49
  evangelical counsels of, 74, 90
  ideal (only), 53, 60, 61, 74, 155, 176
  in Orthodoxy, 177
  not generally a Jewish concern, 7
  See also wholeness.

perfectionism, 2, 3n4, 43n18, 47–50, 53, 54, 62, 108, 153, 181
Pharisees, 78–80
Pietism, 179
pistis christou, 101n23
Platonism, middle, 68–69, 166n24, 168, 169, 175

righteous(ness), 11, 15, 16, 18–20, 24–26, 54–55, 62, 73, 78–79, 120, 135, 178, 183–84. *See also* justify/justification.

salvation, 2, 11, 35–36, 101
Sermon on the Mount, 73–80
  addressees, 76–77
  antitheses, 77–78
shalem, 17, 41
sin/to sin,
  as Israel's stubbornness, 31
  deliberate/habitual, 33–34, 55, 57, 155
  juxtaposed with wholeness in OT, 35–37
  original
    in Orthodoxy, 37–38n34,

    in OT and Judaism, 37–38
    in rabbinic literature, 31n17,
  single act brings eternal loss, 63
  tolerated in OT, 34
  universal, 35–38, 132–37, 140, 151
sinless(ness), 83, 152, 153, 154, 155, 156, 169, 171n44, 175, 178, 180–81
  at the resurrection, 120–21, 157
  of Christ. *See* Christ, sinless.
Small Catechism (Lutheran), 2

tamam (and cognates), 14–17, 19
  as pattern of life, 26
  Greek translations of in LXX, 40–42
  near-synonym of righteous(ness), 19n20
  not merely external behavior, 16
  not sinlessness, 28
  used explicitly of a woman, 52
  used for unblemished animals, 14–15
teleios (and cognates), 5n10, 40n5, 41, 60–61, 91, 92, 105, 119, 120, 150, 188
  formal vs. ethical sense, 67
  in class. Greek, 66
  semantic overlap with *tamim*, 41, 42n11
theosis, 169, 170, 177
Torah (law), 16, 19, 28, 33, 60, 62, 77, 78, 79, 81n27, 89, 96–97, 122, 152
  able to be obeyed, 27, 30, 49, 124–38, 184, 186
  unable to bring perfection, 145–47
  works of (*erga nomou*), 96–97

Vulgate, 82

wholeness.
  and judgment (according to deeds), 112–13, 185

Subject Index

and love, 27, 49, 75, 78, 80–82, 107, 113, 119–20, 125–26, 157, 158, 176, 180–81
and wealth, 91–92
as divine intent for humans, 15, 16, 19, 20, 120–21, 140, 149, 188
as human flourishing or happiness, 62, 68, 187–88
as life pattern, 26, 33–34
eschatological, 108, 110–12, 121, 150, 155, 170, 175
expected in biblical tradition, 15n12, 16, 28, 107, 109, 112, 115, 122, 126, 149, 183, 186
humanly attainable, 26–28, 123–32, 184
in LXX, 40–42
juxtaposed with sinfulness in OT, 35–37
See also perfect and perfection.

yashar, 16, 19, 183

Author Index

Alexander, Philip, 62
Allison, Dale, 75
Antony (Saint), 171
Aquinas, (Saint) Thomas, 176
Aristotle, 66–67
Arminius, Jacobus, 180
Augustine (Saint), 38n36, 174–76, 180

Barclay, John M. G., 47, 51, 99
Behr, John, 165, 167
Bell, Richard H., 136
Betz, Hans Dieter, 81
Blosser, Benjamin P., 169
Bonaventure (Saint), 176
Brown, Peter, 175
Burgess, Stanley M., 169, 176

Calvin, John, 178
Campbell, Douglas A., 64
Carter, Warren, 91
Clement (of Alexandria), 163, 164, 166–69, 177
Clement (of Rome), 164
Coverdale, Myles, 83
Cranford, Michael, 94

Das, A. Andrew, 127
    and OT requirement of
        perfection, 29–33
    on DSS, 44–46
    on Jubilees, 53
    on 2 Bar, 54
    on Philo, 61
    on rabbinic lit., 63–64
Delling, Gerhard, 66
Dunn, James D. G., 100, 128, 139

Feldmeier, Reinhard, 81
Flew, R. Newton, 161, 169
Francke, August Hermann, 179

Garlington, Don, 96–97, 99

Hagner, Donald, 76, 89
Harnack, Adolf von, 166
Harrington, Daniel J., 90
Hartin, Patrick J., 19, 45, 66, 150
Hays, Richard B., 91, 92, 96

Irenaeus, 165

Kaminski, Carol, 15
Kirk, Kenneth E., 161
Koester, Craig R., 149
Kushner, Harold, 16

Laato, Timo, 123, 132
Lapide, Pinchas, 77
Levison, John R., 124
Loewe, Herbert M. J., 62–63
Louth, Andrew, 164, 174, 176
Luther, Martin, 2, 93, 103, 178–79

Matlock, R. Barry, 95
Minns, Denis, 165
Moore, George F., 11
Moule, Handley C. G., 128

Author Index

Origen, 169–71, 177

Pelagius, 123, 175
Peterson, David, 141, 148
Philo, 60–61, 68, 163
Plato, 67–68, 163, 166
Plessis, Paul Johannes du, 5, 41, 42, 46
Potterie, Ignace de la, 156

Sanders, Edward P., 95
   on perfection in Pal. Judaism, 11–12
   on perfection in DSS, 42–44
   perfectionistic legalism in 4 Ezra, 47, 48
   on perfection in rabbinic lit., 62
Schechter, Solomon, 61–62
Schreiner, Thomas, 94
Scott, Mark S. M., 170
Solomon (King), 25–26
Sprinkle, Preston, 123n4
Staniloae, Dumitru, 177

Thielman, Frank, 126–27
Toews, John, 37
Tyndale, William, 83, 84

Umbach, Helmut, 73

Völker, Walther, 169

Walters, John R., 47
Wernle, Paul, 73
Wesley (and Wesleyan perfection), 74–75, 84, 180–81
Windisch, Hans, 73, 173–74
Wycliffe, John, 82–83

Yinger, Kent, 34, 97

Ziesler, John, 134

Ancient Sources Index

OLD TESTAMENT

Gen
3	37–38
6:9	15
17:1	23

Exod
15:26	32n22
29:37–38	111n24
34:6	81

Lev
19:18	78, 80
22:21	21n28
26:14	32n24
26:15	32n23

Deut
6:24–25	33
9:27	31
10:12–13	184
18:13	23
27–30	30–31
27:26	29–32, 97–98
28:1	32
30:11	27, 184

2 Sam
22:21–25	35
22:23	28

1 Kgs
11:1–13	25–26

2 Kgs
18:12	32n23
20:3	24

1 Chron
29:19	28

2 Chron
16:9	23

Job
9:21–22	24

Ps
1:1–6	24–25
14:1–3	135–36
18:20–24	27
18:20–23	24
18:23	124
18:32	28
26:1–12	27
36:1	136
51:2–5	35
143:2	137

Jer

11:2–5 · · · 99

OT APOCRYPHA AND PSEUDEPIGRAPHA

2 Bar
9:1 · · · 54n64
21:11 · · · 54

4 Ezra
7:33 · · · 51
7:46 · · · 48
7:47–48 · · · 50
7.88–89 · · · 47–52
7:104–5 · · · 51
7:138–40 · · · 50, 51
8:1 · · · 51

Apoc. Sedr.
15:3 · · · 58

Jub
5:19 · · · 53
10:17 · · · 52
15:4 · · · 53
23:10 · · · 52
27:17 · · · 52
35:12 · · · 52
36:23 · · · 52

LAE
18:1 · · · 58–59

Pss. Sol.
17:36 · · · 55n65

Pr. Man.
8 · · · 55–56

Sir
15:15 · · · 89n47

T. Ab.
10:13 · · · 57

T. Iss.
7:1–6 · · · 57–58

T. Zeb.
1:4 · · · 59

T. Levi
10:2 · · · 59

Tob
3:14 · · · 58

NEW TESTAMENT

Matt
5–7 · · · 75–80
5:19 · · · 78
5:43–47 · · · 79, 80
5:48 · · · 80–86, 178–79
19:16–22 · · · 87–88
19:16 · · · 89
19:20 · · · 89–90
19:21 · · · 86–92, 171
23:2–3 · · · 79n17
23:4 · · · 79

Mark
2:27 · · · 79
10:17–22 · · · 87–88
10:17 · · · 89
10:18 · · · 89
10:21 · · · 89n47

Ancient Sources Index

Luke
1:45	149n18
6:36	81n28
6:40	84
14:33	91n52
18:18–23	87–88

Acts
21:24	89n47
23:1	127
24:16	127

Rom
2:13,	129–32
2:25–27	132
3:10–12	134–37
3:20	124
3:23	124, 133–34
7	137–38
8:3–4	125
8:7	124
12:2	118
13:8–10	125

1 Cor
1:8	111n25
2:6	84, 105–7
13:10	118–19
14:20	107
15:51–54	121

2 Cor
3:18	158
12:9	105n4, 108n12
13:9	85
13:11	85

Gal
3:1–5	102
3:3	85, 109–10
3:6–9	102
3:10	93–103
3:15–18	102–3
5:3	98n15

Eph
6:2	125
6:13	124
4:12	84
4:13	85, 115–17

Phil
1:6	109n19
2:15	112, 126
3:6	89n47, 126–28
3:12–16	107–9
3:12	86
3:15	85
3:21	121

Col
1:22–23	114
1:28	85, 110–13
3:14	119–20
4:12	85, 113–15

1 Thess
2:10	126
3:13	126

1 Tim
6:13–14	126n11

2 Tim
3:17	85

Heb
2:10	142–43
4:5	142
5:8–9	142, 143–44
5:14	145
6:1	85, 145
7:11	148–49
7:19	145, 149
7:28	142, 144–45
9:11	145n7
9:13	146
10:1	86, 145

10:14–18	147
10:14	86, 146
10:22	146
11:39–40	147, 149
12:2	147–48
12:23	148
13:21	85

Jas

1:2–4	149–50
2:10	152
3:2	86, 150–52

1 Pet

5:10	85

1 John

1:8–10	153
1:9	155
1:10	153
2:5	157
2:29	158
3:2	121n55, 157–58
3:4–10	154–56
3:6	158
4:12	157
4:17	157
4:18	157
5:18	152–56

∼

DEAD SEA SCROLLS

1QH

XII.29–30	43

1QS

I, 9–10	80n22
XI, 2–3	46
XI, 10–11	46

∼

PHILO

Deus 116–118	163n9, 60n84
Ebr. 94	60n84
Gig. 61–62	163
Leg. 3.131	60
QG 1.97	163

∼

RABBINIC WRITINGS

b. Qidd. 40b	62
b. Sanh. 81a	63–64
m. Sanh. 10.1	63
m. Qidd. 1.10	152

∼

GRECO-ROMAN WRITINGS

Seneca

Ben. 4.26.1	80

∼

EARLY CHRISTIAN WRITINGS

Athanasius

Vit. Ant. 2.2–3	170–71

Augustine

Confessions

9.10.23–25	174–75

City of God

15.26	176

Ancient Sources Index

Clement (of Alexandria)

Abr.	31–32
Paed.	
1.4.3	169n34
1.9.75.2	168
1.94.1	169n34
2.5.46.1	167–68
Somn. 2.234	163
Strom.	
4.3	166–67
4.23.147—149.8	168
4.26	167n27
7.3.17	167
7.7.40.1–2	168

Clement (of Rome)

1 *Clem.*	
2:3	164
49–50	164

Irenaeus

Haer.	
4.38	165n16
5.1.1	165n16
5.6.1	165n19

Origen

Contra Celsum 4.29	170
Hom. Num. 27.6	170–71

www.ingramcontent.com/pod-product-compliance
Lightning Source LLC
Chambersburg PA
CBHW022016220426
43663CB00007B/1106